The
HIKERS GUIDE to O'AHU
Revised Edition

The
HIKERS GUIDE to O'AHU
Revised Edition

Stuart M. Ball, Jr.

 A Latitude 20 Book

University of Hawai'i Press

HONOLULU

© 2000 University of Hawai'i Press
All rights reserved
Printed in the United States of America

05   04   03   5   4   3

Library of Congress Cataloging-in-Publication Data
Ball, Stuart M., 1948–
    The hikers guide to O'ahu / Stuart M. Ball, Jr. —
Rev. ed.
       p. cm.
    "A Latitude 20 book."
    Includes bibliographical references and index.
    ISBN 0–8248–2305–2 (pbk. : alk. paper)
    1. Hiking—Hawaii—Oahu—Guidebooks.
2. Oahu (Hawaii)—Guidebooks.   I. Title.
GV199.42.H32 O143 2001
919.69'30442—dc21   00–036880

⚄ Maps by Manoa Mapworks

Designed by Santos Barbasa Jr.

Printed by Data Reproductions Corporation

CONTENTS

Color illustrations follow p. 114

ACKNOWLEDGMENTS

Lynne Masuyama, my wife, joined me on many of the hikes in this book. She is an ideal hiking partner, providing support, guidance, and good company.

For their advice and assistance I would also like to thank Fred Boll, Steve Brown, Bill Gorst, John Hall, John Hoover, Mabel Kekina, Bill Melemai, Grant Oka, Ken Suzuki, Patrick Rorie, Dayle Turner, and Jim Yuen.

INTRODUCTION

O'ahu is truly a paradise for hikers. While tourists and local people alike flock to the beaches, the mountains remain surprisingly deserted. This book aims to change that just a little. It will take you where few people go, to lush valleys, cascading waterfalls, and windswept ridges and sea cliffs.

This guidebook includes most of the day hikes on O'ahu, eighty-seven to be exact. Fifty of them are open to the public and are described in detail. The remaining thirty-seven are closed hikes and thus rate only a brief description in Appendix 1.

Each open hike has a section on highlights, directions to the trailhead, and a detailed description of the route. A narrative section covers points of interest and major hazards along the trail. As applicable, there are short notes about the plants, birds, geology, history, and legends of the area. Each hike also has its own topographic map keyed to the route description.

As you will see, this guidebook is very detailed. The information in it, however, is neither perfect nor up to date because of changing conditions. A landowner may revise his access policy. New housing construction may alter the approach to a trailhead. A winter storm may cause a landslide that blocks the route. Do not rely entirely on this book; use your own judgment and common sense as well.

Good luck and good hiking!

CHANGES IN THE REVISED EDITION

Those of you who have used my original guide will notice some major changes in this revised edition. I have added six new open hikes: Wiliwilinui, Mount Olympus, Puʻu Pia, Makapuʻu Point, Maunawili Falls, and Pūpūkea Summit. Because of access problems and/or disuse, five previously open hikes have been transferred to the closed list: Waikakalaua, Sacred Falls, Kawailoa Ridge, Palikea, and ʻŌhikilolo. I have also combined three hikes with others: Waʻahila-Kolowalu into Mount Olympus, Old Pali Road into Likeke, and Tripler Ridge into Puʻu Keahi a Kahoe. Kawai Iki is mentioned only briefly in the ʻŌpaeʻula hike.

I have made major route changes in the following hikes: Koko Crater, Schofield-Waikāne, Olomana, Koʻolaupoko (now Maunawili), Kahana Valley, Koloa Gulch, Pālehua (now Pālehua-Palikea), Puʻu Kaua, Kānehoa-Hāpapa, Kalena, Waiʻanae Kaʻala, and Waiʻanae Kai.

Each open hike now has a highlights section. The trailhead directions include the nearest bus stop. The route descriptions have been completely rechecked and revised. Expanded notes sections include information on plants, birds, geology, and history along the trail.

For updated route and access information, visit my website at www.hgea.org/~lmasu.

HIKING TIPS

Climate

Oʻahu has two seasons, summer (May to October) and winter (November to April). Summer is the warmer and drier season. Daytime temperatures at sea level are in the 80s, and nighttime temperatures are in the 70s. Trade winds from the northeast blow steadily to cool the Islands. The trades, however, do produce cloud buildup over the mountains and some rain there.

Winter is the cooler and wetter season. Daytime temperatures at sea level are in the 70s and low 80s, and nighttime temperatures are in the 60s and low 70s. The winds are more variable in strength and direction, sometimes coming from the south or west. Southerly Kona winds produce mainland-type weather—clear skies or heavy cloud cover and rain.

Clothing

For short, easy hikes, wear:

   hiking boots, running or walking shoes (with tread)
   socks
   tabis (Japanese reef walkers), for gulch hikes
   lightweight pants or shorts: cotton, cotton blend, or nylon (no jeans)
   lightweight shirt, short or long sleeve: nylon, cotton, or cotton blend
   rain jacket: breathable fabric
   hat, broad-brimmed

For long, difficult hikes, add:

   light sweater or jacket: wool or synthetic fabric
   work gloves

Equipment

For short, easy hikes, bring:

   daypack
   1 liter water

food
sunscreen

For long, difficult hikes, add:
 extra water
 extra food
 first-aid kit
 space blanket
 flashlight and extra bulb and batteries
 whistle
 compass
 topographic map

Pack It Out

Most of the hikes in this book are trash free. Let's keep them that way. Pack out all your trash, including cigarette butts, gum wrappers, orange peels, and apple cores.

Heiau

Heiau are early Hawaiian places of worship with stone or earth platforms. Do not disturb *heiau,* other ancient sites, or artifacts you may come upon while hiking. In addition, do not build new *ahu* (rock cairns) because they may confuse other hikers and archaeologists.

Clidemia hirta

Clidemia is an aggressive weed that overgrows many of the trails in the wet sections of the Ko'olau and Wai'anae Ranges. The shrub is easily recognizable by its heavily creased, elliptical leaves. Mature plants have hairy, blue berries containing lots of tiny seeds.

 Clidemia is spread by birds and, yes, hikers. Carefully clean the soles and sides of your boots after hiking in infested areas.

 In some locations *Clidemia* is under control because of a fungus introduced by Dr. Eduardo Trujillo of the University of Hawai'i. Under the direction of the Division of Forestry and Wildlife, volunteers spray the shrub with a solution containing the fungus.

Emergencies

Don't have any! Seriously, come prepared with the right clothing and equipment. Bring along this book and follow the hike description closely. Memorize key junctions. Constantly be aware of the route you are traveling. You can never be lost if you know where you came from. Above all, use your common sense and good judgment.

Always tell someone where you are hiking and when you will be out. Make sure they know to call the emergency number (911) and ask for Fire Rescue if you don't call or show up on time.

The mountains are a dangerous place for exhausted, disoriented, and/or injured hikers. If you do get into serious trouble, settle down for the night and wait for rescue. You did let someone know where you were hiking, right? You did bring your sweater and space blanket, right?

Hazards

There are hazards in hiking, as in any sport. Described below are the main hazards you should be aware of while hiking on Oʻahu. With the right clothing and equipment, and good judgment on your part, you should be able to avoid or minimize these hazards and have an enjoyable outing.

Too Hot

Hiking on Oʻahu is usually a hot, sweaty experience. Drink plenty of water throughout the hike because it is very easy to become dehydrated. Prolonged lack of water can lead to heat exhaustion and heat stroke.

The need for water on a hike varies from person to person. As a general rule, take 1 liter of water on the short, easy hikes. Take 2 or more liters on the long, difficult hikes. If you have to ration or borrow water, you didn't bring enough.

The sun on Oʻahu is very strong, even in winter. During midday wear a broad-brimmed hat and use lots of sunscreen.

Too Cold

Hiking on Oʻahu can sometimes be a wet, cold experience. A winter Kona storm with high winds and heavy rainfall can make you very cold very quickly. Insufficient or inappropriate clothing leads to chilling, which leads to hypothermia.

Always bring a rain jacket to protect you from wind and rain. Most of the time you won't even take it out of your pack, but bring it anyway! On the long ridge hikes take a light wool or synthetic-fabric sweater or jacket that will keep you warm even when wet.

Leptospirosis

Leptospirosis is a bacterial disease found in freshwater ponds and streams contaminated with the urine of rats, mice, or mongooses. The bacteria can enter the body through the nose, mouth, eyes, or open cuts.

The incubation period is generally 1 to 3 weeks. Symptoms resemble those of the flu—fever, chills, sweating, head and muscle aches, weakness, diarrhea, and vomiting. If you develop the symptoms during the incubation period, see your doctor immediately and mention that you have been exposed to stream water. If left untreated, the symptoms may persist for a few days to several weeks. In rare cases the disease may become more severe and even lead to death.

You can take several precautions to prevent leptospirosis. First, never drink any stream water unless you have adequately boiled, filtered, or chemically treated it. That's easy. None of the hikes in this book is so long that you cannot bring all the water you need with you. Second, on the stream hikes wear long pants to avoid getting cut and don't go swimming. That's harder for some people to do. Only you can decide how much risk you are willing to take.

High Streams

O'ahu streams can rise suddenly during heavy rainstorms. Do not cross a fast-flowing stream if the water is much above your knees. Wait for the stream to go down. It is far better to be stranded for half a day than to be swept away.

Narrow Trail

O'ahu is known for its knife-edge ridges and sheer cliffs. Trails in those areas tend to be very narrow with steep drop-offs on one or both sides. Often, the footing is over loose, rotten rock or slick mud.

If narrow sections make you feel overly uneasy, don't try them. There is no shame in turning back if you don't like what you see.

Rock Falls

Rock falls occur sporadically in the O'ahu mountains. Most are small or take place away from the trail or when no one is around. Because of the steep slopes above, the narrow gulch hikes are particularly susceptible to rock falls. Because they occur with little or no warning, there is not much you can do about them. If caught in a rock fall, protect your head with your arms and pack and hope for the best.

Goat/Pig/Bird Hunters

On the hikes in the state forest reserves you may meet goat, pig, or bird hunters. They are friendly people, and their dogs generally are, too. They use hiking routes to access hunting areas; however, the hunt usually takes place off trail. Stay away from areas where you hear shots being fired or dogs barking.

Marijuana (paka lōlō) Growers

The danger from marijuana growers and their booby traps is much exaggerated. The growers do not plant their plots near recognized trails. All of the hikes in this book travel on established routes. Stay on the trail, and you should have no paka lōlō problems.

Hurricanes

Hurricane season on O'ahu is usually from June to December. Before starting a hike during that period, check the weather report to make sure no hurricanes are in the vicinity.

A Final Caution

The hazards just described are the main ones you may encounter, but the list is by no means all inclusive. Like life in general, hiking on O'ahu carries certain risks, and no hike is ever completely safe. YOU HAVE TO DECIDE HOW MUCH RISK YOU ARE WILLING TO TAKE.

HIKE CATEGORIES

Type

There are three types of hikes on Oʻahu: ridge, valley, and foothill. Ridge hikes climb a ridge to the summit of a mountain or a mountain range. Valley hikes follow a valley bottom upstream. In both types the route out is usually the same as the route in.

Foothill hikes cut across the topography. They cross a ridge, descend into a valley, and so on. They do this at lower elevations where the topography is relatively gentle. Foothill hikes are usually loop hikes.

There are two types of trails on ridge hikes: graded and ungraded. An ungraded trail sticks to the crest of the ridge with all of its ups and downs. A graded trail is built into the side of the ridge just below its top. Although avoiding drastic elevation changes, a graded trail works into and out of every ravine along the flank of the ridge.

Length

Length is the distance covered on the entire hike. If the hike is point to point, the length is one way. If the hike is out and back, the length is round trip. If the hike is a loop, the length is the complete loop.

Length is measured on the U.S. Geological Survey topographic maps. The plotted distance is then increased by 10 to 20 percent and rounded to the nearest mile. The percentage increase attempts to account for trail meandering too small to be shown on the map.

None of the trails on Oʻahu has been measured precisely.

To convert the length to kilometers, multiply the miles by 1.609.

Elevation Gain

Elevation gain includes only significant changes in altitude. No attempt is made to account for all the small ups and downs along the route. Measurements are taken from the U.S. Geological Survey topographic maps and then rounded to the nearest 100 feet.

To convert the elevation gain to meters, multiply the feet by 0.305.

Danger

Danger rates the extent of two major hazards, narrow trail for: ridge and foothill hikes, and flash flooding for valley hikes. Both hazards have caused serious injuries or deaths of hikers in the past. For ridge and foothill hikes, the rating is based on the length and difficulty of narrow trail sections over steep slopes. For valley hikes, the rating is based on the frequency and severity of flash floods.

The categories are low, medium, and high. A rating of low or medium does not imply that the hike is completely safe from those two hazards.

Suitable for

Use this index to determine which hikes best match your ability. The categories are novice, intermediate, and expert. Novices are beginning hikers. Experts are experienced hikers. Intermediates are those in between.

Novice hikes generally follow a short, well-graded, and well-marked trail with gradual elevation changes and few hazards. Expert hikes have a long, rough, sometimes obscure route with substantial elevation changes and multiple hazards. Most hikes fall between those two extremes. Some are even suitable for everyone because they start out easy and then get progressively harder the farther you go.

How difficult a hike seems to you depends on your hiking experience and physical fitness. An experienced, conditioned hiker will find the novice hikes easy and the expert hikes difficult. An out-of-shape beginner may well find some of the novice hikes challenging.

Use this index only as a rough guide. Read the route description and notes to get a better feel for the hike.

Location

Location tells the general area of the hike. The nearest town or subdivision is given. Also mentioned is the state park or state forest reserve where the hike is found.

Topo Map

Topo map refers to the U.S. Geological Survey quadrangle that shows the area of the hike. All maps referenced are in the 7.5-minute topographic series with a scale of 1:24,000 and a contour interval of 40 feet.

You can purchase topographic maps directly from the Geological Survey. The address is USGS Information Services, P.O. Box 25286, Denver, CO 80225.

In Honolulu, topo maps are available from Pacific Map Center at 560 N. Nimitz Hwy, Suite 206A; phone 545-3600.

Access

There are two categories of access: open and conditional.

You may do Open hikes anytime without restriction.

You may do Conditional hikes subject to the terms required by the landowner. They usually include obtaining verbal or written permission. You may have to sign a liability waiver. In addition, there may be restrictions on the size and composition of the group and the time when you can do the hike. If you do not adhere to the landowner's conditions, you are trespassing.

The outdoor organizations mentioned in Appendix 2 offer a good means of doing conditional hikes. The organization gets the required permissions, saving you time and trouble. Check their schedules.

In addition to the hikes described in detail in this book, there are numerous hikes that are currently closed to the general public. See Appendix 1 for a list and brief description of them.

Highlights

Highlights briefly describes the hike and its major attractions.

Trailhead Directions

Trailhead directions are detailed driving instructions from down-town Honolulu to the start of the hike. If you are at all familiar with O'ahu, these directions should be sufficient to get you to the trailhead. If you are unfamiliar with the island, bring along a copy of Bryan's O'ahu Sectional Maps or James A. Bier's O'ahu Reference Maps to supplement the directions. Both show the start of many of the hikes. You can purchase either map at local bookstores and tourist shops.

For some hikes the directions stop short of the actual trailhead. There are two reasons for suggesting that you do some extra road walking. First, in certain areas it is generally safer to park your car on a main road rather than at the trailhead. Wherever you park, never leave valuables in your vehicle.

Second, the dirt roads leading to some of the trailheads are narrow, rough, and often muddy. The directions assume that you have a two-wheel-drive car and the road is dry. With a four-wheel-drive vehicle you may be able to get closer to the trail-head. On the other hand, if the road is wet, you may not even be able to drive as far as the directions recommend.

The directions also mention the bus route number and the stop nearest the trailhead. For route and schedule information, phone The Bus at 848-5555.

Route Description

This section provides a detailed description of the route that the hike follows. Noted are junctions, landmarks, and points of interest. Also mentioned are specific hazards, such as a rough, narrow trail section. Out-and-back hikes are described on the way in. Loop hikes and point-to-point hikes are described in the preferred direction.

Each hike has its own map. The solid line shows the route. The letters indicate important junctions or landmarks and are keyed to the route description. For example, map point A is always the point where you start the hike.

The maps are reproductions of the U.S. Geological Survey

quadrangles for the immediate area of the hike. As in the originals, the scale is 1:24,000, and the contour interval is 40 feet.

Hawaiian words are sometimes used in this section to describe the route. They are listed below with their English definition.

makai	seaward; toward the ocean
mauka	inland; toward the mountains
pali	cliff
pu'u	hill or peak

The word *contour* is sometimes used in the route description as a verb (that is, to contour). It means to hike roughly at the same elevation across a slope. Contouring generally occurs on trails that are cut into the flank of a ridge and work into and out of each side gulch.

Notes

The notes section provides additional information about the hike to make it safer and more enjoyable. Included are comments about trail conditions, major hazards, and the best time of day or year to take the hike. Also mentioned are scenic views, deep swimming holes, ripe fruit, and hungry mosquitoes. In addition, there are short notes about the plants, birds, geology, history, and legends of the area. At the end is a brief description of any alternatives to the basic route.

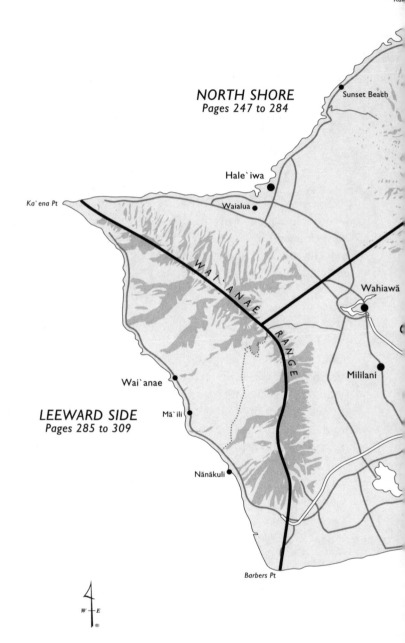

NORTH SHORE
Pages 247 to 284

Sunset Beach

Hale`iwa

Ka`ena Pt

Waialua

Wahiawā

W A I `A N A E

Mililani

Wai`anae

R A N G E

LEEWARD SIDE
Pages 285 to 309

Mā`ili

Nānākuli

Barbers Pt

Ka

W — E

Cartography by Manoa Mapworks, Inc.

0		5		10 miles

0	5	10	15 kilometers

O`AHU

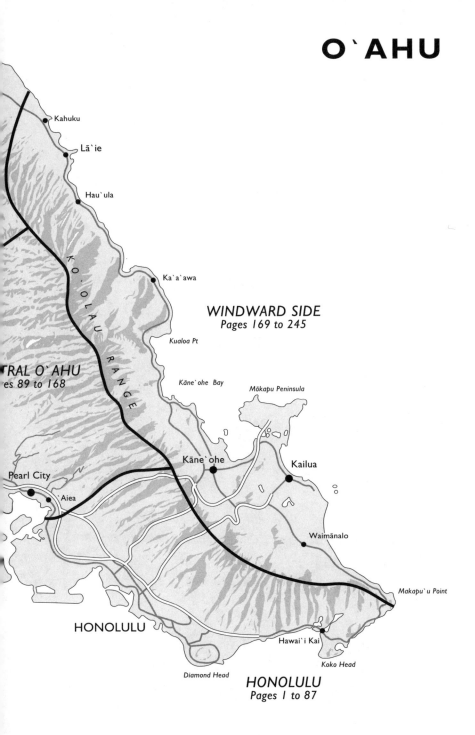

Kahuku

Lā`ie

Hau`ula

KO`OLAU RANGE

Ka`a`awa

WINDWARD SIDE
Pages 169 to 245

Kualoa Pt

RAL O`AHU
es 89 to 168

Kāne`ohe Bay

Mōkapu Peninsula

Pearl City

Kāne`ohe

Kailua

`Aiea

Waimānalo

Makapu`u Point

HONOLULU

Hawai`i Kai

Koko Head

Diamond Head

HONOLULU
Pages 1 to 87

HIKE SUMMARY

Hike	Location	Type	Length (miles)	Elev. Gain (feet)	Access	Suitable for Nov.	Int.	Exp.	Narrow Spots	Views	Swimming	Native Plants/Birds
Honolulu												
1. Koko Crater	Hawai'i Kai	Ridge	2	1,200	Open	X			X	X		
2. Kuli'ou'ou Ridge	Kuli'ou'ou	Ridge	5	1,800	Open	X	X			X		X
3. Kuli'ou'ou Valley	Kuli'ou'ou	Valley	2	300	Open	X						X
4. Hawai'iloa Ridge	Hawai'i Loa	Ridge	5	1,500	Cond.	X	X			X		X
5. Wiliwilinui	Wai'alae Iki	Ridge	5	1,300	Cond.	X	X			X		X
6. Lanipō	Maunalani Heights	Ridge	7	2,000	Open		X			X		X
7. Mount Olympus	St. Louis Heights	Ridge	6	1,500	Open		X			X		X
8. Pu'u Pia	Mānoa	Foothill	2	500	Open	X				X		
9. 'Aihualama-'Ōhi'a	Mānoa	Foothill	8	1,700	Open	X	X			X	X	
10. Makiki-Tantalus	Makiki	Foothill	8	1,500	Open	X	X			X		X
11. Nu'uanu-Judd	Nu'uanu	Foothill	5	1,000	Open	X	X			X	X	
12. Kamanaiki	Kalihi	Ridge	5	1,400	Open	X	X			X		X
13. Bowman	Fort Shafter	Ridge	12	2,400	Open		X	X	X	X		X
14. Pu'u Keahi a Kahoe	Moanalua	Ridge	11	2,600	Cond.		X	X	X	X		X
15. Moanalua Valley	Moanalua	Valley	11	1,500	Cond.	X	X			X	X	
Central O'ahu												
16. 'Aiea Loop	'Aiea	Foothill	5	900	Open	X	X			X		
17. 'Aiea Ridge	'Aiea	Ridge	11	1,800	Open	X	X	X		X		X
18. Kalauao	'Aiea	Valley	4	700	Open	X	X				X	
19. Waimano Ridge	Pearl City	Ridge	15	1,700	Open		X	X		X		X
20. Waimano Valley	Pearl City	Valley	2	400	Open	X						
21. Waimano Pool	Pacific Palisades	Valley	3	700	Open	X	X				X	
22. Mānana	Pacific Palisades	Ridge	12	1,700	Open		X	X		X		X
23. Pu'u Kaua	Kunia	Ridge	3	1,900	Cond.		X	X		X		X
24. Kānehoa-Hāpapa	Schofield Barracks	Ridge	6	1,500	Cond.		X	X	X	X		X

No.	Name	Location	Type	No.	Elev.	Cond.							
25.	Kalena	Schofield Barracks	Ridge	5	2,100	Cond.		X	X	X		X	X
26.	Schofield-Waikāne	Wahiawā	Ridge	14	1,200	Cond.		X	X	X		X	X
27.	Wahiawā Hills	Wahiawā	Foothill	5	1,300	Cond.	X	X		X	X	X	
28.	Poamoho Ridge	Helemano	Ridge	12	1,100	Cond.		X	X	X		X	X
Windward Side													
29.	Makapuʻu Point	Makapuʻu	Ridge	3	600	Open	X	X	X			X	
30.	Olomana	Maunawili	Ridge	6	1,600	Cond.	X	X	X	X	X	X	
31.	Maunawili Falls	Maunawili	Valley	3	400	Open	X		X			X	X
32.	Maunawili	Maunawili	Foothill	10	600	Open	X		X			X	
33.	Likeke	Nuʻuanu Pali	Foothill	7	600	Open	X		X			X	
34.	Puʻu Manamana	Kahana	Ridge	4	2,100	Open	X	X	X	X	X	X	X
35.	Kahana Valley	Kahana	Valley	6	400	Open		X	X		X	X	X
36.	Puʻu Piei	Kahana	Ridge	3	1,700	Open	X	X	X	X		X	
37.	Hauʻula-Papali	Hauʻula	Foothill	7	1,500	Open	X	X	X			X	
38.	Maʻakua Gulch	Hauʻula	Valley	6	900	Open		X	X		X	X	X
39.	Koloa Gulch	Lāʻie	Valley	8	1,300	Cond.		X	X		X	X	X
40.	Lāʻie	Lāʻie	Ridge	12	2,200	Cond.		X	X	X	X	X	X
North Shore													
41.	Kaunala	Pūpūkea	Foothill	6	500	Cond.	X	X	X		X	X	
42.	Pūpūkea Summit	Pūpūkea	Ridge	9	900	Cond.	X	X	X	X	X	X	X
43.	Kawainui	Haleʻiwa	Valley	6	800	Cond.	X	X				X	X
44.	ʻŌpaeʻula	Haleʻiwa	Valley	2	200	Cond.	X	X					X
45.	Dupont	Waialua	Ridge	11	4,100	Cond.		X	X	X	X	X	X
46.	Mokulēʻia	Mokulēʻia	Ridge	7	2,000	Open		X	X			X	
Leeward Side													
47.	Pālehua-Palikea	Makakilo	Ridge	2	400	Cond.	X	X	X		X	X	X
48.	Waiʻanae Kaʻala	Waiʻanae	Ridge	8	3,500	Open	X	X	X	X		X	X
49.	Waiʻanae Kai	Waiʻanae	Foothill	6	2,200	Open		X	X	X		X	X
50.	Kuaokalā	Kaʻena	Foothill	6	1,200	Cond.		X	X			X	

HONOLULU

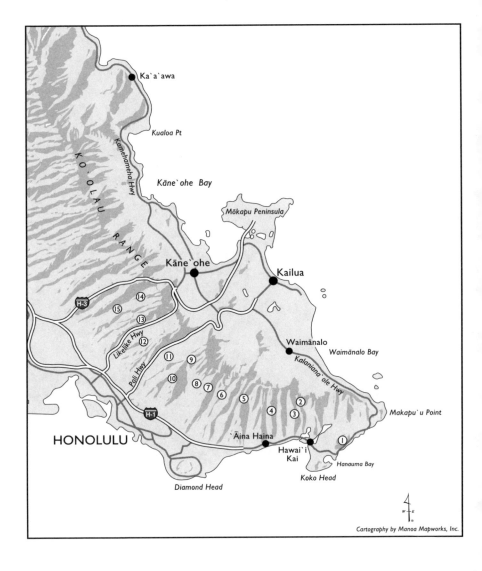

Ka`a`awa

Kualoa Pt

KO`OLAU RANGE

Kamehameha Hwy

Kāne`ohe Bay

Mōkapu Peninsula

Kāne`ohe

Kailua

H-3

⑭
⑮
⑬
⑫
Likelike Hwy

Waimānalo

Waimānalo Bay

Kalaniana`ole Hwy

Pali Hwy

⑪
⑨
⑩
⑧
⑦
⑥
⑤
②
③
④

Makapu`u Point

H-1

HONOLULU

`Āina Haina

Hawai`i Kai

①

Hanauma Bay

Koko Head

Diamond Head

Cartography by Manoa Mapworks, Inc.

1 Koko Crater (Kohelepelepe)

Type:	Ungraded ridge
Length:	2-mile round trip
Elevation Gain:	1,200 feet
Danger:	Medium
Suitable for:	Intermediate
Location:	Koko Head Regional Park
Topo Map:	Koko Head
Access:	Open

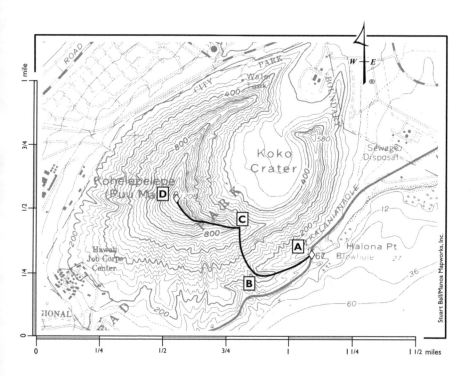

Highlights

This short, windy hike climbs a steep-sided volcanic cone. Along the way are a narrow rock arch and a chance at whale watching. At the top are a panoramic view of east O'ahu and the remains of an incline railway.

Trailhead Directions

At Ward Ave. get on Lunalilo Fwy (H-1) Koko Head bound (east).

As the freeway ends, continue straight on Kalaniana'ole Hwy (Rte 72).

The highway narrows to two lanes past Koko Marina Shopping Center in Hawai'i Kai.

Pass the entrance to Hanauma Bay Beach Park on the right.

Turn right at Hālona blowhole lookout and park in the large lot there (elevation 40 feet) (map point A).

Bus: Route 22 to Sandy Beach Park. Walk back 0.4 mile along Kalaniana'ole Hwy to the blowhole parking lot.

Route Description

From the parking lot walk back along the highway toward Hanauma Bay.

As the guardrail on the right ends, bear right and up onto a spur ridge of tuff.

Angle up a sloping ledge on the right side of the ridge.

Gain the ridgeline and climb gradually along it. Look for the low-lying native shrub 'ilima papa with its yellow orange flowers.

The ridge curves to the right and levels off briefly (map point B).

Ascend very steeply across a natural arch.

Continue steep climbing through scrub koa haole trees.

Reach a junction at the rim of Koko Crater (Kohelepelepe) (map point C). Turn left and up along the rim. Memorize that junction for the return trip.

Climb steeply to the top of a triangular rock formation.

Traverse a narrow, rocky section. Stay on top of the ridge and watch your footing.

Bear right around a large, balanced rock.

Negotiate another narrow stretch.

Jog left and then right through a band of gray rock.

The angle of ascent eases through scrub Christmas berry and koa haole. Be careful of barbed wire on the ground.

Pass two small concrete buildings on the right and some downed utility poles on the left. Watch for the native shrub 'a'ali'i.

Reach Pu'u Ma'i, the highest point on the crater rim (elevation 1,208 feet) (map point D). At the top is a metal viewing platform and the remains of an incline railway and a radar site.

Notes

Koko Crater is the volcanic cone overlooking Hālona (peering place) blowhole and Sandy Beach. The exhilarating climb to its open summit is short and superb, but not for everyone because of several windy, narrow stretches. If the route looks too steep and scary, try the Makapu'u Point loop just down the road.

Take this hike during winter (November–April) when temperatures are cooler and the sun less intense. Migrating humpback whales are also on view then. Don't forget the two essentials for this hike—sunscreen and binoculars.

Most of the hike is a steep scramble over crumbly rock and loose dirt. The precipitous crossing of a natural arch is the most difficult part of the climb. Use the footholds chiseled into the rock and the cables, if there are any. Tread gingerly through the narrow sections along the rim. Don't let the wind catch you off balance. Finally, take your time on the way down.

On the trail look for the low-lying native shrub 'ilima papa. It has oblong, serrated leaves, about 1 inch long. The yellow orange flowers strung together make a regal *lei* (garland), in both ancient and modern Hawai'i.

Koko Crater is a horseshoe-shaped double cone built by eruptions from two nearby vents. Much of the spewed ash landed downwind, forming a distinct summit on the southwest side of the crater. Over the years the ash hardened into tuff, the porous, stratified rock that you are walking on. Both Koko Crater and Diamond Head are remnants of the last volcanic activity on O'ahu, known as the Honolulu Series.

While on the crater rim, scan the ocean for humpback whales.

They migrate from the North Pacific to the Hawaiian Islands, arriving in October and leaving in May. The whales congregate off the leeward coast of Maui and occupy themselves calving, nursing, breeding, and generally horsing around.

Before reaching the top, watch for the native shrub 'a'ali'i. It has shiny, narrow leaves and red seed capsules. Early Hawaiians used the leaves and capsules in making *lei*. When crushed or boiled, the capsules produced a red dye for decorating *kapa* (bark cloth).

At the summit is a 360-degree view of east O'ahu. From the ocean clockwise are Hanauma (curved) Bay, Koko Head (Kuamo'o Kāne), and the leeward coast to Diamond Head and Waikīkī (spouting water). Completing the panorama are the Ko'olau (windward) Range ending at Makapu'u (bulging eye) Point, Mānana (Rabbit) Island, and Sandy Beach. Across Kaiwi (the bone) Channel is the neighbor island of Moloka'i. On a clear day you can also see the islands of Maui and Lāna'i.

At the summit are several concrete platforms and buildings, including the upper terminal of an incline railway. The site was likely a radar complex for controlling coastal batteries during World War II. The railway provided comfortable transportation to the top for soldiers manning the radars. An electric winch and a stout cable pulled a tram up the tracks. The cars featured angled seats that leveled out on the steep gradient below the summit.

The old Hawaiian name for Koko Crater is Kohelepelepe or the inner lips of the vagina. According to a racy legend, the pig demigod Kamapua'a hotly pursued the goddess of fire Pele on the Big Island. The goddess Kapo, Pele's sister, detached her *kohe* (vagina) and flung it to eastern O'ahu to divert Kamapua'a. The trick apparently worked because the pig demigod followed the so-called traveling vagina and left Pele alone. The vaginal imprint became the crater known as Kohelepelepe.

2 Kuli'ou'ou Ridge

Type:	Ungraded ridge
Length:	5-mile round trip
Elevation Gain:	1,800 feet
Danger:	Low
Suitable for:	Novice, Intermediate
Location:	Kuli'ou'ou Forest Reserve above Kuli'ou'ou
Topo Map:	Koko Head
Access:	Open

Highlights
This popular hike climbs a dry, shady ridge to the top of the Ko'olau Range. Along the way are some native plants and a stately forest of Cook pines. From the summit lookout are superb views of the windward coast.

Trailhead Directions
At Ward Ave. get on Lunalilo Fwy (H-1) Koko Head bound (east).

As the freeway ends, continue straight on Kalaniana'ole Hwy (Rte 72).

Drive by 'Āina Haina and Niu Valley Center.

Pass Holy Trinity Catholic Church on the right.

Turn left on Kuli'ou'ou Rd. and head into Kuli'ou'ou Valley.

The road jogs left and then right.

Pass Kuli'ou'ou Neighborhood Park on the right. The park has rest rooms and drinking water.

At the Dead End sign turn right on Kala'au Pl.

Park on the street just before it ends at a turnaround circle (elevation 260 feet) (map point A).

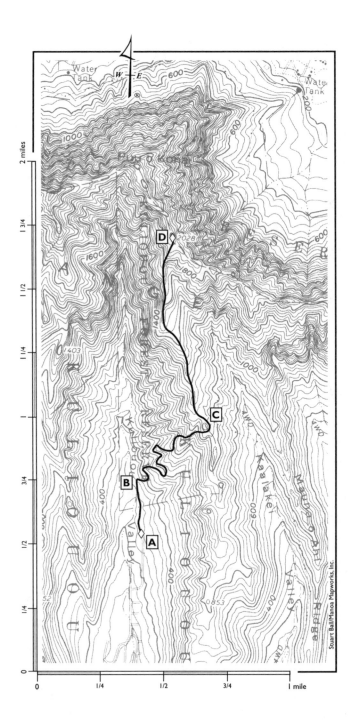

Bus: Route 1 to Kalaniana'ole Hwy and Kuli'ou'ou Rd. Walk 1.3 miles along Kuli'ou'ou Rd. and Kala'au Pl. to the trailhead.

Route Description

At the back of the circle take the one-lane, paved road on the left leading down to Kuli'ou'ou Stream.

Before crossing the stream, bear right on a grassy road by a utility pole.

Enter a clearing with a lone Christmas berry tree in the middle.

The road narrows and becomes the Kuli'ou'ou Valley Trail.

Cross a small gully.

Contour above the stream through an introduced forest of Christmas berry, koa haole, and guava. Laua'e ferns and native 'ūlei shrubs cover the ground.

Reach a signed junction by some small boulders (map point B). Turn sharp right and up on the Kuli'ou'ou Ridge Trail. (The valley trail continues straight.) Just after the junction look for noni, a small tree with large, shiny green leaves and warty fruits.

Climb gradually up the side of the valley on ten long switchbacks. After the first one are good views of Kuli'ou'ou Valley. Between the second and third switchbacks the trail splits twice. Keep right each time. After the eighth one the trail enters a grove of ironwood trees.

Ascend straight up a side ridge briefly.

Bear right off the side ridge and continue climbing via two short switchbacks.

Just before the top, work up a gully lined with ironwoods.

Reach the ridgeline (map point C) and turn left up the ridge. Memorize that junction for the return trip.

Climb steadily up the ridge on its right side.

After regaining the ridgeline, wind through a stand of large Cook pines.

Skirt an eroded spot.

Shortly afterward pass two covered picnic tables on the right.

The trail climbs steeply and then levels off briefly in a lovely area lined with stately pines.

Ascend steadily along the left side of the broad ridge through Cook pines and ironwoods.

Break out into the open. On the left you can see the sheer walls of Kuli'ou'ou Valley. Along the route are the native trees 'ōhi'a and lama.

The ridge narrows, and the trail becomes rough and eroded in spots. Look to the left for an unusual view of the back side of Diamond Head. To the right are Koko Crater (Kohelepelepe) and Koko Head (Kuamo'o Kāne) overlooking Hawai'i Kai and Maunalua Bay.

Climb steeply on plastic steps.

Reach the Ko'olau summit at an eroded hill (elevation 2,028 feet) (map point D).

Notes

Kuli'ou'ou Ridge is a popular route to the summit of the Ko'olau Range. The hike is reasonably short, mostly shady, and usually mud free. Novices can climb the graded switchbacks to the pic-nic tables. More experienced hikers can head for the summit lookout with its superb view of the windward coast.

Before you start the hike, a few cautions are in order. Look out for mountain bikers and trail runners on the switchback section. Beyond the picnic tables the trail becomes steep and eroded in spots. Watch your footing, especially on the descent. In the worst areas plastic steps have been installed to slow the erosion and stabilize the trail.

On the valley trail, look for the sprawling native shrub 'ūlei in the sunny sections. It has small, oblong leaves arranged in pairs; clusters of white, roselike flowers; and white fruit. Early Hawaiians ate the berries and used the tough wood for making digging sticks, fish spears, and 'ūkēkē (the musical bow).

Along the ridge near the picnic tables are several groves of tall Cook pines. They have overlapping, scalelike leaves about 1/4 inch long, rather than true needles. The pines were planted in the 1930s for reforestation. Discovered by Captain James Cook, they are native to New Caledonia (Isle of Pines) in the South Pacific between Fiji and Australia.

Beyond the pines the trail climbs through a more open native forest of 'ōhi'a and lama trees. 'Ōhi'a has oval leaves and clusters of delicate red flowers. Early Hawaiians used the flowers in *lei* (garlands) and the wood in outrigger canoes. The hard, durable wood was also carved into god images for *heiau* (religious sites).

Lama has oblong, pointed leaves that are dark green and leathery. Its fruits are green, then yellow, and finally bright red when fully ripe. Lama was sacred to Laka, goddess of the hula. Early Hawaiians used the hard, light-colored wood in temple construction and in hula performances.

After the steep final climb, relax on the summit and take in the magnificent view. In front of you is the broad sweep of Waimānalo (potable water) Bay. To the right the sheer summit ridge ends at Makapu'u (bulging eye) Point. Offshore is Mānana Island, a seabird sanctuary. Along the coast to the left is Kailua (two seas) Bay, stretching to Mōkapu (taboo district) Peninsula. Pu'u o Kona (hill of leeward) is the flat-topped peak on the summit ridge to the left. Wafting up on the trade winds is the earthy odor from the Waimānalo dairies and farms below.

Kuli'ou'ou means sounding knee, referring to the sound made by the *pūniu* (knee drum). Early Hawaiians made the drum out of a coconut shell. They cut off the top portion and covered it with the stretched skin of the surgeonfish, kala. The *pūniu* was tied to the right thigh of the player, just above the knee.

The Kuli'ou'ou Valley hike also starts from the same trailhead. That short, pleasant walk makes an attractive alternative for beginning hikers.

3 Kuliʻouʻou Valley

Type:	Valley
Length:	2-mile round trip
Elevation Gain:	300 feet
Danger:	Low
Suitable for:	Novice
Location:	Kuliʻouʻou Forest Reserve above Kuliʻouʻou
Topo Map:	Koko Head
Access:	Open

Highlights
This short, uncrowded hike explores a lovely leeward valley. The stream there is usually dry, so the walk is a quiet one, the stillness broken only by the sigh of the wind and the song of the white-rumped shama. Along the trail you may glimpse the native bird ʻelepaio.

Trailhead Directions
At Ward Ave. get on Lunalilo Fwy (H-1) Koko Head bound (east).

As the freeway ends, continue straight on Kalanianaʻole Hwy (Rte 72).

Drive by ʻĀina Haina and Niu Valley Center.

Pass Holy Trinity Catholic Church on the right.

Turn left on Kuliʻouʻou Rd. and head into Kuliʻouʻou Valley.

The road jogs left and then right.

Pass Kuliʻouʻou Neighborhood Park on the right. The park has rest rooms and drinking water.

At the Dead End sign turn right on Kalaʻau Pl.

Park on the street just before it ends at a turnaround circle (elevation 260 feet) (map point A).

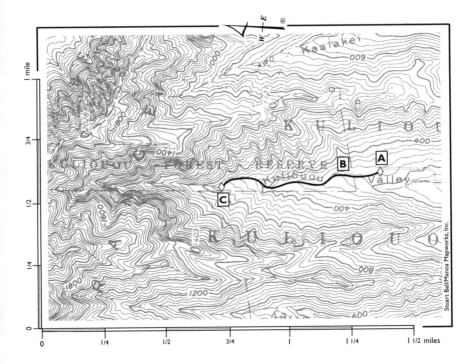

Bus: Route 1 to Kalaniana'ole Hwy and Kuli'ou'ou Rd. Walk 1.3 miles along Kuli'ou'ou Rd. and Kala'au Pl. to the trailhead.

Route Description

At the back of the circle take the one-lane, paved road on the left leading down to Kuli'ou'ou Stream.

Before crossing the stream, bear right on a grassy road by a utility pole.

Enter a clearing with a lone Christmas berry tree in the middle.

The road narrows and becomes the Kuli'ou'ou Valley Trail.

Cross a small gully.

Contour above the intermittent stream through an introduced forest of Christmas berry, koa haole, and guava. Laua'e ferns and native 'ulei shrubs cover the ground.

Reach a signed junction by some small boulders (map point B). Continue straight on the Kuli'ou'ou Valley trail. (On the right the Kuli'ou'ou Ridge Trail switchbacks up the side of the valley.)

Cross several more small gullies. Look for kukui and noni trees there.

The trail descends briefly to Kuli'ou'ou Stream.

Climb steadily under arching Christmas berry and guava on a rocky trail.

Pass a small waterfall and pool on the left.

At a second waterfall reach the end of the improved trail (elevation 520 feet) (map point C).

Notes

Kuli'ou'ou Valley is the perfect hike for beginners. The walk is short and shady on a well-groomed and graded path. Most hikers take the nearby ridge trail, leaving the valley uncrowded and peaceful. Unfortunately, the route does have some mosquitoes despite the usually dry conditions. If you want to see the stream running, take this hike on the day after a heavy rainstorm in winter.

Kuli'ou'ou means sounding knee, referring to the sound made by the *pūniu* (knee drum). Early Hawaiians made the drum out of a coconut shell. They cut off the top portion and covered it with the stretched skin of the surgeonfish, kala. The *pūniu* was tied to the right thigh of the player, just above the knee.

On the trail look for the sprawling native shrub 'ūlei in the sunny sections. It has small, oblong leaves arranged in pairs; clusters of white, roselike flowers; and white fruit. Early Hawaiians ate the berries and used the tough wood for making digging sticks, fish spears, and 'ūkēkē (the musical bow).

In the forest look and listen for the white-rumped shama. It is black on top with a chestnut-colored breast and a long black-and-white tail. The shama has a variety of beautiful songs and often mimics other birds. A native of Malaysia, the shama has become widespread in introduced forests such as this one.

Lining the gullies are kukui trees. Their large, pale green leaves resemble those of the maple, with several distinct lobes. Early Polynesian voyagers introduced kukui into Hawai'i. They used the wood to make gunwales and seats for their outrigger canoes. The flowers and sap became medicines to treat a variety of ailments. Early Hawaiians strung the nuts together to make *lei hua* (seed or nut garlands). The oily kernels became house candles and torches for night spearfishing.

Watch for the 'elepaio, a small native bird. It is brown on top and white underneath with a black throat and a dark tail, usually cocked. The bird roams the forest understory catching insects on the fly or on vegetation. 'Elepaio are very curious, which is why you can sometimes see them.

Although the improved trail ends at the second waterfall, farther exploration upstream is possible. The path, however, quickly becomes rough and ill defined. Eventually it disappears altogether as the valley walls close in. Walk in the streambed until a high waterfall blocks the way.

The Kuli'ou'ou Ridge hike starts from the same trailhead. That popular climb offers an appealing route to the Ko'olau (windward) summit for intermediate hikers.

4 Hawai'iloa Ridge

Type:	Ungraded ridge
Length:	5-mile round trip
Elevation Gain:	1,500 feet
Danger:	Low
Suitable for:	Novice, Intermediate
Location:	Honolulu Watershed Forest Reserve above Hawai'i Loa
Topo Map:	Koko Head
Access:	Conditional; show an ID and sign a liability waiver at the security station on Pu'u 'Ikena Dr.

Highlights
This popular hike mostly rambles along a gently rolling ridge. Near the end, however, is a stiff climb to the scenic Ko'olau summit. Along the way are intriguing native dryland and rain forest plants.

Trailhead Directions
At Ward Ave. get on Lunalilo Fwy (H-1) Koko Head bound (east).

As the freeway ends, continue straight on Kalaniana'ole Hwy (Rte 72).

Pass 'Āina Haina Public Library on the left.

By Kawaiku'i Beach Park, turn left on Pu'u 'Ikena Dr. To make the left turn, bear right initially and then cross Kalaniana'ole at the traffic light.

Stop at the security station and check in.

Ascend steadily through Hawai'i Loa Ridge subdivision.

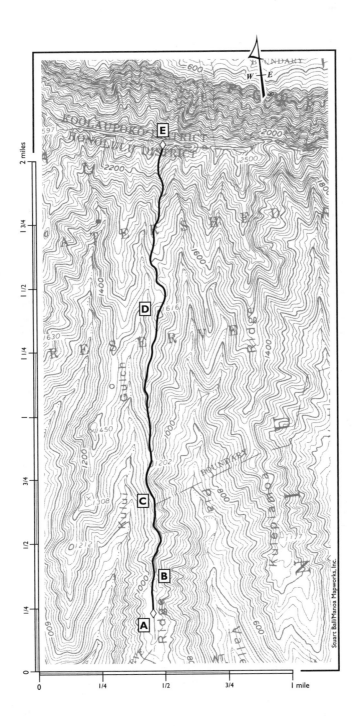

At the top of the subdivision, Pu'u 'Ikena narrows and is lined with ironwood trees.

The road ends at a water tank marked Hawai'i Loa 1125 Reservoir.

Park in the lot on the right just past the water tank (elevation 1,100 feet) (map point A).

Bus: Route 1 to Kalaniana'ole Hwy and Pu'u 'Ikena Dr. Walk 1.8 miles up Pu'u 'Ikena Dr. to the trailhead.

Route Description

From the lot, walk *mauka* (inland) crossing a gravel jogging path.

Behind a chain pick up a dirt road along the crest of Hawai'iloa Ridge. Among the Christmas berry and strawberry guava trees are the native shrubs 'ūlei and pūkiawe.

After crossing a rocky, eroded section, the dirt road ends (map point B). To the right are views of Koko Crater (Kohelepelepe) and Koko Head (Kuamo'o Kāne).

Continue on an ungraded trail as the ridge narrows briefly.

Walk through three stands of ironwoods.

Traverse a relatively level section of the ridge (map point C). Ignore a side trail on the right. Look for the native lama tree and 'akoko and 'ilima shrubs.

Ascend gradually through a long stretch of guava (waiawī). The trail briefly follows several wires, the remains of an old fence line. Watch for an occasional native alahe'e tree.

Cross another relatively level section and then descend gradually, still through guava.

After passing a downed koa trunk, resume the ascent through a dark guava forest.

Reach a distinct, moss-covered knob (map point D). To the side is a partial view of the summit.

The guava ends shortly afterward. Keep right and descend steeply through uluhe ferns.

Work to the left side of the ridge through native koa and 'ōhi'a trees.

Turn right and up to regain the ridgeline.

As the ridge flattens, work left again through uluhe.

By several guava trees, swing right across the broad ridge.

Bear left up an eroded slope to regain the distinct crest of the ridge.

Climb steadily along the open ridge. Look for native kōpiko trees and naupaka kuahiwi shrubs.

The angle of ascent increases markedly. Some of the steep sections have plastic steps to stabilize the trail and make the going easier. On the left is a lone lapalapa tree with its fluttering leaves.

As the top nears, the vegetation thickens.

Reach the Ko'olau summit at a small knob (elevation 2,520 feet) (map point E).

Notes

This popular hike comes in two parts. The first is an enjoyable walk on a gently rolling ridge. The second is a steep, slippery climb to the Ko'olau summit. Many hikers do the first part and then turn around at the moss-covered knob. The scramble to the top, however, is well worth the effort for the marvelous views and native plants en route.

Although ungraded, the trail in the first part is mostly dry and wide. Look out for small guava stumps along the path. In the second part the trail is eroded and slippery in spots. The very steep stretches have plastic steps to stabilize the treadway and make the going easier. Nevertheless, watch your footing constantly, especially on the return.

Along the short road section are the native shrubs 'ūlei and pūkiawe. Sprawling 'ūlei has small, oblong leaves arranged in pairs; clusters of white, roselike flowers; and white fruit. Early Hawaiians ate the berries and used the tough wood for making digging sticks, fish spears, and 'ūkēkē (the musical bow). Pūkiawe has tiny, rigid leaves and small white, pink, or red berries.

Before entering the guava tree tunnel, look for the native shrub 'akoko. It has rounded, oblong leaves arranged in pairs. The branches are dark brown and jointed with white rings. Early Hawaiians used the milky sap mixed with charcoal to stain their outrigger canoe hulls.

For much of the hike the trail is lined with guava trees (waiawī). They have glossy, light green leaves and smooth brown bark. Unfortunately their yellow fruit has a tart, bitter taste. Cattle, grazing in the adjacent valleys, probably spread the guava to the ridge top.

In the stands of guava watch for the 'elepaio, a small native bird. It is brown on top and white underneath with a black throat and a dark tail, usually cocked. The bird roams the forest understory catching insects on the fly or on vegetation. 'Elepaio are very curious, which is why you can sometimes see them.

While climbing to the summit, take a breather and look leeward. From left to right you can see Koko Crater (Kohelepelepe), Koko Head (Kuamo'o Kāne), Diamond Head, and Waikīkī (spouting water). In the distance is the Wai'anae (mullet water) Range.

Want another excuse to take a break? Look for kōpiko, a native member of the coffee family. It has leathery, oblong leaves with a light green midrib. Turn the leaf over to see a row of tiny holes (piko [navel]) on either side of the midrib. The kōpiko produces clusters of little white flowers and fleshy, orange fruits.

At the top you can see the windward coast from Kualoa (long back) Point to Waimānalo (potable water). The triple-peaked mountain just to the left is Olomana (forked hill) with Mōkapu (taboo district) Point behind. Along the summit ridge to the left is Kōnāhuanui (large fat testicles), the highest peak in the Ko'olau (windward) Range. To the right along the summit is flat-topped Pu'u o Kona (hill of leeward).

For a more challenging outing, combine the Hawai'iloa Ridge and Wiliwilinui hikes. Go up Hawai'iloa, turn left along the Ko'olau summit ridge, and then go down Wiliwilinui. The summit section is for experienced hikers only because the trail is narrow, overgrown, and sometimes socked in.

5 Wiliwilinui

Type:	Ungraded ridge
Length:	5-mile round trip
Elevation Gain:	1,300 feet
Danger:	Low
Suitable for:	Novice, Intermediate
Location:	Honolulu Watershed Forest Reserve above Wai'alae Iki
Topo Map:	Koko Head
Access:	Conditional; pick up a parking permit at the guard station on Laukahi St.

Highlights
This short, popular hike follows a dirt road and then a steep trail to the Ko'olau summit. Along the trail portion is a fair assortment of native forest plants. At the top are spectacular views of both sides of the island.

Trailhead Directions
At Ward Ave. get on Lunalilo Fwy (H-1) Koko Head bound (east).

As the freeway ends, continue straight on Kalaniana'ole Hwy (Rte 72).

Just past Kalani High School turn left on Laukahi St.

Drive up through Wai'alae Iki subdivision.

Stop at the guard station for Wai'alae Iki V and get a parking permit.

At the road end turn left on 'Oko'a St.

The road narrows after going through a small circle.

Park in the small lot on the right just before the road is blocked by a chain (elevation 1,180 feet) (map point A).

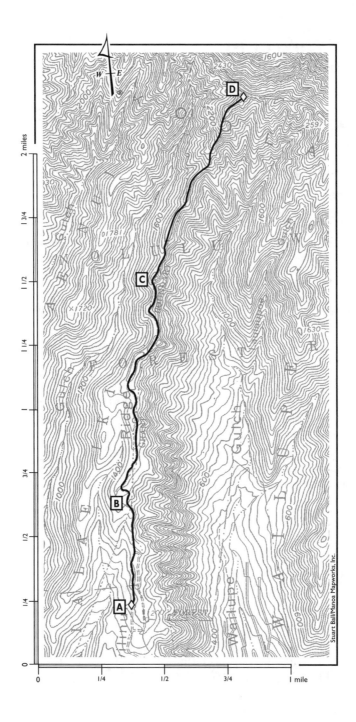

Bus: Route 21 to Laukahi St. and Lālea Pl. Walk 1.1 miles up Laukahi and 'Oko'a St. to the trailhead.

Route Description
Go around the chain and proceed up the one-lane paved road through Formosa koa.

The paved road ends at a water tank.

Continue straight on a dirt road, which climbs Wiliwilinui Ridge. The road is lined with guava (waiawī) and ironwood trees.

Utility lines come in on both sides and parallel the ridge (map point B). To the right is a good view of Koko Crater (Kohelepelepe) and Koko Head (Kuamo'o Kāne).

The road goes over three small humps. Pass several stands of Cook pines.

Contour left around a large knob on the ridge.

Go around another knob through native koa trees.

The road ends at a vehicle turnaround (map point C).

Pick up the Wiliwilinui Trail on the left.

Climb steadily on dirt steps to a group of utility poles.

Stroll through a pleasant, level section. Look for native 'ōhi'a and kōpiko trees and naupaka kuahiwi shrubs with their white half-flowers.

Ascend to a second group of utility poles on a small knob.

Begin the final climb to the summit. The very steep sections of the trail are deeply rutted. Watch your footing, especially if the ground is slick.

Pass a lone loulu palm on the left.

The angle of ascent decreases past a utility relay station.

Reach the Ko'olau summit at a small knob (elevation 2,480 feet) (map point D).

Notes
With its road, utility lines, and relay station this popular hike is hardly a wilderness experience. Nevertheless, it is the most easily accessible route to the Ko'olau summit. Along the trail section are magnificent views and some interesting native plants.

Wiliwilinui (large wiliwili tree) combines a pleasant road walk with a steep ridge climb. Built by the U.S. Army in 1941, the road is wide and well graded, although slick and muddy in spots. Watch for mountain bikers. The trail has several steep, deeply rutted sections near the top. Watch your footing, especially on the return.

Much of the dirt road is lined with guava trees (waiawī). They have glossy, light green leaves and smooth brown bark. Unfortunately their yellow fruit has a tart, bitter taste. Cattle, grazing in the adjacent valleys, probably spread the guava to the ridge top.

Along the road watch for the 'elepaio, a small native bird. It is brown on top and white underneath with a black throat and a dark tail, usually cocked. The bird roams the forest understory catching insects on the fly or on vegetation. 'Elepaio are very curious, which is why you can sometimes see them.

Near the road end native koa and 'ōhi'a trees begin to replace the guava and other introduced species. Koa has sickle-shaped foliage and pale yellow flower clusters. Early Hawaiians made surfboards and outrigger canoe hulls out of the beautiful red brown wood. Today it is made into fine furniture. 'Ōhi'a has oval leaves and clusters of delicate red flowers. Early Hawaiians used the flowers in lei (garlands) and the wood in outrigger canoes. The hard, durable wood was also carved into god images for heiau (religious sites).

Along the trail look for the native shrub naupaka kuahiwi. It has light green, toothed leaves and white half-flowers. The unusual appearance of the flowers has given rise to several unhappy legends. According to one, a Hawaiian maiden believed her lover unfaithful. In anger she tore all the naupaka flowers in half. She then asked him to find a whole flower to prove his love. He was, of course, unsuccessful and died of a broken heart.

From the summit are superb views of both sides of the island. In front is the windward coast from Kualoa (long back) Point to Waimānalo (potable water). The triple-peaked mountain dead ahead is Olomana (forked hill) with Mōkapu (taboo district) Point behind. Along the summit ridge to the left is Kōnāhuanui (large fat testicles), the highest peak in the Ko'olau (windward)

Range. To leeward are Koko Head (Kuamoʻo Kāne), Diamond Head, and Waikīkī (spouting water). In the distance is the Waiʻanae (mullet water) Range.

At the top look down and left for a small group of native loulu palms clinging to the cliff. They have rigid, fan-shaped fronds in a cluster at the top of a ringed trunk. Early Hawaiians used the fronds for thatch and plaited the blades of young fronds into fans and baskets. On the way down look for a lone loulu on the right after the relay station.

For a more challenging outing, combine the Wiliwilinui and Lanipō hikes. Go up Wiliwilinui, turn left along the Koʻolau summit ridge, and then go down Lanipō. You can also turn right along the summit ridge and go down Hawaiʻiloa Ridge. The summit connectors are for experienced hikers only because the trail is narrow, overgrown, and sometimes socked in.

6 Lanipō (Mauʻumae)

Type:	Ungraded ridge
Length:	7-mile round trip
Elevation Gain:	2,000 feet
Danger:	Low
Suitable for:	Intermediate
Location:	Honolulu Watershed Reserve above Maunalani Heights
Topo Map:	Honolulu, Koko Head
Access:	Open

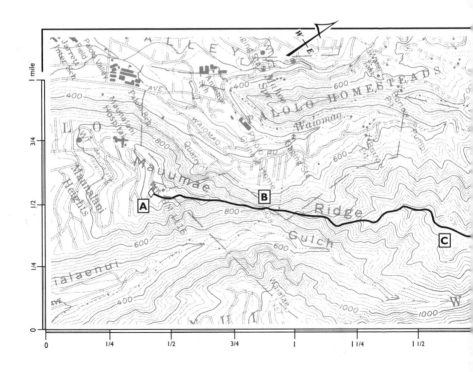

Highlights

This up-and-down hike follows the crest of Mau'umae Ridge to the Ko'olau summit. Along the route you see a rich variety of native plants and a hidden volcanic crater. From the lookout on Kainawa'aunui peak is a splendid view of much of the windward coast.

Trailhead Directions

At Ward Ave. get on Lunalilo Fwy (H-1) Koko Head bound (east).

Take the Koko Head Ave. exit (26A) in Kaimukī.

At the top of the off-ramp, turn left on Koko Head Ave.

Cross Wai'alae Ave.

At the first stop sign turn left, still on Koko Head Ave.

At the next stop sign turn right on Sierra Dr.

Switchback up the ridge to Maunalani Heights.

Pass Maunalani Community Park on the right and Maunalani

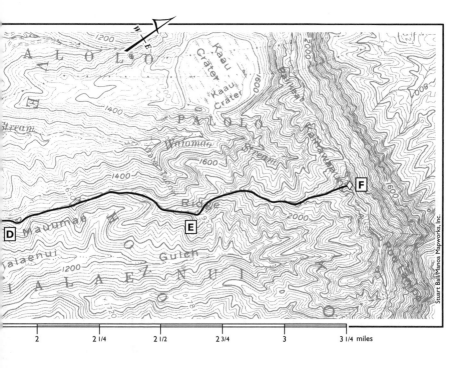

Nursing Center on the left. The park has rest rooms and drinking water.

At the end of Sierra Dr. by the last bus stop bear right and up on Maunalani Circle.

The road swings left in a broad arc.

On the right look for a chain-link fence enclosing a Board of Water Supply tank.

Park on the street next to the fence (elevation 1,040 feet) (map point A).

Bus: Route 14 to the end of Sierra Dr. Walk 0.2 mile up Maunalani Circle to the trailhead.

Route Description

Walk back down the road to a signed junction at the corner of the fence. Turn left on the Mauʻumae Trail, which follows a narrow right-of-way between two chain-link fences. The passageway is directly across from the garage of 4970 Maunalani Circle.

At the end of the fences keep left through a small grove of ironwood trees.

Reach the crest of Mauʻumae Ridge and bear right along it.

Descend moderately along the mostly open ridge. There is one rocky section. Along the trail are Formosa koa trees and the native dryland shrubs ʻūlei, ʻaʻaliʻi, and ʻilima.

Pass a utility pole on the left (map point B).

Begin a long climb interspersed with two dips. On the left is Pālolo Valley and on the right, Waiʻalae Nui Gulch.

After the second dip ascend steeply through native koa trees. At this point the ridge is quite massive and well forested.

After a pleasant level section through ironwood trees, climb steeply again on a badly eroded trail.

Stroll through a lovely stretch of koa and ʻiliahi trees.

Ascend a flat, grassy knob with a 360-degree view (map point C). Look behind you for an unusual view of the back side of Diamond Head. Along the coast to the left is Maunalua Bay and Koko Head (Kuamoʻo Kāne) and Koko Crater (Kohelepelepe).

The vegetation gradually changes from dryland to rain forest.

Native 'ōhi'a trees form a loose canopy, and uluhe ferns cover the ground.

Climb a second, shady knob topped by two Cook pines (map point D).

Traverse a long, relatively level section with many small ups and downs. The path leaves the ridgeline for short periods.

As the trail resumes serious climbing, pass a lookout on the left above a landslide. Across Pālolo Valley is Ka'au Crater, nestled below the Ko'olau summit ridge. A waterfall cascades from the lip of the crater.

The ridge narrows, and the vegetation thins.

After a stiff climb reach a flat, open knob with a panoramic view (map point E).

Descend off the knob, passing a spindly Cook pine.

Ascend steeply on a rutted trail to a broad hump. From its top you can see the last stretch of the hike.

Descend the back side of the hump and go left around a slippery, exposed spot.

Begin the final climb to the summit along the open, windswept ridge. On the right is a magnificent 'ōhi'a tree, which seems to be partly sheltered from the trade winds.

As the top nears, the trail steepens and becomes severely eroded.

Reach the Ko'olau summit at a peak called Kainawa'aunui (elevation 2,520 feet) (map point F). Look for dwarf kōpiko trees in the area.

Notes

Lanipō is the classic O'ahu ridge hike. It offers a challenging climb, breathtaking windward views, and a surprising variety of native plants. As a bonus, you get to see a little-known volcanic crater and a lovely waterfall.

Start early to avoid the hot sun in the open lower section of the Mau'umae (wilted grass) Trail. Watch your footing constantly because the ungraded route is often rough, sometimes muddy, and occasionally narrow. The middle section of the trail may be overgrown with grass and scratchy uluhe ferns. The upper section is wet and cool, with vegetation stunted by the wind.

Some hikers are put off by the initial rocky descent, which, of course, must be climbed on the way back in the hot afternoon. Don't be discouraged! The native plants and the spectacular views farther in are well worth the extra effort.

On the trail look for the native dryland shrubs 'a'ali'i and 'ilima. 'A'ali'i has shiny, narrow leaves and red seed capsules. Early Hawaiians used the leaves and capsules in making lei (garlands). When crushed or boiled, the capsules produced a red dye for decorating kapa (bark cloth). 'Ilima has oblong, serrated leaves, about 1 inch long. The yellow orange flowers strung together make a regal lei, in both ancient and modern Hawai'i.

In the dry lower section of the trail, koa is the most common native tree. It has sickle-shaped foliage and pale yellow flower clusters. Early Hawaiians made surfboards and outrigger canoe hulls out of the beautiful red brown wood. Today it is made into fine furniture.

Less common along the trail is 'iliahi, the native sandalwood tree. Its small leaves are dull green and appear wilted. 'Iliahi is partially parasitic, with outgrowths on its roots that steal nutrients from nearby plants. Early Hawaiians ground the fragrant heartwood into a powder to perfume their kapa. Beginning in the late 1700s, sandalwood was indiscriminately cut down and exported to China to make incense and furniture. The trade ended around 1840 when the forests were depleted of 'iliahi.

In the wetter middle section of the trail, native 'ōhi'a gradually replaces koa as the dominant tree. 'Ōhi'a has oval leaves and clusters of delicate red flowers. Early Hawaiians used the flowers in lei and the wood in outrigger canoes. The hard, durable wood was also carved into god images for heiau (religious sites).

From the lookout above the landslide you can see Ka'au (forty), a circular crater at the base of the Ko'olau summit ridge. The crater was probably formed by steam explosions when rising molten rock encountered groundwater. Both Ka'au and Diamond Head Craters are remnants of the last volcanic activity on O'ahu, known as the Honolulu Series.

According to Hawaiian legend, the demigod and trickster Māui wanted to join all the islands together. From Ka'ena (the heat) Point he threw a great hook toward Kaua'i, hoping to snare the island. Initially the hook held fast, and Māui gave a mighty tug on the line. A huge boulder, known as Pōhaku o Kaua'i, dropped at his feet. The hook sailed over his head and fell in Pālolo Valley, forming Ka'au Crater. The crater may have been named after Ka'auhelemoa, a supernatural chicken that lived in the valley.

Near the top look for kōpiko, a native member of the coffee family. It has leathery, oblong leaves with a light green midrib. Turn the leaf over to see a row of tiny holes (*piko* [navel]) on either side of the midrib. The kōpiko produces clusters of little white flowers and fleshy, orange fruits.

From the summit lookout on Kainawa'aunui are some impressive windward views. In front is Olomana (forked hill) with its three peaks. To the right is the broad sweep of Waimānalo (potable water) Bay. Farther along the coast are Kailua (two seas) and Kāne'ohe (cutting husband) Bays, separated by Mōkapu (taboo district) Peninsula. You can also see the sheer Ko'olau (windward) summit ridge from flat-topped Pu'u o Kona (hill of leeward) on the right to twin-peaked Kōnāhuanui (large fat testicles) on the left.

To reach the actual peak of Lanipō (dense), turn right along the Ko'olau summit ridge. For a more challenging outing, continue past Lanipō and go down the Wiliwilinui Trail. The summit section is for experienced hikers only because it is steep, narrow, overgrown, and sometimes socked in.

7 Mount Olympus (Awaawaloa)

Type:	Ungraded ridge
Length:	6-mile round trip
Elevation Gain:	1,500 feet
Danger:	Low
Suitable for:	Novice, Intermediate
Location:	Honolulu Watershed Reserve above St. Louis Heights
Topo Map:	Honolulu
Access:	Open

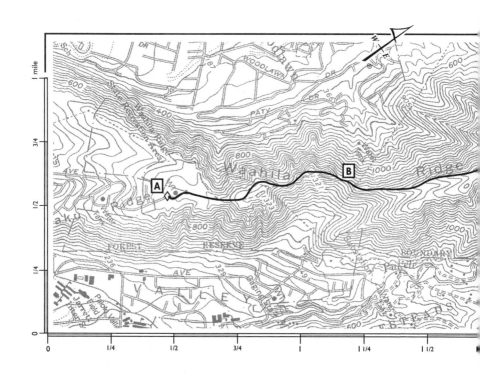

Highlights
In back of Mānoa Valley is the massive peak of Olympus (Awaawaloa). This hike to its broad summit follows mist-shrouded Waʻahila Ridge. Along the way are impressive views and interesting native plants.

Trailhead Directions
At Ward Ave. get on Lunalilo Fwy (H-1) Koko Head bound (east).

Take the King St. exit (25A).

Turn left underneath the freeway onto Waiʻalae Ave.

At the second traffic light, by the Chevron gas station, turn left on St. Louis Dr.

Switchback up St. Louis Heights.

A block before St. Louis Dr. ends, turn right on Peter St.

Turn left on Ruth Pl. at the bus turnaround circle.

Enter Waʻahila Ridge State Recreation Area.

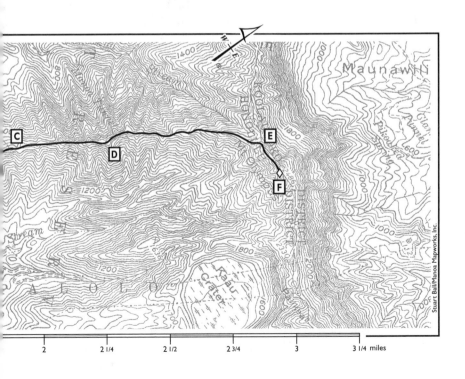

Park in the lot at the road end (elevation 1,080 feet) (map point A). The recreation area has rest rooms uphill to the right.

Bus: Route 14 to Peter St. and Ruth Pl. Walk 0.4 mile along Ruth Pl. and through the recreation area to the trailhead.

Route Description

Take the paved path at the back of the parking lot.

Almost immediately cross another paved walkway and continue straight on the wide Wa'ahila Ridge Trail through tall Cook pines.

Pass a small water tank on the left.

Climb steadily through ironwood and strawberry guava trees.

Just before a level clearing turn left and down to bypass a utility line tower.

Descend steeply through ironwoods and then cross an open, windswept saddle. Mānoa Valley is on the left, and Pālolo Valley on the right. Look for the native shrub 'ilima.

Climb over three small, but rough, humps on Wa'ahila Ridge. Among the Christmas berry and silk oak trees is the native tree alahe'e.

Bear right to bypass a large knob with utility poles on top (map point B).

Climb gradually through solid strawberry guava, passing several banyan trees on the left.

The trail becomes a wide, open avenue through native 'ōhi'a and koa trees.

Reach a grassy lookout where a side ridge comes in on the right. *Makai* (seaward) are Diamond Head, Waikīkī, and downtown Honolulu.

Reach a signed junction (map point C). Bear right and up on a narrow trail along the main ridge. (To the left the wide Kolowalu Trail heads down a side ridge into Mānoa Valley.)

Climb steeply to a knoll. On top are kī (ti) plants and native 'ōhi'a 'āhihi trees.

Descend a short rock face with the aid of a makeshift ladder. You can bypass the rock face using a steep trail on the right.

Ascend to a second knoll with good views of the back of Mānoa Valley (map point D). Across the valley are the wooded volcanic cinder cones of Round Top and Tantalus (Puʻu ʻŌhiʻa). Along the Koʻolau summit are the peaks of Kōnāhuanui and Olympus (Awaawaloa).

The ridge levels, and the strawberry guava gives way to native forest. Look for kōpiko trees along the trail.

Climb steadily on the now open ridge to a knob below the summit.

Cross a short, level section and then begin the final push to the top.

Climb steeply, at times on a very eroded trail.

Reach the Koʻolau summit at a small overlook (map point E). Turn right along the summit ridge.

Pass a second overlook and go over a small hump.

Reach the lush, broad summit of Mount Olympus (Awaawaloa) (elevation 2,486 feet) (map point F).

Notes

Mount Olympus is the imposing peak along the Koʻolau summit on the east side of Mānoa (vast) Valley. Early Hawaiians called the mountain Awaawaloa (long valley). Perhaps because of its commanding presence, students at Punahou, a nearby private school, renamed the peak after the mythical home of the Greek gods. Although the effort required to reach the top is hardly Olympian, the climb does provide a challenge for intermediate hikers. The exciting finish along the open, windswept summit ridge is particularly memorable.

The route as far as the grassy overlook is a popular novice hike. Although ungraded, the trail is wide and well trodden, for the most part. Take care on the rooty and rocky spots, especially if you are new to hiking. Beyond the Kolowalu (eight creeping) Trail junction the trail becomes rough, narrow, and sometimes muddy. It may be overgrown with scratchy uluhe ferns and Clidemia shrubs. Watch your footing at all times.

The hike starts in a grove of tall Cook pines planted in 1931–1932 for reforestation. They have overlapping, scalelike leaves about 1/4 inch long, rather than true needles. Discovered by Captain James Cook, they are native to New Caledonia (Isle of Pines) in the South Pacific between Fiji and Australia.

Past the pines the trail is lined with strawberry guava trees (waiawī ʻulaʻula). They have glossy, dark green leaves and smooth brown bark. Their dark red fruit is delicious, with a taste reminiscent of strawberries. The guavas usually ripen in August and September. Pickings may be slim along the trail, however, because of its popularity. The strawberry guava is a native of Brazil but was introduced to Hawaiʻi from England in the 1800s.

In the forest understory look and listen for the white-rumped shama. It is black on top with a chestnut-colored breast and a long black-and-white tail. The shama has a variety of beautiful songs and often mimics other birds. A native of Malaysia, the shama has become widespread in introduced forests such as this one.

Past the windswept saddle are a few native alaheʻe trees. Their oblong leaves are shiny and dark green. Alaheʻe has fragrant white flowers that grow in clusters at the branch tips. Early Hawaiians fashioned the hard wood into farming tools, and hooks and spears for fishing.

At the top of the knoll past the Kolowalu Trail junction, look for native ʻōhiʻa ʻāhihi trees. They have narrow, pointed leaves with red stems and midribs. Their delicate red flowers grow in clusters and are similar to those of the more common ʻōhiʻa. ʻŌhiʻa ʻāhihi is found only in the Koʻolau (windward) and Waiʻanae (mullet water) Mountains on Oʻahu.

When the strawberry guava finally ends, look for kōpiko, a native member of the coffee family. It has leathery, oblong leaves with a light green midrib. Turn the leaf over to see a row of tiny holes (piko [navel]) on either side of the midrib. The kōpiko produces clusters of little white flowers and fleshy, orange fruits.

After the steep climb enjoy the remarkable views from the overlooks along the Koʻolau summit. Over 2,000 feet down lies the windward side of the island. Slightly to the right is triple-peaked Olomana. To the left along the sheer, fluted flanks of the summit ridge is Kōnāhuanui (large fat testicles), the highest peak in the Koʻolau Range. For a view into Kaʻau (forty) Crater and of

Lanipō (dense) peak, walk to the far side of the broad summit of Olympus.

At the summit is a lush thicket of native vegetation. Look for hāpu'u tree ferns with delicate, sweeping fronds. Their trunks consist of roots tightly woven around a small central stem. The brown fiber covering the young fronds of hāpu'u is called *pulu*. Also in evidence are 'ōlapa trees and pū'ahanui (kanawao) shrubs.

For a shorter, but tougher approach to Mount Olympus, take the Kolowalu Trail. It starts in Mānoa Valley and climbs to the junction with the Wa'ahila Ridge Trail. See the Pu'u Pia (arrow-root hill) hike for driving instructions to the trailhead.

8 Pu'u Pia

Type:	Foothill
Length:	2-mile round trip
Elevation Gain:	500 feet
Danger:	Low
Suitable for:	Novice
Location:	Honolulu Watershed Forest Reserve above Mānoa
Topo Map:	Honolulu
Access:	Open

Highlights
This short, delightful walk climbs Pu'u Pia, a rounded hill toward the back of Mānoa Valley. From the bench at the top there are scenic views of the valley and the ridges and peaks surrounding it.

Trailhead Directions
Get on S. King St. Koko Head bound (east).
   Turn left on Punahou St.
   Pass Punahou School on the right and enter Mānoa Valley.
   The road splits and narrows to two lanes. Take the right fork onto E. Mānoa Rd.
   Pass Mānoa Market Place on the right.
   Toward the back of the valley the road splits. Take the right fork, still on E. Mānoa Rd.
   At the road end turn left on Alani Dr.
   Park on Alani Dr. just before its intersection with Woodlawn Dr. (elevation 370 feet) (map point A).

Bus: Route 6 to Alani Dr. and Woodlawn Dr.

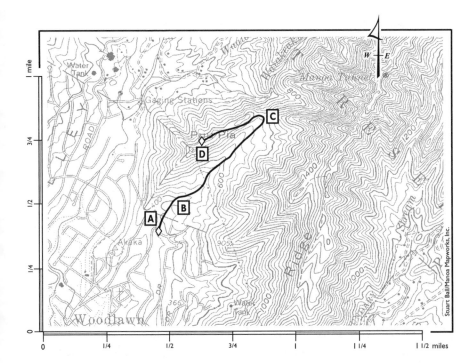

Route Description

Continue along Alani Dr. on foot. The paved one-lane road soon turns to gravel and then dirt after passing the last house.

Climb over a wire across the road.

Parallel an intermittent stream on the left.

Reach a signed junction in a clearing with a lone albizia tree and a shelter (map point B). Keep left on the road, which is the Pu'u Pia Trail. (The wide path to the right is the Kolowalu Trail, which ascends to Wa'ahila Ridge.)

Climb gradually along the side of a wide gulch through eucalyptus, paperbark, and other introduced trees. Look and listen for the white-rumped shama.

Cross several small intermittent streams coming in from the right.

Swing left around the back of the gulch past some tall ironwood trees (map point C). Ignore side trails to the left and right.

Ascend gradually along the left side of Pu'u Pia through native koa trees.

Gain the ridgeline and bear left up it through strawberry guava. At a clearing is a lone naupaka kuahiwi shrub.

Reach the top of Pu'u Pia at a bench (elevation 880 feet) (map point D). A makeshift trail continues briefly along the ridge to two utility poles.

Notes

Pu'u Pia (arrowroot hill) is another good hike for beginners. The trail is short and well groomed, and the climbing is gradual. The views of Mānoa (vast) Valley are well worth the minimal effort required to get to the top.

Pia or arrowroot is a perennial herb introduced to Hawai'i by early Polynesian voyagers. Its large, lobed leaves resemble those of a papaya. Pia produces a tall flower stalk and an underground tuber similar to a potato. Early Hawaiians used powdered starch from the tuber as a thickening for *haupia* (coconut pudding).

On the trail look and listen for the white-rumped shama. It is black on top with a chestnut-colored breast and a long black-and-white tail. The shama has a variety of beautiful songs and often mimics other birds. A native of Malaysia, the shama has become widespread in introduced forests such as this one.

Along the Pu'u Pia ridge are native naupaka kuahiwi shrubs and koa trees. Naupaka kuahiwi has light green, toothed leaves and white half-flowers. Koa has sickle-shaped foliage and pale yellow flower clusters. Early Hawaiians made surfboards and outrigger canoe hulls out of the beautiful red brown wood. Today it is made into fine furniture.

From the summit bench is a 360-degree view around Mānoa Valley. Facing the ocean, you can see the University of Hawai'i and Waikīkī (spouting water). On the left Wa'ahila (Mānoa rain) Ridge climbs to Mount Olympus (Awaawaloa) on the Ko'olau (windward) summit ridge. On the ridge to the right are the wooded volcanic cinder cones of Round Top and Tantalus (Pu'u 'Ōhi'a). At the back of the valley is Kōnāhuanui (large fat testicles), the highest peak in the Ko'olau Range.

For a more difficult ridge hike, take the Kolowalu (eight creeping) Trail. It branches off the Pu'u Pia Trail at the shelter and ascends steeply to Wa'ahila Ridge. From there you can climb Mount Olympus or follow the ridge *makai* (seaward) to Wa'ahila State Recreation Area.

9 'Aihualama-'Ōhi'a
(via Mānoa Falls)

Type:	Foothill
Length:	8-mile round trip
Elevation Gain:	1,700 feet
Danger:	Low
Suitable for:	Novice, Intermediate
Location:	Honolulu Watershed Forest Reserve above Mānoa
Topo Map:	Honolulu
Access:	Open

Highlights

This hike climbs to the top of Tantalus (Pu'u 'Ōhi'a) from Mānoa Valley. Along the way is lovely Mānoa (Waihī) Falls with its small swimming hole. On Tantalus are a surprising variety of native plants and some panoramic views.

Trailhead Directions

Get on S. King St. Koko Head bound (east).

Turn left on Punahou St.

Pass Punahou School on the right and enter Mānoa Valley.

The road splits and narrows to two lanes. Take the left fork onto Mānoa Rd.

At the stop sign proceed straight across the intersection on a much wider Mānoa Rd.

Pass Mānoa Elementary School on the right.

Park on Mānoa Rd. just before it narrows at the intersection with Wa'akaua St. (elevation 280 feet) (map point A).

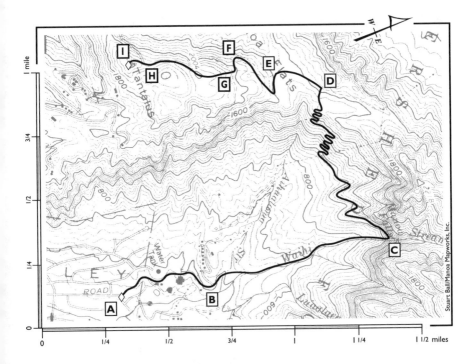

Bus: Route 5 to Mānoa Rd. and Kumuone St. Walk 0.5 mile to the start of the hike.

Route Description

Continue along Mānoa Rd. on foot.

Walk underneath the pedestrian overpass at the entrance to Paradise Park.

Follow the main road as it curves left and then right around the lower parking lot of the park.

As the paved road turns left to Harold L. Lyon Arboretum, proceed straight on a gravel road (map point B).

The road narrows and becomes Mānoa Falls Trail. On the left is a hau tree tangle.

Cross 'Aihualama Stream on a bridge.

Swing left to parallel Waihī Stream.

Bear right and ford a side stream.

Cross a muddy, rooty stretch. Stay on the trail to minimize erosion.

Ascend gradually alongside Waihī Stream. On the left is another hau tangle. Above are introduced albizia trees with their whitish bark and layered branches. The trail is paved with rocks in several spots.

Climb more steeply now as the valley narrows. You can see the top of Mānoa Falls through the trees.

Go through a bamboo grove.

Just before the falls, reach a signed junction with the 'Aihualama Trail in a grove of mountain apple trees. For now, continue the short distance to lovely Mānoa (Waihī) Falls and its small swimming hole (map point C).

Backtrack to the signed junction. Turn right and up on the 'Aihualama Trail. The path is narrow and rocky at first but soon widens.

Work in and out of three gulches cut into the side of Mānoa Valley. The third gulch has a small stream. Look for yellow ginger and red heliconia in this section.

Break out into the open near some utility lines. Below is Lyon Arboretum. Beyond, Mānoa Valley stretches to the ocean.

Climb the side of the valley on fourteen switchbacks. Kī (ti) plants line the trail. After the eighth switchback are two concrete posts. Between nine and thirteen a dense stand of cinnamon trees blots out the daylight.

At the top of the ridge turn right, through a bamboo forest.

Reach a signed junction with the Pauoa Flats Trail (map point D). Turn left on it. (To the right the flats trail leads to Nu'uanu Valley overlook.) Memorize that junction for the return trip.

Begin crossing Pauoa Flats on a very rooty trail.

Reach another signed junction. Continue straight on the flats trail. (To the right the Nu'uanu Trail leads down to the Judd Trail and Nu'uanu Valley.)

Right after the Nu'uanu Trail junction, the trail forks. Keep left, still on the flats trail.

Reach a signed junction (map point E). Continue straight on the flats trail. (To the right the Kalāwahine Trail connects with the Mānoa Cliff Trail and Tantalus Dr.)

Climb gradually up the flank of Tantalus on one long, lazy switchback. The trail is lined with fragrant white and yellow ginger and colorful kāhili ginger.

By some native 'ōhi'a trees reach a signed junction with a posted trail map (map point F). Turn left on the Mānoa Cliff Trail. (To the right the cliff trail leads to Tantalus Dr.) Look for a native kōpiko tree, identified by marker no. 19, just beyond that junction on the left.

Contour around the side of Tantalus.

Reach another signed junction (map point G). Turn sharp right and up on the Pu'u 'Ōhi'a Trail. (The cliff trail continues straight, to Round Top Dr.) Right before and after that junction are several native white hibiscus trees, known as koki'o ke'oke'o.

Ascend gradually through 'ōhi'a and koa trees and then bamboo. On the right you can see Nu'uanu Pali between the peaks of Lanihuli and Kōnāhuanui.

Go around to the right of a Hawaiian Telephone installation.

Turn right on a one-lane paved road.

The road dips and then climbs gradually.

Reach an intersection (map point H). Take the road on the left heading up Tantalus. (The road on the right leads down to Tantalus Dr. The Pu'u 'Ōhi'a Trail continues on the left, descending steeply to Tantalus Dr.)

The road ends at a second Hawaiian Telephone installation with a tower.

Take the path by a short utility pole.

Reach the summit of Tantalus (Pu'u 'Ōhi'a) (elevation 2,013 feet) (map point I). The concrete base of a triangulation station provides a good viewing platform. Look for native 'ōhi'a 'āhihi trees *mauka* (inland) of the summit.

Notes

The 'Aihualama-'Ōhi'a hike combines a pleasant walk in Mānoa (vast) Valley with a steady climb to the top of Tantalus (Pu'u 'Ōhi'a). The short stroll to the falls at the back of the valley is popular with tourists and local people alike, especially on weekends. Few people go beyond the falls because of the long ascent to the ridge top. Around Tantalus you may see some hikers because there are other, easier routes to the summit.

This hike uses five of the eighteen different trails in the Honolulu *mauka* trail system. Because of the many trails in the area, the route has numerous junctions, which come fast and furiously. Fortunately, all are signed, and most are obvious. Memorize the key junctions for the return trip.

The trails making up this hike are generally well graded, although muddy and rooty in spots. The 'Aihualama (eat lama fruit) Trail climbs out of the valley on long, lazy switchbacks. Because of heavy traffic, the wet and eroded sections of the Mānoa Falls Trail have been improved with gravel, plastic steps, and wooden walkways. The upgraded trail allows you to keep just ahead of the hungry mosquitoes in the valley.

The falls trail initially passes a tangled grove of hau trees with large, heart-shaped leaves. Their flowers are bright yellow with a dark red center and resemble those of a hibiscus. Early Hawaiians used the wood for kites and canoe outriggers, the bark for sandals, and the sap as a laxative.

Mānoa Falls makes a refreshing rest stop or a good turnaround point for novice hikers. Early Hawaiians aptly named the falls Waihī (trickling water). If you can't resist, take a quick dip in the small pool there. Otherwise, wait until the return trip when you are really hot and tired. If it is late July, you may get some delicious mountain apples ('ōhi'a 'ai) from the grove in front of the falls.

Lining the middle switchbacks of the 'Aihualama Trail are kī (ti) plants. They have shiny leaves, 1–2 feet long, that are arranged spirally in a cluster at the tip of a slender stem. Early Polynesian voyagers introduced ti to Hawai'i. They used the leaves for house thatch, skirts, sandals, and raincoats. Food to be cooked in an *imu* (underground oven) was first wrapped in ti leaves. A popular sport with the commoners was *ho'ohe'e kī* or ti-leaf sledding. The sap from ti plants was used to stain canoes and surfboards.

Near the junction of the Mānoa Cliff and Pu'u 'Ōhi'a Trails, look for the native hibiscus koki'o ke'oke'o. It is a small tree with dark green, oval leaves. Its large flowers have white petals and pink to red stamens.

To the left of the Hawaiian Telephone access road is a small volcanic crater, mostly hidden by vegetation. An explosive eruption from that crater formed a cinder cone downwind, the summit of Tantalus. Lava from that eruption flowed across the flats and down into upper Pauoa Valley. Both Tantalus and Diamond Head Craters are remnants of the last volcanic activity on O'ahu, called the Honolulu Series.

From the top of Tantalus is a 360-degree view. To leeward you can see Diamond Head, Waikīkī (spouting water), Pearl Harbor, and, in the distance, the Wai'anae (mullet water) Range. *Mauka* (inland) is Tantalus Crater, and beyond is the Ko'olau (windward) summit. From left to right along the ridge is Pu'u Keahi a Kahoe (hill of Kahoe's fire), Lanihuli (turning royal chief), Nu'uanu Pali (cool height cliff), Kōnāhuanui (large fat testicles), and Olympus (Awaawaloa).

Mauka of the Tantalus summit are several native 'ōhi'a 'āhihi trees. They have narrow, pointed leaves with red stems and midribs. Their delicate red flowers grow in clusters and are similar to those of the more common 'ōhi'a. 'Ōhi'a 'āhihi is found only in the Ko'olau and Wai'anae Mountains on O'ahu.

For a shorter hike from the same trailhead, turn right on the Pauoa Flats Trail to the Nu'uanu Valley overlook. For an exciting traverse, combine the 'Aihualama-'Ōhi'a and Nu'uanu-Judd hikes. Go up 'Aihualama to the valley overlook and then down Nu'uanu-Judd. Leave a car at each trailhead or take the bus.

10 Makiki-Tantalus

Type:	Foothill
Length:	8-mile loop
Elevation Gain:	1,500 feet
Danger:	Low
Suitable for:	Novice, Intermediate
Location:	Honolulu Watershed Forest Reserve above Makiki
Topo Map:	Honolulu
Access:	Open

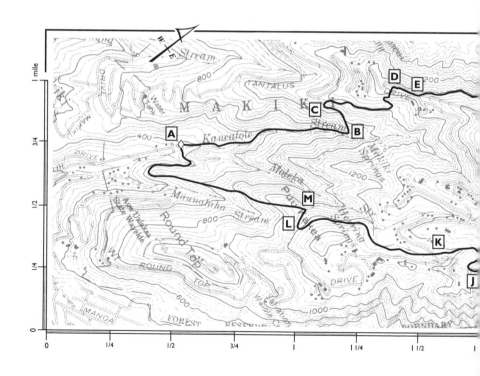

Highlights
This elongated loop hike circles Tantalus (Puʻu ʻŌhiʻa) peak. Along the roundabout route are introduced songbirds and a surprising variety of native forest plants. From scenic overlooks are views of three valleys and the Koʻolau Range.

Trailhead Directions
Get on S. King St. Koko Head bound (east).

Turn left on Keʻeaumoku St.

After going over the freeway, turn right on Wilder Ave.

Take the first left on Makiki St.

After crossing Nehoa St. at the first traffic light, bear left on Makiki Heights Dr.

As the road switchbacks to the left, continue straight on an unnamed paved road.

Enter the Makiki Forest Recreation Area.

Pass the Hawaiʻi Nature Center on the right.

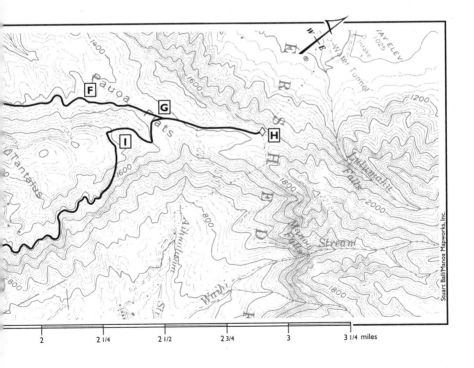

Park on the side of the road just before a gate blocks further progress (elevation 360 feet) (map point A). Rest rooms are behind the Hawai'i Nature Center office on the right just before the gate.

Bus: Route 4 to Wilder Ave. and Makiki St. Walk 1.0 mile up Makiki St. and Makiki Heights Dr. to the recreation area.

Route Description

Just before the gate is a signed junction. Continue along the road through the gate to the Kanealole Trail. (To the right is the Maunalaha Trail, which is the return leg of the loop.)

Pass the Forestry and Wildlife District Office and base yard.

The pavement ends, and the road becomes the wide Kanealole Trail.

Ascend gradually next to Kanealole Stream. In the gulch on the right are kukui trees and tangled hau groves. Listen for the Japanese bush warbler.

Under a kukui tree reach a signed junction at the end of the Kanealole Trail (map point B). Turn left and up on the Makiki Valley Trail. (To the right the valley trail crosses the stream and contours to Round Top Dr.)

Climb steadily up a ridge on two switchbacks past huge mango trees.

At the third switchback reach a signed junction (map point C). Turn sharp right and up on the Nahuina Trail. (The valley trail continues straight, through a large fallen trunk, and eventually reaches Tantalus Dr.)

Contour along the side of the ridge, crossing several gullies.

Climb gradually on four switchbacks. Kī (ti) plants line the trail, and a native koa tree arches overhead.

At the ridge top reach a signed junction at the end of Nahuina Trail (map point D). Turn right on paved Tantalus Dr.

At the end of the stone wall on the left reach another signed junction (map point E). Bear left off the road onto the Kalāwahine Trail. (The one-lane paved road just to the right of the trail leads up to the top of Tantalus.)

Begin to contour along the flank of Tantalus (Puʻu ʻŌhiʻa), working into and out of numerous gulches. Look and listen for the white-rumped shama in the introduced forest.

Pass a wooden bench on the left and go through a grove of coffee trees with their shiny leaves.

Reach a signed junction (map point F). Keep left on the Kalāwahine Trail. (The Mānoa Cliff Trail curves right and contours around Tantalus.)

The path swings right and climbs briefly to Pauoa Flats.

In the flats reach a signed junction at the end of the Kalāwahine Trail (map point G). Turn left on the Pauoa Flats Trail. (The flats trail to the right is the return portion of the loop.)

Almost immediately reach another signed junction. Continue straight on the flats trail. (To the left the Nuʻuanu Trail heads down into Nuʻuanu Valley and connects with the Judd Trail.)

In a bamboo grove reach a third signed junction. Continue straight on the flats trail. (To the right the ʻAihualama Trail leads down to Mānoa Falls.)

Walk through dark cinnamon trees on a muddy trail.

Reach windy Nuʻuanu Valley overlook (elevation 1,640 feet) (map point H). Nearby are some native ʻōhiʻa ʻāhihi trees and naupaka kuahiwi shrubs with their white half-flowers.

Retrace your steps past the ʻAihualama and Nuʻuanu Trail junctions to the junction with the Kalāwahine Trail (map point G). Now continue straight on the flats trail.

Climb gradually up the flank of Tantalus on one long, lazy switchback. The trail is lined with fragrant white and yellow ginger and colorful kāhili ginger.

By some native ʻōhiʻa trees reach a signed junction with a posted trail map (map point I). Turn left on the Mānoa Cliff Trail. (To the right the cliff trail leads back to the Kalāwahine Trail.) Look for a native kōpiko tree, identified by marker no. 19, just beyond that junction on the left.

Reach another signed junction. Continue straight on the cliff trail. (To the right the Puʻu ʻŌhiʻa Trail leads to the top of Tantalus.)

Begin contouring around Tantalus (Puʻu ʻŌhiʻa), working into and out of several small gulches. Watch for native māmaki trees and the white hibiscus, kokiʻo keʻokeʻo.

Pass a viewpoint with a bench on the left. At the back of Mānoa Valley you can see two waterfalls. Across the valley are Puʻu Pia and Mount Olympus (Awaawaloa).

Pass the remains of the Mānoa Cliff Bamboo Rest Bench on the right in a grove of bamboo.

The Mānoa Cliff Trail ends at a signed switchback. Turn right and up on the connector trail to Round Top Dr. (map point J).

Ascend briefly to cross a broad ridge through strawberry guava.

Descend into a small gulch and bear left down it. The trail widens and is lined with plastic planks.

Cross paved Round Top Dr. to reach a signed junction at a small parking lot (map point K). Continue straight and down on the Moleka Trail.

Descend gradually through bamboo, paralleling Moleka Stream, but well above it.

Climb briefly on two switchbacks up the side of Puʻu Kākea on a narrow trail.

By a banyan tree reach a signed junction at the end of the Moleka Trail (map point L). Turn right on the wide Makiki Valley Trail. (To the left the valley trail contours back to Round Top Dr.)

By a posted trail map and a bench reach a signed junction with the ʻUalakaʻa and Maunalaha Trails (map point M). Take the latter by bearing slightly left and down. (The ʻUalakaʻa Trail requires a sharp left and leads to Round Top Dr. To the right the valley trail contours to Tantalus Dr.)

Descend steeply through eucalyptus, first on the left side of the ridge and then on the ridgeline itself. The trail is rocky and rooty.

Bear right off the ridgeline by several Cook pines.

Descend the slope on two switchbacks following a line of pines.

Walk downstream briefly, passing *loʻi* (*kalo* or taro terraces).

Cross Kanealole Stream on a bridge.

Reach the signed junction near the nature center office and the gate (map point A).

Notes

Makiki-Tantalus is a grand sightseeing tour on O'ahu's best-developed trail network. The hike uses eight of the eighteen different trails in the Honolulu *mauka* trail system. Because of the many trails in the area, the route has numerous junctions, which come fast and furiously. Fortunately, all are signed, and most are obvious. Follow the narrative closely to stay on course.

The trails making up this hike are generally wide and well graded, although muddy and rooty in spots. On the return watch your step on the narrow sections of the Moleka Trail. Take your time descending the rocky, rooty Maunalaha (flat mountain) Trail.

Along the Mānoa (vast) Cliff Trail are small signs identifying some of the native and introduced plants. The signs are keyed to an inexpensive pamphlet, Mānoa Cliff Trail Plant Guide, available from the Hawai'i Nature Center office at the start of the hike.

Past the forestry base yard on the Kanealole Trail, listen for the Japanese bush warbler (uguisu), a bird often heard, but rarely seen. Its distinctive cry starts with a long whistle and then winds down in a series of notes. The bush warbler is olive brown on top with a white breast and a long tail.

The gulches along the loop are often lined with kukui trees. Their large, pale green leaves resemble those of the maple, with several distinct lobes. Early Polynesian voyagers introduced kukui into Hawai'i. They used the wood to make gunwales and seats for their outrigger canoes. The flowers and sap became medicines to treat a variety of ailments. Early Hawaiians strung the nuts together to make *lei hua* (seed or nut garlands). The oily kernels became house candles and torches for night spearfishing.

While contouring around Tantalus (Pu'u 'Ōhi'a) on the Kalāwahine (the day of women) Trail, look and listen for the white-rumped shama. It is black on top with a chestnut-colored breast and a long black-and-white tail. The shama has a variety of beautiful songs and often mimics other birds. A native of Malaysia, the shama has become widespread in introduced forests such as this one.

From the windy overlook at the end of the Pauoa Flats Trail you can look down into Nuʻuanu (cool height) Valley with its reservoir. The massive peak across the valley is Lanihuli (turning royal chief). The saddle to the right of Lanihuli is Nuʻuanu Pali (cliff). You can see the windward coast through the gap in the Koʻolau (windward) summit ridge. To the right of the Pali is mist-shrouded Kōnāhuanui (large fat testicles) (elevation 3,105 feet), the highest point in the Koʻolau Range.

Near the overlook are several native ʻōhiʻa ʻāhihi trees. They have narrow, pointed leaves with red stems and midribs. Their delicate red flowers grow in clusters and are similar to those of the more common ʻōhiʻa. ʻŌhiʻa ʻāhihi is found only in the Koʻolau and Waiʻanae (mullet water) Mountains on Oʻahu.

One of the more common native trees along the Mānoa Cliff Trail is the hibiscus, kokiʻo keʻokeʻo. It has dark green, oval leaves and large white flowers with pink to red stamens. The showy flowers frequently fall right on the trail.

Also on the cliff trail is māmaki, a small native tree. It has leathery, light green leaves with toothed margins and prominent veins. Along the stems are the white, fleshy fruits. Early Hawaiians used the bark and sap in making *kapa* (bark cloth). They also steeped the leaves to prepare a tea as a tonic.

There are several variations to the route as described. You can, of course, do the hike in the opposite direction if you don't mind reading the narrative in reverse. For a shorter loop, turn right on the Mānoa Cliff Trail to eliminate the extension to the Nuʻuanu Valley overlook. For a mini loop, turn right on the Makiki Valley Trail and then right again on the Maunalaha Trail. Other hikes in the Makiki-Tantalus area are ʻAihualama-ʻŌhiʻa and Nuʻuanu-Judd.

11 Nu'uanu-Judd

Type:	Foothill
Length:	5-mile round trip
Elevation Gain:	1,000 feet
Danger:	Low
Suitable for:	Novice, Intermediate
Location:	Honolulu Watershed Forest Reserve above Nu'uanu
Topo Map:	Honolulu
Access:	Open

Highlights
This hike combines a valley loop with a ridge climb. At the end is a windy overlook of Nu'uanu Valley and Pali. On the return is lovely Jackass Ginger (Ilanawai) pool.

Trailhead Directions
At Punchbowl St. get on Pali Hwy (Rte 61 north) heading up Nu'uanu Valley.
Pass Queen Emma Summer Palace on the right.
Bear right on Nu'uanu Pali Dr.
As the road forks, keep right, still on Nu'uanu Pali Dr.
Cross a stream on a stone bridge.
Pass Polihiwa Pl. and then several houses on the left.
On the right look for several concrete barriers just before a small bridge spanning a reservoir spillway.
Park off the road before or after the bridge (elevation 720 feet) (map point A).

Bus: Route 4 to Nu'uanu Pali Dr. and Kimo Dr. Walk 0.7 mile along Nu'uanu Pali Dr. to the trailhead.

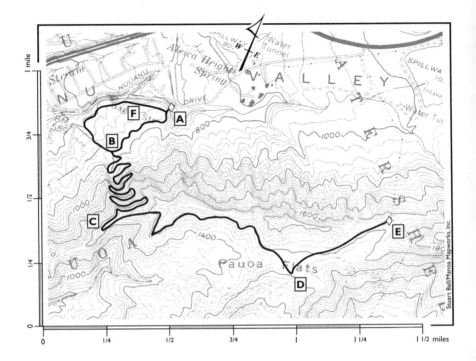

Route Description

Go around the barriers and walk across a flat clearing formerly used as a parking lot.

Descend to Nu'uanu Stream through ironwood trees on the unmarked Judd Trail.

Cross the stream immediately upon reaching it. (Do not take the trail heading downstream along the near bank.)

On the far bank reach a signed junction in a bamboo grove. Continue straight on the wide trail heading away from the stream. (The trail on the right along the stream is the return leg of the Judd loop.)

Turn right and contour into and out of several small gullies through eucalyptus and Cook pines. Ignore side trails heading upslope or down to the stream.

Enter the Charles S. Judd Memorial Grove of Cook pines.

As the trail descends, bear left into a shallow gully and cross it.

Almost immediately reach a signed junction (map point B). Turn left and up on the Nu'uanu Trail. (The Judd loop continues straight downhill and is the route on the return.)

Ascend gradually up the side of Nu'uanu Valley on eighteen (count 'em) switchbacks. After the thirteenth, leave the Cook pines behind. After the fifteenth, pass a rock cliff dripping with water. Along the trail are kī (ti) plants.

After passing a banyan tree, reach the top of a ridge (map point C). Turn left along it.

Climb steadily on a wide, grassy trail under native koa and 'ōhi'a trees. On the right across Pauoa Valley is Tantalus (Pu'u 'Ōhi'a), a wooded volcanic cone. On the left are views of Nu'uanu Valley, Honolulu, and, in the distance, the Wai'anae Range.

At a small clearing, bear right off the ridgeline.

Contour along the right side of the ridge. Look for the native shrubs maile and naupaka kuahiwi.

Descend gradually toward Pauoa Flats. The trail widens as it enters the flats.

Reach a signed junction at the end of the Nu'uanu Trail (map point D). Turn left on the Pauoa Flats Trail. (To the right the flats trail connects with the Mānoa Cliff Trail.)

In a bamboo grove reach another signed junction. Continue straight on the flats trail. (To the right the 'Aihualama Trail leads down to Mānoa Falls.)

Walk through dark cinnamon trees on a muddy trail.

Reach windy Nu'uanu Valley overlook (elevation 1,640 feet) (map point E). Nearby are some native 'ōhi'a 'āhihi trees and naupaka kuahiwi shrubs.

Retrace your steps along the Pauoa Flats and Nu'uanu Trails.

At the junction with the Judd Trail turn left to complete the loop (map point B).

Descend the ridge in a series of gentle switchbacks. Ignore a side trail on the left.

Emerge from the Cook pines and cross two gullies with tangled hau groves.

Swing right and contour well above Nu'uanu Stream along the edge of the pine grove.

Reach an obscure junction marked by a small metal stake. Keep left toward the stream.

Below on the left is Jackass Ginger (Ilanawai) pool (map point F). Take the makeshift trail down to the pool.

After a cooling swim, climb back up from the pool and turn left on the main trail heading upstream.

Contour above the stream briefly and then descend to it.

Pass a large banyan tree on the far bank and go through a bamboo grove.

Reach the initial junction and stream crossing.

Turn left, recross Nu'uanu Stream, and climb the far bank to the main road (map point A).

Notes

Most people just take the short Judd loop, go for a swim in Jackass Ginger pool, and call it a day. If you have a little more ambition and stamina, try the less-popular Nu'uanu extension up the side of the valley. The views from the ridge top and the overlook are well worth the climb.

The two trails making up this hike are generally well graded, although muddy and rooty in spots. Completed in 1991, the Nu'uanu Trail climbs out of the valley on long, lazy switchbacks. The many side trails can make the Judd loop difficult to follow, especially on the return along the stream. If you lose the official trail, keep heading upstream until you reach the initial crossing by the bamboo grove. Watch your step crossing the stream and watch your backside for marauding mosquitoes.

On the initial section of the Judd loop is a large grove of Cook pines. They have overlapping, scalelike leaves about 1/4 inch long, rather than true needles. Discovered by Captain James Cook, the pines are native to New Caledonia (Isle of Pines) in the South Pacific between Fiji and Australia. The grove and the loop trail are named after Charles S. Judd, the Territorial Forester during the 1930s when the pines were planted.

On top of the ridge look back into lower Nu'uanu Valley, the site of a pivotal battle in Hawaiian history. In 1795 Kamehameha, chief of the Big Island, invaded O'ahu, landing a large force at Waikīkī. Opposing him was an army massed in

Nu'uanu Valley under the direction of Kalanikupule, chief of O'ahu and Maui. The first engagement took place at Pū'iwa (startled) near the present Judd St. Kamehameha attacked the confident defenders who were protected by a long rock wall. The battle was hotly contested until the invaders brought up a field cannon. Its accurate fire shattered rocks in the wall and killed a key commander. The startled O'ahu warriors broke ranks and retreated up the valley, closely pursued by the attackers. Gradually the retreat turned into a rout. Some defenders escaped up the sides of the valley. Most, including Kalanikupule, made a last stand at Nu'uanu Pali and were killed or driven over the cliff there. With the victory Kamehameha extended his control over all the Hawaiian islands.

Along the ridge section are the native shrubs naupaka kuahi-wi and maile. Naupaka has light green, toothed leaves and white half-flowers. Maile has shiny, pointed leaves, tangled branches, and fruit resembling a small olive. The fragrant leaves and bark make a distinctive open-ended *lei* (garland), in both ancient and modern Hawai'i.

From the windy viewpoint at the end you can look down into Nu'uanu (cool height) Valley with its reservoir. The massive peak across the valley is Lanihuli (turning royal chief). The saddle to the right of Lanihuli is Nu'uanu Pali (cliff). You can see the windward coast through the gap in the Ko'olau (windward) summit ridge. To the right of the Pali is mist-shrouded Kōnāhuanui (large fat testicles) (elevation 3,105 feet), the highest point in the Ko'olau Range.

Near the overlook are several native 'ōhi'a 'āhihi trees. They have narrow, pointed leaves with red stems and midribs. Their delicate red flowers grow in clusters and are similar to those of the more common 'ōhi'a. 'Ōhi'a 'āhihi is found only in the Ko'olau and Wai'anae (mullet water) Mountains on O'ahu.

On the way back stop for a swim at lovely Jackass Ginger pool. Its original name is Ilanawai (tranquil water); the stream tumbles over rapids into a deep, placid swimming hole. In the early 1900s local youths renamed the pool after a nearby donkey and the surrounding yellow ginger.

There are two good variations to the route as described. To

climb Tantalus (Pu'u 'Ōhi'a), turn right on the Pauoa Flats Trail and follow the route narrative of the 'Aihualama-'Ōhi'a hike. For an exciting traverse, combine the Nu'uanu-Judd and 'Aihualama-'Ōhi'a hikes. Go up Nu'uanu to the valley overlook and then down 'Aihualama past Mānoa (vast) Falls. Leave a car at each trailhead or take the bus.

12 Kamanaiki

Type:	Ungraded ridge
Length:	5-mile round trip
Elevation Gain:	1,400 feet
Danger:	Low
Suitable for:	Novice, Intermediate
Location:	Honolulu Watershed Forest Reserve above Kalihi
Topo Map:	Honolulu
Access:	Open

Highlights
This hike climbs partway up the ridge on the right side of Kalihi Valley. From lookouts en route and at the end are scenic views of the valley and the Koʻolau summit ridge. Along the way is a surprising variety of native plants.

Trailhead Directions
At Punchbowl St. get on Lunalilo Fwy (H-1) heading ʻewa (west).

Take Likelike Hwy (exit 20A, Rte 63 north) up Kalihi Valley.

At the sixth traffic light, by the pedestrian overpass, turn right on Nalaniʻeha St.

Cross Kalihi Stream on a bridge.

Park on the street near the intersection with Kalihi St. (elevation 240 feet) (map point A).

Bus: Route 7 to Kalihi St. and Nalaniʻeha St.

Route Description
Turn left on Kalihi St. by the Kalihi Uka pumping station.

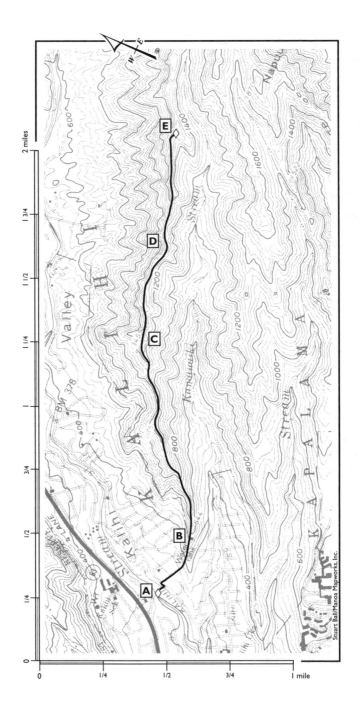

Almost immediately turn right on Manaiki Pl.

At the road end take the concrete stairway straight ahead between two houses. The stairway is just to the left of a utility pole.

Climb steeply up the stairs to the ridgeline.

Bear left on a trail heading up the ridge through an ironwood grove. Lining the route are small kolomona trees with their bright yellow flowers.

Ascend two more flights of stairs to a water tank (map point B).

Keeping the tank on the left, continue up the ridge under ironwoods.

Break out into the open past scattered Formosa koa trees and then climb steeply over a hill.

Ascend over a second hill through a stand of tall Sydney blue gum.

Emerge from the forest into a grassy area dotted with native koa and 'ōhi'a trees. Look for the native shrub naupaka kuahiwi.

Reach a small, eroded knob with good views up and down Kalihi Valley (map point C).

Traverse a narrow windswept section with Christmas berry trees.

Reach a second, less distinct knob by several rose apple trees.

Continue along the ridge past a small ironwood grove to another viewpoint (map point D). Look for maile, a native twining shrub.

Traverse another windswept section on a sometimes narrow trail. Among the 'ōhi'a and strawberry guava trees is the native herb ko'oko'olau.

Climb steadily to a flat-topped hill covered with guava. A cable is provided for assistance at the steepest part. On the far side of the hill are several 'iliahi (sandalwood) trees.

Ascend gradually through scratchy uluhe ferns.

Pass a tall ironwood tree on the left.

Shortly afterward reach a clearing on top of a broad hill (elevation 1,560 feet) (map point E). On the right is an uluhe-covered side ridge. On the left are commanding views of the back of Kalihi Valley and the Ko'olau summit.

Notes

This hike climbs partway up the ridge between Kalihi (the edge) and Kamanaiki (the small branch) Valleys. The route provides a good introduction to the pleasures and pitfalls of ungraded ridge hiking on O'ahu—superb views and intriguing native plants, but also steep climbs and narrow sections. The only real negative is the noise from vehicles on Likelike Hwy below.

The route up the ridge is straightforward and easy to follow. The ungraded trail, however, has several stiff climbs and a few narrow spots. Some sections may be overgrown with introduced shrubs, such as oī (Jamaica vervain), and bristly native uluhe ferns. Watch your step because the vegetation can hide steep drop-offs. Novices should hike as far as feels comfortable and then turn around.

The hike initially ascends through introduced forest. Easily recognized is Sydney blue gum, with its smooth, blue gray bark and very narrow, pointed leaves. The tree is a member of the eucalyptus family and a native of Queensland, Australia. Beginning in the 1930s, blue gum was planted extensively on O'ahu for reforestation.

In the open area past the blue gum is the native shrub naupaka kuahiwi. It has light green, toothed leaves and white half-flowers. The unusual appearance of the flowers has given rise to several unhappy legends. According to one, a Hawaiian maiden believed her lover unfaithful. In anger she tore all the naupaka flowers in half. She then asked him to find a whole flower to prove his love. He was, of course, unsuccessful and died of a broken heart.

After the first viewpoint look for two more native shrubs, maile and ko'oko'olau. Maile has shiny, pointed leaves, tangled branches, and fruit resembling a small olive. The fragrant leaves and bark make a distinctive open-ended lei (garland), in both ancient and modern Hawai'i. Ko'oko'olau is an herb related to the daisy and sunflower families. It has pointed, serrated leaves and flower heads with yellow petals. Early Hawaiians steeped the leaves to make a tea used as a tonic.

Just past the flat-topped hill are a few native 'iliahi (sandalwood) trees. Their small leaves are dull green and appear wilted.

'Iliahi is partially parasitic, with outgrowths on its roots that steal nutrients from nearby plants. Early Hawaiians ground the fragrant heartwood into a powder to perfume their *kapa* (bark cloth). Beginning in the late 1700s, sandalwood was indiscriminately cut down and exported to China to make incense and furniture. The trade ended around 1840 when the forests were depleted of 'iliahi.

From the viewpoints along the ridge you can look down into two valleys, Kamanaiki on the right and Kalihi on the left. *Mauka* the Ko'olau (windward) summit ridge rises abruptly in the back of Kalihi Valley. Along the top are the peaks of Pu'u Kahuauli (dark site hill) on the left and massive Lanihuli (turning royal chief) in front. To leeward you can see west Honolulu and the 'Ewa (crooked) plain.

13 Bowman

Type:	Ungraded ridge
Length:	12-mile round trip
Elevation Gain:	2,400 feet
Danger:	Medium
Suitable for:	Intermediate, Expert
Location:	Honolulu Watershed Forest Reserve above Fort Shafter
Topo Map:	Honolulu, Kāne'ohe
Access:	Open

Highlights
This strenuous hike climbs to the Ko'olau summit from Kalihi Valley. Along the sometimes narrow ridge are incredible views and interesting native plants. Near the top is a hair-raising scramble up the flank of a volcanic cone.

Trailhead Directions
At Punchbowl St. get on Lunalilo Fwy (H-1) heading 'ewa (west).

Take Likelike Hwy (exit 20A, Rte 63 north) up Kalihi Valley.

At the sixth traffic light, by the pedestrian overpass, turn left on Nalani'eha St.

At its end, turn left on Kula Kōlea Dr.

At the next intersection turn right on Nā'ai St.

Park on the street near its end (elevation 320 feet) (map point A).

Bus: Route 2 to School St. and Likelike Hwy. Walk 1.5 miles along Likelike Hwy to the trailhead. Route 7 to Kalihi St. and

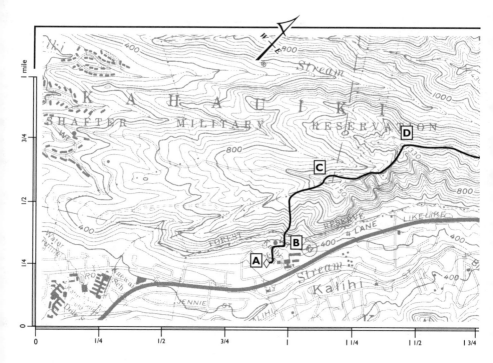

Nalaniʻeha St. Walk 0.5 mile along Nalaniʻeha St. to Likelike Hwy and the trailhead.

Route Description

Continue along Nāʻai St. on foot.

At its end by Kalihi Elementary School, turn left on Hālina St.

Just before it ends at a water tank, turn right into the school playing field and head for the basketball courts.

Between the red and yellow backboards turn left up the side of the ridge on a trail (map point B).

Cross a low retaining wall.

Ascend straight up toward a utility pole.

At the pole bear left and contour briefly.

Resume steep climbing, first through an open area, and then through mixed ironwoods and Christmas berry. The native shrub ʻūlei carpets the ground in the sunny sections; lauʻae ferns cover the shady areas.

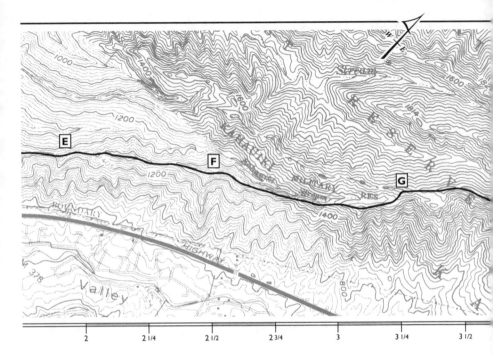

The trail levels off somewhat through an ironwood grove. Keep to the left in this section.

Cross an open grassy area.

The trail ends at a junction with a dirt road. Turn right on the road. Memorize the junction for the return trip.

Climb steeply on the road following the utility lines.

At the crest of the ridge reach a junction with Radar Hill Rd. (map point C). Turn right on it. (To the left the road is semi-paved and leads down to Fort Shafter.)

The overgrown dirt road skirts a hump in the ridge, dips, and then climbs steeply to the left.

At the ridge top reach a junction (map point D). Turn right on the Bowman Trail. (The road swings left toward a power-line tower.)

Almost immediately pass a small concrete building on the right.

Keep left while descending briefly through an ironwood grove.

Pass United States Military Reservation (USMR) marker no. 22 on the left.

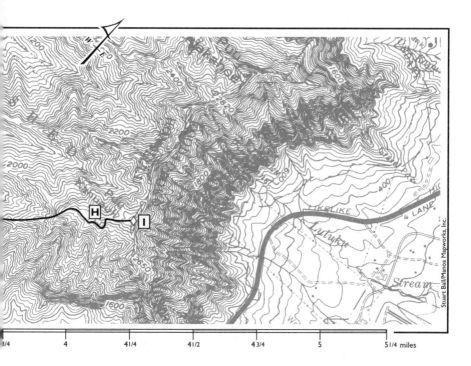

Enter a long stretch of guava (waiawī) trees.

Pass marker no. 21 on the right at the top of a hill (map point E). An opening nearby provides a view of the entire ridge to be climbed.

Cross a level section through mixed introduced forest.

Climb briefly to a second hill with two rocks on top.

Pass two large banyan trees on the left.

Walk under a lovely canopy of native lama trees.

Enter the native rain forest dominated by koa and 'ōhi'a trees. In the understory are naupaka kuahiwi shrubs and uluhe ferns.

Ascend gradually to a third hill. Marker no. 20 is on the right (map point F). There are good views up Kalihi Valley toward the Ko'olau summit.

Come abreast of the last house in Kalihi Valley.

Traverse a series of short, steep descents, passing marker no. 19 on the left.

Cross a narrow, but level, section, inching to the right of a rock face.

Ascend steeply with the aid of a cable.

Shortly afterward pass marker no. 18 on the left in an iron-wood grove.

Climb gradually to marker no. 17 at the top of a hill.

Walk through a relatively level section lined with native hapu'u tree ferns and 'ie'ie. Overhead arch huge koa trees.

Reach the head of Kahauiki Valley. Keep right and up along the ridge.

Descend briefly and then climb steeply through uluhe.

Reach the junction of the two ridges forming the head of Kahauiki Valley (map point G). Bear right to continue to the Ko'olau summit.

Begin climbing gradually toward Pu'u Kahuauli. Along the summit ridge to the right are the peaks of Lanihuli and Kōnāhuanui. Look for the native tree kōpiko and 'ōhi'a with yellow blossoms.

After a steep ascent reach a junction under a spreading koa tree. Continue straight along the main ridge on the grassy trail. (The faint trail on the prominent side ridge to the right leads down to Likelike Hwy.)

Bear right to contour around a distinctive hump in the ridge.

Past the hump turn sharp left up the ridge.

Climb the steep side of Kamanaiki cone with the aid of a cable.

Bear left across the precipitous face of the cone on a narrow, slippery trail (map point H).

Switchback once and resume steep climbing. Again, cables are provided for the worst sections.

The ridge broadens and the angle of ascent eases. Take in the panoramic leeward view. You can see the top of Diamond Head, downtown Honolulu, and Pearl Harbor. In the distance is the Wai'anae Range.

The muddy trail winds through stunted 'ōhi'a trees. Watch for the native shrub pū'ahanui (kanawao) with its creased and toothed leaves.

Climb a small, grassy gully with exposed rock on the right.

At the end of the gully turn right along the ridge.

Bear left, following the ridge. Look for the native tree 'ōlapa with its fluttering leaves.

Reach the Ko'olau summit at Pu'u Kahuauli (elevation 2,740 feet) (map point I).

Notes

Bowman is the most difficult of the ungraded ridge trails in the Ko'olau (windward) Range. The hike starts with a stiff climb, follows a narrow up-and-down ridge, and culminates in the spectacular ascent of the Kamanaiki cone. The only detraction is the noise from vehicles on Likelike Hwy below. The trail was named after Colonel Donald S. Bowman, commander of Fort Shafter during part of World War I.

Start early to avoid the hot sun on the initial climb to the Bowman Trail. Walk gingerly through the narrow, crumbly sections along the ridge. Overgrowing vegetation may mask some dangerous spots. On the final climb test all cables before using them. Turn around if you don't feel comfortable with the exposure.

On the Bowman Trail past the guavas (waiawī) look for lama trees, a remnant of the native dryland forest. Lama has oblong, pointed leaves that are dark green and leathery. Its fruits are green, then yellow, and finally bright red when fully ripe. Lama was sacred to Laka, goddess of the hula. Early Hawaiians used the hard, light-colored wood in temple construction and in hula performances.

Farther along the ridge begins the native rain forest dominated by koa and 'ōhi'a trees. Koa has sickle-shaped foliage and pale yellow flower clusters. Early Hawaiians made surfboards and outrigger canoe hulls out of the beautiful red brown wood. Today it is made into fine furniture.

'Ōhi'a has oval leaves and clusters of delicate red flowers. Early Hawaiians used the flowers in *lei* (garlands) and the wood in outrigger canoes. The hard, durable wood was also carved into god images for *heiau* (religious sites).

Before the final climb watch for kōpiko, a native member of the coffee family. It has leathery, oblong leaves with a light green midrib. Turn the leaf over to see a row of tiny holes (*piko* [navel]) on either side of the midrib. The kōpiko produces clusters of little white flowers and fleshy, orange fruits.

The steep, cabled section climbs Kamanaiki cone, a remnant of the last volcanic activity on Oʻahu, known as the Honolulu Series. During the eruption lava poured from the cone down both sides of the ridge into Kalihi and Manaiki Valleys.

After climbing the cables, calm down by looking for the native shrub pūʻahanui (kanawao), a relative of hydrangea. It has large, serrated, deeply creased leaves and clusters of delicate pink flowers. Early Hawaiians used the plants for medicinal purposes.

Near the summit is the native tree ʻōlapa. Its leaves are opposite, oblong and flutter in the slightest wind. In a special hula stance named after the tree, dancers mimic the exquisite movements of the leaves. Early Hawaiians used the bark, leaves, and purple fruit to make a blue black dye to decorate their *kapa* (bark cloth).

The view from the top is world class or no class depending on the weather. On a clear day you can see the windward coast from Kāneʻohe (cutting husband) Bay to Makapuʻu (bulging eye) Point. Over 2,000 feet below are Hoʻomaluhia Botanical Garden with its lake and Kāneʻohe town. The mist-shrouded peak along the summit to the left is Puʻu Keahi a Kahoe (hill of Kahoe's fire). To the right, across Kalihi (the edge) Valley, is massive Lanihuli (turning royal chief). In the distance on the right is triple-peaked Olomana (forked hill).

For a more challenging outing, combine the Bowman and Puʻu Keahi a Kahoe hikes. From Bowman turn left along the Koʻolau summit ridge and then descend either side of the Keahi a Kahoe loop. The summit connector is for experienced hikers only because it is narrow, overgrown, and frequently socked in.

Alternate access to Bowman is available through Fort Shafter on Radar Hill Rd. However, you must get written permission from the Army. See the Schofield-Waikāne hike for the address.

14 Pu'u Keahi a Kahoe

Type:	Ungraded ridge
Length:	11-mile loop
Elevation Gain:	2,600 feet
Danger:	High
Suitable for:	Intermediate, Expert
Location:	Honolulu Watershed Forest Reserve above Moanalua
Topo Map:	Kāne'ohe
Access:	Conditional; open to individuals and organized groups with permission. Contact Moanalua Gardens, 1352 Pineapple Pl., Honolulu, HI 96819 (phone 833-1944).

Highlights
Pu'u Keahi a Kahoe is the mist-shrouded peak in back of Moanalua (Kamananui) Valley. This challenging climb to its summit features narrow, windswept ridges and sheer cliffs. Along the loop are lofty lookouts and a rich variety of native trees and shrubs.

Trailhead Directions
At Punchbowl St. get on Lunalilo Fwy (H-1) heading 'ewa (west).

Near Middle St. keep left on Rte 78 west (exit 19B, Moanalua Rd.) to 'Aiea.

Take the exit marked Moanalua Valley–Red Hill.

From the off-ramp turn right on Ala Aolani St. heading into Moanalua Valley.

The road ends at Moanalua Valley Park. The park has rest rooms and drinking water.

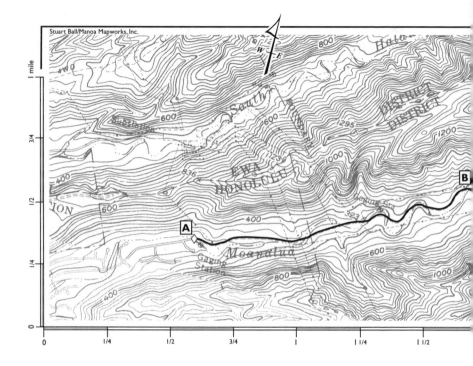

Park on the street just before the park entrance (elevation 240 feet) (map point A).

Bus: Route 16 to Ala Aolani and Ala Lani Streets (weekday mornings and afternoons only). Walk 0.4 mile along Ala Aolani St. to the park.

Route Description
Enter Moanalua Valley Park and proceed along the dirt/gravel road at the back of the parking lot.

Walk around a locked gate to the right.

On the left by a huge monkeypod tree pass a muddy driveway leading to the Douglas Damon house site (marker no. 3).

Cross Moanalua (Kamananui) Stream seven times on stone bridges. Look and listen for the white-rumped shama in the introduced forest.

On the right at the seventh crossing is Pōhakukaluahine, a

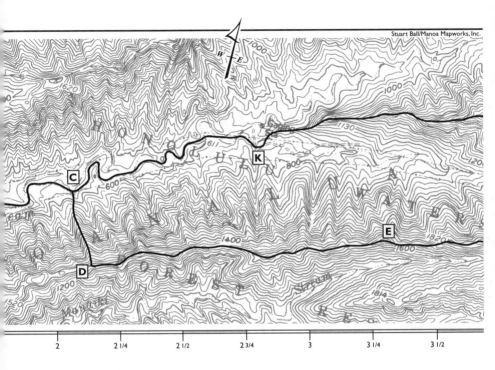

Stuart Ball/Manoa Mapworks, Inc.

large boulder covered with petroglyphs (map point B) (marker no. 10).

Around the bend from the petroglyph rock and before the next stream crossing, reach a junction (marker no. 11). Continue straight on the dirt road. (To the right a short loop trail leads up to the May Damon house site.)

Ford the stream four times. Along the stream are kukui trees and tangled groves of hau.

The road gradually climbs, passing a more open, grassy area on the right.

As the road levels off, reach an obscure junction just before marker no. 12 (map point C). Turn right and climb the low, eroded embankment onto a trail through yellow strawberry guava (waiawī lena).

Keep left and up through two patches of uluhe ferns.

Ascend steadily up a side ridge in solid guava.

The ridge becomes rocky, rooty, and better defined.

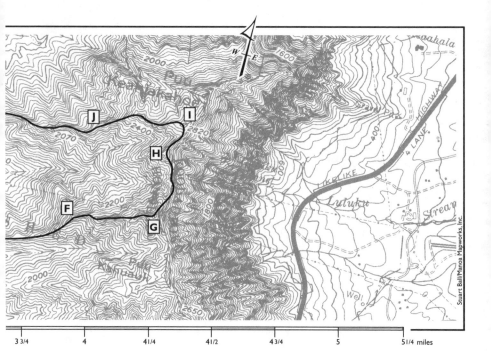

Bear right off the ridgeline to avoid a rock face.

Climb steeply on the sometimes narrow side ridge.

At the ridge top reach a junction with the Tripler (Kauakaulani) Ridge Trail (map point D). Turn left on it. (To the right the trail heads down the main ridge to a U.S. Army housing area above Tripler Medical Center.)

Traverse a relatively gentle section through strawberry guava. Look for an occasional native lama tree.

Climb gradually over a series of small humps in the ridge. The guava gradually gives way to a native forest of koa and 'ōhi'a trees. In the understory are the native shrubs maile and naupaka kuahiwi.

Pass a small landslide on the left.

Climb sharply over two humps with a level section in between (map point E). From the tops are good views of the remaining route up Tripler Ridge, across the summit, and down Keanaakamanō, the middle ridge.

Descend briefly and then resume the ascent past a huge land-slide on the left. Look for native kōpiko and 'ōhi'a 'āhihi trees along the trail.

Negotiate a particularly steep, narrow section.

Reach a junction just before a small, flat clearing marked by a metal pipe (map point F). Continue straight along the main ridge. (To the left an old Hawaiian Electric access trail descends into Moanalua Valley.)

As the vegetation hunkers down, climb steeply to a false summit.

Cross a short level stretch and then ascend gradually over several small humps. Along the trail are native kūkaemoa (alani) and pū'ahanui (kanawao) shrubs.

Reach the Ko'olau summit at a flat, grassy knob (elevation 2,760 feet) (map point G).

Turn left along the summit, passing a power-line tower.

Descend steeply on the narrow ridge. Look for native lapalapa trees.

Cross a level section marked by several metal posts.

Reach a junction where the posts diverge. Keep left and up following the red posts. Native 'ōhelo shrubs with their red berries cling to the cliff.

Pass a lone metal rod on the left.

Bear left around the embankment on the far side of another power-line tower. Native loulu palms loom out of the mist.

Climb steeply past an abandoned radar.

Reach the top of Kaho'omoe'ihikapulani peak (map point H) and descend its back side, still on the summit ridge.

Traverse a relatively level, but extremely narrow and rough section. Watch for the native shrub 'ohe naupaka with its yellow, tube-shaped flowers.

Ascend very steeply on grass, keeping to the edge of the ridge.

Reach the flat summit of Maunakapu (elevation 2,820 feet) (map point I) with its benchmark.

There the trail splits. Take the left fork heading down Keanaakamanō, the middle ridge of Moanalua (Kamananui) Valley. (The right fork continues a short distance along the summit ridge to the top of Pu'u Keahi a Kahoe and the Ha'ikū Stairs.)

The ridge narrows and is severely windswept.

The ridge widens briefly (map point J). Keep to the left to avoid going down a side ridge.

Descend steeply, bear right, and then descend very steeply.

The ridge alternately widens and contracts. Watch out for narrow spots hidden by vegetation.

Pass a small landslide on the right.

Descend steeply and then climb past a rock outcrop.

Resume the descent through huge koa trees and strawberry guava thickets.

Pass a large native 'iliahi (sandalwood) tree on the right.

Swing right and then left through uluhe ferns and more guava.

Cross Moanalua Stream to reach a junction with the dirt road (map point K). Turn right on the road. (To the left the road leads to the start of the Hawaiian Electric access trail.)

Almost immediately reach a junction marked by two boulders on the right. Continue straight on the road. (To the right is the stream trail, which is part of the Moanalua Valley hike.)

Ford the stream six times.

Pass a wide vehicle turnaround area (marker no. 13). On the left a trail leads up to an overlook of the entire valley.

Reach the original junction near marker no. 12 (map point C).

Follow the road back to Moanalua Valley Park (map point A).

Notes

Pu'u Keahi a Kahoe is the mist-shrouded peak in back of Moanalua (Kamananui) Valley. The demanding climb to its summit starts and finishes with a pleasant stroll in the valley. In between is a walk on the wild side. If you are an experienced hiker, try the entire loop and find out why it's known as a "wow" hike.

Keahi a Kahoe more than lives up to its expert rating. The trails making up the loop are steep, narrow, and unimproved. The upper sections are slippery, windswept, and frequently socked in. Watch your footing constantly, whether over rock, roots, or mud. Some trail sections may be overgrown with *Clidemia* shrubs and scratchy uluhe ferns. The vegetation can mask narrow spots, making them doubly dangerous.

Pu'u Keahi a Kahoe means the hill of Kahoe's fire. In ancient times two brothers left their parents and settled on the windward side. Pahu was a fisherman and lived near Kāne'ohe Bay. Kahoe was a *kalo* (taro) farmer in Ha'ikū (sharp break) Valley. The two often traded gifts, poi for fish. Stingy Pahu, however, always gave Kahoe the leftover bait fish, rather than the fresh catch. Kahoe eventually learned of his brother's deceit from their sister.

Soon afterward the crops failed, and the fish mysteriously disappeared. Those with some food took to cooking at night to conceal the smoke from their hungry neighbors. Kahoe continued to cook during the day because the smoke from his *imu* (underground oven) only appeared at the very top of the *pali* (cliff) near a pointed peak. Starving Pahu knew the smoke was from *keahi a Kahoe* but did not dare approach his brother for food.

Along the road look and listen for the white-rumped shama. It is black on top with a chestnut-colored breast and a long black-and-white tail. The shama has a variety of beautiful songs and often mimics other birds. A native of Malaysia, the shama has become widespread in introduced forests such as this one. Until the 1920s, the owners grazed cattle in the valley, resulting in the destruction of much of the original native vegetation.

On Tripler (Kauakaulani) Ridge past the long stretch of guava look for kōpiko and 'ōhi'a āhihi trees. Kōpiko is a native member of the coffee family. It has leathery, oblong leaves with a light green midrib. Turn the leaf over to see a row of tiny holes (*piko* [navel]) on either side of the midrib. The kōpiko produces clusters of little white flowers and fleshy, orange fruits.

Native 'ōhi'a 'āhihi trees have narrow, pointed leaves with red stems and midribs. Their delicate red flowers grow in clusters and are similar to those of the more common 'ōhi'a, which you saw on the way up. 'Ōhi'a 'āhihi is found only in the Ko'olau (windward) and Wai'anae (mullet water) Mountains on O'ahu.

Closer to the Ko'olau summit are the native shrubs pū'ahanui (kanawao) and kūkaemoa (alani). Pū'ahanui, a relative of hydrangea, has large, serrated, deeply creased leaves and clusters of delicate pink flowers. Kūkaemoa (chicken dung) shrubs have curled, dark green leaves, which give off a slight anise odor. The fruits resemble miniature cauliflowers or chicken droppings.

The views all along the summit ridge are spectacular, if the weather cooperates. Over 2,000 feet straight down are Kāne'ohe town and Ho'omaluhia Botanical Garden. You can see the windward coast from Kāne'ohe (cutting husband) to Waimānalo (potable water) Bays. The triple-peaked mountain on the right is Olomana (forked hill). On the way down the whole of Moanalua (Kamananui) Valley spreads out in front of you. In the distance are Pearl Harbor and the Wai'anae Range.

The native plants along the summit are as intriguing as the views are spectacular. Look for lapalapa trees, loulu palms, and 'ohe naupaka shrubs. Lapalapa has roundish leaves arranged in groups of three that flutter in the slightest wind. Early Hawaiians used the bark, leaves, and purple fruit to make a blue black dye to decorate their *kapa* (bark cloth). The leaves also make a distinctive *lei* (garland).

Loulu palms have rigid, fan-shaped fronds in a cluster at the top of a ringed trunk. Early Hawaiians used the fronds for thatch and plaited the blades of young fronds into fans and baskets. 'Ohe naupaka has narrow, pointed leaves growing in clumps at the end of the branches. The distinctive tube-shaped flowers are bright yellow orange.

There are several variations to the loop as described. You can, of course, do the complete hike in reverse. Intermediates can try either side of the loop and then return the same way. The old Hawaiian Electric trail provides alternate access to Tripler Ridge. The route starts on the left just before the dirt road crosses the stream and ends at a vehicle turnaround. The trail, however, is badly eroded and may be overgrown.

For a more challenging loop, combine the Pu'u Keahi a Kahoe and Bowman hikes. At the top of Tripler (Kauakaulani) Ridge turn right along the Ko'olau summit and then descend Bowman. The summit connector is for experienced hikers only because it is narrow, overgrown, and frequently socked in. For a less difficult outing, try the Moanalua Valley hike that starts from the same trailhead. The notes section of that hike describes some of the numbered points of interest in the valley.

15 Moanalua (Kamananui) Valley

Type:	Valley
Length:	11-mile round trip
Elevation Gain:	1,500 feet
Danger:	Low
Suitable for:	Novice, Intermediate
Location:	Honolulu Watershed Forest Reserve above Moanalua
Topo Map:	Kāneʻohe
Access:	Conditional; open to individuals and organized groups with permission. Contact Moanalua Gardens, 1352 Pineapple Pl., Honolulu, HI 96819 (phone 833-1944).

Highlights
This classic stream hike winds through a lovely valley rich in historical sites and legends. Along the way are a small swimming hole, a boulder covered with petroglyphs, and over forty stream crossings. Near the end a short climb leads to a windward overlook on the Koʻolau summit ridge.

Trailhead Directions
At Punchbowl St. get on Lunalilo Fwy (H-1) heading ʻewa (west).

Near Middle St. keep left on Rte 78 west (exit 19B, Moanalua Rd.) to ʻAiea.

Take the exit marked Moanalua Valley–Red Hill.

From the off-ramp turn right on Ala Aolani St. heading into Moanalua Valley.

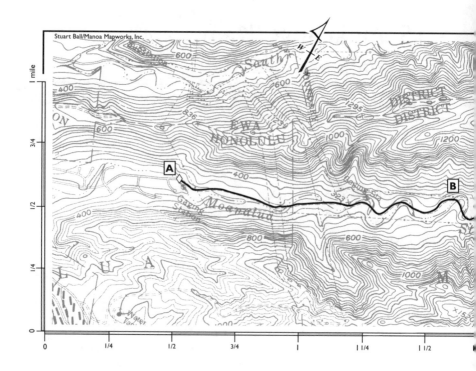

The road ends at Moanalua Valley Park. The park has rest rooms and drinking water.

Park on the street just before the park entrance (elevation 240 feet) (map point A).

Bus: Route 16 to Ala Aolani and Ala Lani Streets (weekday mornings and afternoons only). Walk 0.4 mile along Ala Aolani St. to the park.

Route Description

Enter Moanalua Valley Park and proceed along the dirt/gravel road at the back of the parking lot.

Walk around a locked gate to the right.

On the left by a huge monkeypod tree pass a muddy driveway leading to the Douglas Damon house site (marker no. 3).

Cross Moanalua (Kamananui) Stream seven times on stone bridges. The original cobblestones of the old carriage road

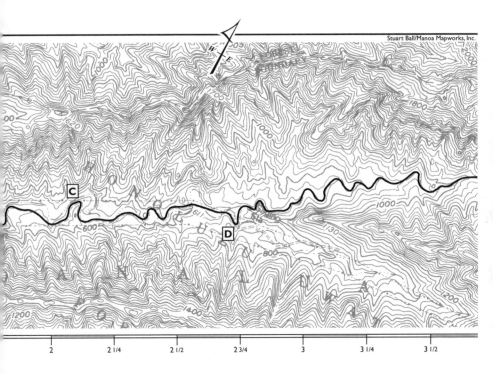

remain intact on the bridge approaches at the fifth and seventh crossings. Look and listen for the white-rumped shama in the introduced forest.

On the right under a mango tree at the seventh crossing is Pōhakukaluahine, a large boulder covered with petroglyphs (map point B) (marker no. 10).

Around the bend from the petroglyph rock and before the next stream crossing, reach a junction (marker no. 11). Continue straight on the dirt road. (To the right a short loop trail leads up to the May Damon house site and a view up the valley.)

Ford the stream four times. Along the stream are kukui trees and tangled groves of hau.

Ascend gradually to a wide vehicle turnaround area (map point C) (marker no. 13). On the right a trail leads up to another overlook of the entire valley.

Cross the stream six more times.

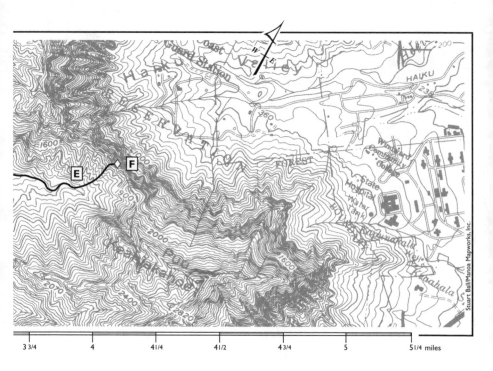

After the sixth ford and as the road curves right, look for two boulders on the left side of the road.

Just past the second boulder turn left off the road onto a trail (map point D). (The road continues to the back of the valley.)

Cross the stream immediately, climb the embankment, and turn left again.

Skirt the foot of Keanaakamanō, the middle ridge, which divides the valley into two drainages.

Pass a stream gauging station on the left.

Cross the left fork of Moanalua Stream twenty-three times! Highlights are as follows: At 6: a small, but delightful pool. Just after the pool is another petroglyph rock on the right. At 8: a dense hau grove. Between 12 and 13: Climb over a small side ridge and then descend steeply back to the stream. Between 14 and 16: two dense hau groves. Keep your head down! After 18: Break out into the open for a short stretch. On the left is a lone loulu palm. After 20: another hau tangle. The stream then splits in two several times. The trail generally hugs the main (left) channel on the islands created by the two braids. Along the trail are lovely Chinese ground orchids. At 21: a tiny pool and waterfall.

After the twenty-third crossing, bear left and up, leaving the stream for good (map point E). Listen for the Japanese bush warbler.

Climb steeply up a spur ridge through uluhe ferns and 'ōhi'a 'āhihi trees. To the right is a waterfall chute at the head of the stream.

Reach the Ko'olau summit at a saddle (elevation 1,660 feet) (map point F). To the right is a flat overlook of Ha'ikū Valley.

Notes

Moanalua Valley is a classic combination hike that includes a valley stroll, a stream walk, and a ridge climb. Along the valley road are some historical sites. By the stream is a delightful, though small, swimming hole. At the ridge top are native plants and windward views. What more could you want?

The historical sites are marked by numbered wooden posts along the road. In 1884 Bernice Pauahi Bishop willed the entire *ahupua'a* (land division) of Moanalua (two camps) to her husband's business partner, Samuel M. Damon. His son, Douglas, built a luxurious mountain house (marker no. 3) in the valley, which is also known as Kamananui (great spiritual power). A cobbled carriage road crossed seven ornate bridges and ended at the house of his daughter, May Damon (marker no. 11). For a detailed explanation of those and other sites, pick up the pamphlet, *A Walk into the Past from Moanalua Gardens* (address at Access, above).

Along the road look and listen for the white-rumped shama. It is black on top with a chestnut-colored breast and a long black-and-white tail. The shama has a variety of beautiful songs and often mimics other birds. A native of Malaysia, the shama has become widespread in introduced forests such as this one. Until the 1920s the owners grazed cattle in the valley, resulting in the destruction of much of the original native vegetation.

At marker no. 10 is Pōhakukaluahine (rock of the old

woman), a sacred boulder covered with ancient petroglyphs. Most of the carvings are human stick figures, although a few resemble bird-men. Also on the boulder are a *kōnane* game board and a winding groove suggesting Moanalua Stream.

Pōhakukaluahine received its name from an old story. Many years ago a small child cried during the consecration of a *heiau* (religious site) in the lower valley. Such offense to the gods was punishable by death, so the grandmother rushed up the valley with the child and hid behind a large boulder. The *mana* (supernatural power) of the rock protected the two from the pursuing warriors. When the noise *kapu* (taboo) was lifted, the grandmother returned the child safely to its parents.

After the vehicle turnaround, start counting stream crossings because the junction with the trail is not obvious. After the sixth ford look for the twin boulders on the left. The junction may be marked with surveyor's ribbon but don't count on it. On the trail watch your footing while rock hopping across the stream. If necessary, slosh through the water. Your boots are eventually going to get wet anyway. As always, do not ford the stream if the water gets much above your knees. Finally, look out for a few wayward mosquitoes.

The stream trail frequently tunnels through tangled hau trees with large, heart-shaped leaves. Their flowers are bright yellow with a dark red center and resemble those of a hibiscus. Early Hawaiians used the wood for kites and canoe outriggers, the bark for sandals, and the sap as a laxative.

While walking along the stream, watch for the 'elepaio, a small native bird. It is brown on top and white underneath with a black throat and a dark tail, usually cocked. The bird roams the forest understory catching insects on the fly or on vegetation. 'Elepaio are very curious, which is why you can sometimes see them.

After the last hau tangle look for the Chinese ground or nun's orchid. Its lovely flowers have tapered petals, which are white on the outside and reddish brown within. The lowest petal is a cream-colored tube with purple marking.

Toward the back of the valley listen for the Japanese bush warbler (uguisu), a bird often heard, but rarely seen. Its distinctive cry starts with a long whistle and then winds down in a series of notes. The bush warbler is olive brown on top with a white breast and a long tail.

On the climb to the saddle the trail is lined with native 'ōhi'a 'āhihi trees. They have narrow, pointed leaves with red stems and midribs. Their delicate red flowers grow in clusters and are similar to those of the more common 'ōhi'a. 'Ōhi'a 'āhihi is found only in the Ko'olau (windward) and Wai'anae (mullet water) Mountains on O'ahu.

From the saddle along the Ko'olau summit the *pali* (cliff) drops straight down into Ha'ikū (sharp break) Valley, where the H-3 freeway runs. The long side ridges enclosing the valley constrict the view somewhat, but you can still see Kāne'ohe (cutting husband) Bay extending to Mōkapu (taboo district) Peninsula. On the steep side ridge to the right is the Ha'ikū Stairs climbing to a small radar on top of Pu'u Keahi a Kahoe (hill of Kahoe's fire).

A short side trip leads to the site of an old plane crash at the bottom of an intermittent waterfall. To get there, leave the trail at the last stream crossing (no. 23) and walk up the streambed. At a fork keep right following the main channel. The wreckage of the plane is strewn along the stream just below the waterfall. At its base is a clearing with a shallow pool.

For a more difficult outing, try the Pu'u Keahi a Kahoe hike that starts from the same trailhead. The route loops along the Ko'olau summit and then descends Keanaakamanō, the middle ridge of Moanalua Valley.

CENTRAL OʻAHU

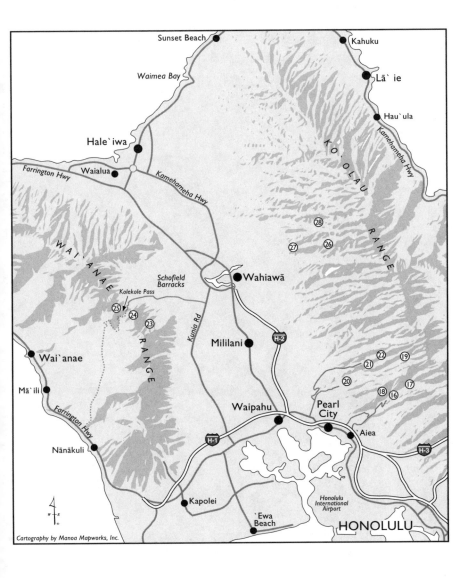

Sunset Beach

Kahuku

Waimea Bay

Lāʻie

Hauʻula

Haleʻiwa

KOʻOLAU RANGE

Farrington Hwy

Waialua

Kamehameha Hwy

Kamehameha Hwy

WAIʻANAE

28

27   26

Schofield
Barracks

Wahiawā

Kolekole Pass

25

24

23

Kunia Rd

Mililani

H-2

22   19

RANGE

Waiʻanae

21

Māʻili

20

18 16   17

Farrington Hwy

Waipahu

Pearl
City

Aiea

H-3

Nānākuli

H-1

Kapolei

Honolulu
International
Airport

ʻEwa
Beach

HONOLULU

N
W E
S

Cartography by Manoa Mapworks, Inc.

16 'Aiea Loop

Type:	Foothill
Length:	5-mile loop
Elevation Gain:	900 feet
Danger:	Low
Suitable for:	Novice
Location:	Keaīwa Heiau State Recreation Area above 'Aiea
Topo Map:	Waipahu, Kāne'ohe
Access:	Open

Highlights
This short, pleasant hike winds through the foothills of the Ko'olau Range. Along the trail you see some native trees and the site of a plane crash. Nearby is Keaīwa *heiau*, an early Hawaiian medicine center.

Trailhead Directions
At Punchbowl St. get on Lunalilo Fwy (H-1) heading 'ewa (west).

Near Middle St. keep left on Rte 78 west (exit 19B, Moanalua Rd.) to 'Aiea.

While descending Red Hill, take the exit marked Hālawa-Stadium.

At the end of the long off-ramp continue straight on Ulunē St.

At the road end turn right on 'Aiea Heights Dr.

Pass 'Aiea High School on the left.

Climb gradually through 'Aiea Heights subdivision.

Reach the entrance to Keaīwa Heiau State Recreation Area.

Drive past the *heiau* and the camping area to the upper lot and

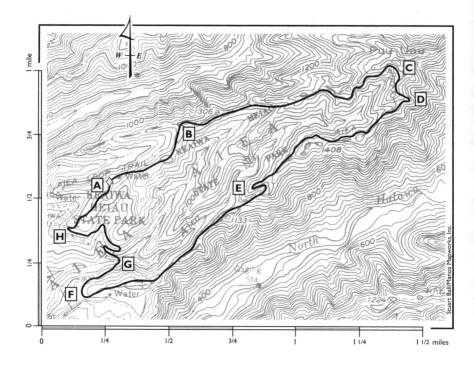

park there (elevation 1,080 feet) (map point A). At the trail-head are rest rooms and drinking water.

Bus: Route 11 to 'Aiea Heights Dr. and Ka'amilo St. Walk 2.0 miles along 'Aiea Heights Dr. and through the recreation area to the trailhead. Route 74 goes farther up 'Aiea Heights Dr., but it only runs on weekday mornings and afternoons.

Route Description
At the back of the upper lot take the 'Aiea Loop Trail.

Pass a small water tank on the right.

Enter a grove of Sydney blue gum trees.

Cross an open, eroded area. On the right is a view of Diamond Head and Honolulu.

Pass a power-line tower above and to the right. Strawberry guava trees line the trail.

Shortly afterward reach a junction (map point B). Continue

straight on the loop trail. (The side trail to the left leads down to Kalauao Stream and is described in the Kalauao hike.)

Pass a second power-line tower on the left.

Contour on the right side of the ridge just below its top.

Reach a small, grassy clearing with a bench. From there is a good view of the Wai'anae Range in the distance. The flat-topped mountain is Ka'ala, the highest point on O'ahu.

Continue contouring well below the ridgeline for a stretch.

Duck under a huge tree trunk spanning the trail.

Right after the trunk the trail curves right and then left.

As it begins to curve right again, reach another junction (map point C). Continue on the wide loop trail to the right. (On the left is the 'Aiea Ridge Trail, which leads to the Ko'olau summit.)

Cross over to the left side of the ridge. You can see the Ko'olau Range through the native koa and 'ōhi'a trees. Look for alahe'e, a small native tree with shiny, dark green leaves.

Reach the farthest point of the loop by a large 'ōhi'a tree with exposed roots (elevation 1,480 feet) (map point D). Just past the 'ōhi'a are two native 'iliahi (sandalwood) trees.

Along the first part of the return leg are views of North Hālawa Valley and the H-3 freeway on the left.

Walk under a shady mango tree and then switch to the right side of the ridge.

Descend gradually, well below the ridgeline, through eucalyptus.

In a gully pass the wing section of a B-24 Army Air Corps bomber on the right. A steep, overgrown trail leads to other wreckage farther down the gully. The plane crashed on 5 May 1944 after taking off from Hickam Field.

Pass a power-line tower above and to the left (map point E). Pass a second one.

Stroll through a grove of Cook pines on a broad trail.

Reach a junction. Keep right on the contour trail. (The eroded trail to the left climbs to a view of Honolulu and Salt Lake.)

Go under some power lines.

Pass another grove of Cook pines.

In a stand of albizia trees reach another junction (map point

F). Bear right on the wide trail. (The left fork leads to Camp Smith.)

Switchback once and descend into a lush gulch. Look for kukui trees and yellow ginger there.

Cross intermittent 'Aiea Stream (map point G) and climb out of the gulch on a rocky, rooty trail with three switchbacks.

Switchback once again past a power-line tower on the left.

The trail levels off and enters the camping area of the park (map point H).

Turn right and climb the steps to the middle parking lot.

Turn right again and walk up the paved road to the upper parking lot (map point A).

Notes

'Aiea Loop is a very popular hike, especially on weekends. The route is reasonably short, mostly shady, and quite scenic. It seems as though everyone who has ever hiked on O'ahu has done the loop. To avoid the crowds, go on a weekday or start early. Many people just walk partway, so the return portion is often less traveled.

The loop is a perfect hike for beginners. Built by the Civilian Conservation Corps in 1935, the trail remains wide and well graded, for the most part. The only rough section is the short climb out of the gulch near the end of the hike. Watch out for other trail users, such as runners, mountain bikers, horseback riders, and wayward mosquitoes.

An inexpensive interpretive pamphlet, 'Aiea Loop Trail and Keaīwa Heiau: Field Site Guide, is available from Moanalua Gardens Foundation. If possible, pick one up at the foundation office before starting the hike. The address is in Appendix 2.

After the first viewpoint, the trail is lined with strawberry guava trees (waiawī 'ula'ula). They have glossy, dark green leaves and smooth brown bark. Their dark red fruit is delicious, with a taste reminiscent of strawberries. The guavas usually ripen in August and September. Pickings are slim along the loop trail, however, because of its popularity. The strawberry guava is a native of Brazil but was introduced to Hawai'i from England in the 1800s.

In the forest look and listen for the white-rumped shama. It is black on top with a chestnut-colored breast and a long black-and-white tail. The shama has a variety of beautiful songs and often mimics other birds. A native of Malaysia, the shama has become widespread in introduced forests such as this one.

Near the farthest point of the loop are some native 'ōhi'a and koa trees. Ōhi'a has oval leaves and clusters of delicate red flowers. Early Hawaiians used the flowers in *lei* (garlands) and the wood in outrigger canoes. The hard, durable wood was also carved into god images for *heiau* (religious sites). Koa has sickle-shaped foliage and pale yellow flower clusters. Early Hawaiians made surfboards and outrigger canoe hulls out of the beautiful red brown wood. Today it is made into fine furniture.

Among the 'ōhi'a and koa is a small native tree, alahe'e. Its oblong leaves are shiny and dark green. Alahe'e has fragrant white flowers that grow in clusters at the branch tips. Early Hawaiians fashioned the hard wood into farming tools, and hooks and spears for fishing.

In the gulch on the way back is a grove of kukui trees. Their large, pale green leaves resemble those of the maple, with several distinct lobes. Early Polynesian voyagers introduced kukui into Hawai'i. They used the wood to make gunwales and seats for their outrigger canoes. The flowers and sap became medicines to treat a variety of ailments. Early Hawaiians strung the nuts together to make *lei hua* (seed or nut garlands). The oily kernels became house candles and torches for night spearfishing.

After completing the loop hike, stop at Keaīwa (mysterious) *heiau* on the way out. The ancient site is a *heiau ho'ōla* or medical center. There *kāhuna lapa'au* (healers) treated patients with herbs from the surrounding gardens. The *heiau* was probably built in the 1500s and was rededicated in 1951.

The hike is described clockwise. You can, of course, take all or part of the loop in either direction. For a valley walk, take the Kalauao hike that starts from the same trailhead. For a longer, tougher outing, try the 'Aiea Ridge hike. It also starts from the same trailhead and leads to the summit of the Ko'olau (windward) Range.

17 'Aiea Ridge

Type:	Ungraded ridge
Length:	11-mile round trip
Elevation Gain:	1,800 feet
Danger:	Low
Suitable for:	Novice, Intermediate, Expert
Location:	Keaīwa Heiau State Recreation Area and 'Ewa Forest Reserve above 'Aiea
Topo Map:	Waipahu, Kāne'ohe
Access:	Open

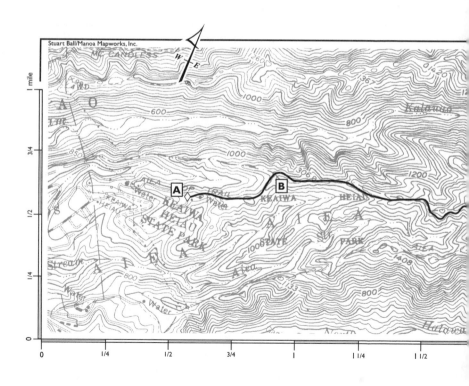

Highlights

This long, wonderful hike follows a mostly open, windswept ridge to the Ko'olau summit. Along the route is an amazing assemblage of native forest plants. On the final climb and at the top are magnificent leeward and windward views.

Trailhead Directions

At Punchbowl St. get on Lunalilo Fwy (H-1) heading *'ewa* (west).

Near Middle St. keep left on Rte 78 west (exit 19B, Moanalua Rd.) to 'Aiea.

While descending Red Hill, take the exit marked Hālawa-Stadium.

At the end of the long off-ramp continue straight on Ulunē St.

At the road end turn right on 'Aiea Heights Dr.

Pass 'Aiea High School on the left.

Climb gradually through 'Aiea Heights subdivision.

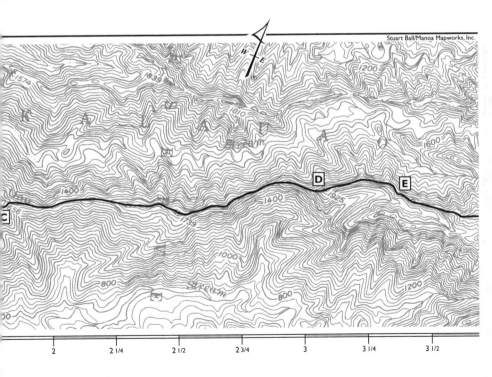

Stuart Ball/Manoa Mapworks, Inc.

Reach the entrance to Keaīwa Heiau State Recreation Area.

Drive past the *heiau* and the camping area to the upper lot and park there (elevation 1,080 feet) (map point A). At the trail-head are rest rooms and drinking water.

Bus: Route 11 to 'Aiea Heights Dr. and Ka'amilo St. Walk 2.0 miles along 'Aiea Heights Dr. and through the recreation area to the trailhead. Route 74 goes farther up 'Aiea Heights Dr., but it only runs on weekday mornings and afternoons.

Route Description

At the back of the upper lot take the 'Aiea Loop Trail.

Pass a small water tank on the right.

Enter a grove of Sydney blue gum trees.

Cross an open, eroded area. On the right is a view of Diamond Head and Honolulu.

Pass a power-line tower above and to the right. Strawberry guava trees line the trail.

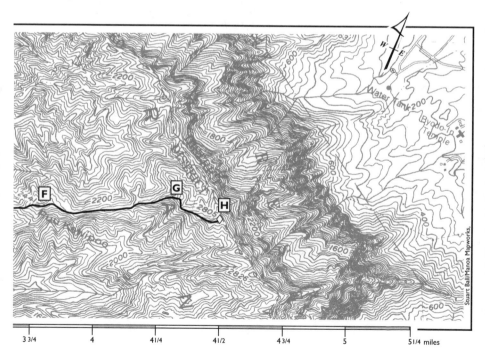

3 3/4   4   4 I/4   4 I/2   4 3/4   5   5 I/4 miles

Shortly afterward reach a junction (map point B). Continue straight on the loop trail. (The side trail to the left leads down to Kalauao Stream and is part of the Kalauao hike.)

Pass a second power-line tower on the left.

Contour on the right side of the ridge just below its top.

Reach a small, grassy clearing with a bench.

Continue contouring well below the ridgeline for a stretch.

Duck under a huge tree trunk spanning the trail.

Right after the trunk the trail curves right and then left.

As it begins to curve right again, reach a junction (map point C). Turn left and up on the 'Aiea Ridge Trail. (The loop trail swings right, descends gradually, and then switches to the left side of the ridge.)

Shortly afterward bear left at the edge of the ridge.

Almost immediately go around to the right of Pu'u 'U'au, a large hill on the ridge. Ignore the side trail on the left, which is the return portion of the extended Kalauao loop.

Regain the ridgeline and traverse a relatively level, but rooty, section under native koa and 'ōhi'a trees. Along the trail are native maile shrubs and alahe'e trees.

Ascend gradually over three gentle hills through more open forest. Look and listen for the Japanese bush warbler and the native 'apapane. Watch for a few native iliahi (sandalwood) trees.

Contour along the right side of the ridge for a short distance.

The trail bears left and then descends briefly, but steeply.

Traverse a lush, narrow section past native hāpu'u tree ferns.

Climb gradually, skirting to the left of a large hill (map point D).

Cross a partially open, level stretch through native kōpiko trees. From a small clearing is a magnificent view *mauka* to the Ko'olau summit.

Descend to a saddle in the ridge (map point E).

Begin the long, gradual climb to Pu'u Kaiwipo'o, the large peak looming ahead.

Pass a small clearing on the right with good views leeward.

After a stiff ascent, reach the top of Kaiwipo'o (elevation 2,441 feet) (map point F).

Descend off Kaiwipo'o and then climb gradually over a series of small humps toward the summit. The ridge is open, windswept, and at times narrow. Look for the native shrubs ko'oko'olau and pū'ahanui (kanawao).

Reach a flat, grassy spot on the left with the first view of the windward side (map point G).

Turn right and down, still on the main ridge, toward a power-line tower. Along the trail are native manono shrubs.

Bear left around the base of the tower.

Climb steadily along the ridge, which levels off near the top.

Reach the Ko'olau summit (elevation 2,805 feet) (map point H) and a sweeping view of the windward coast. Behind the overlook is a native lapalapa tree.

Notes

'Aiea Ridge offers something for everyone except water babies. The hike starts with a pleasant stroll and ends with a wild climb along an open, windswept ridge. In between are intriguing native plants and a chance at glimpsing some native birds. Go as far as you want and then turn around. The only negatives are the power-line tower near the top and the noise from the H-3 freeway below.

Two vastly different trails make up this hike. The popular 'Aiea Loop Trail is wide and well graded. The little-used 'Aiea Ridge Trail is ungraded and rooty and muddy in spots. The first half may be overgrown with scratchy uluhe ferns and *Clidemia* shrubs. Watch out especially for narrow sections hidden by vegetation.

On the ridge trail look for native alahe'e trees and maile shrubs. Alahe'e has shiny, oblong, dark green leaves. Its fragrant white flowers grow in clusters at the branch tips. Early Hawaiians fashioned the hard wood into farming tools, and hooks and spears for fishing. Maile has glossy, pointed leaves, tangled branches, and fruit resembling a small olive. The fragrant leaves and bark make a distinctive open-ended *lei* (garland), in both ancient and modern Hawai'i.

Throughout the hike listen for the Japanese bush warbler (uguisu), a bird often heard, but rarely seen. Its distinctive cry starts with a long whistle and then winds down in a series of notes. The bush warbler is olive brown on top with a white breast and a long tail. If you are very lucky, you may catch a glimpse of a native 'apapane in the forest canopy. It has a red breast and head, black wings and tail, and a slightly curved black bill. In flight the 'apapane makes a whirring sound as it darts from tree to tree searching for insects and nectar.

Along the gently rolling ridge section are a few 'iliahi (sandalwood) trees. Their small leaves are dull green and appear wilted. 'Iliahi is partially parasitic, with outgrowths on its roots that steal nutrients from nearby plants. Early Hawaiians ground the fragrant heartwood into a powder to perfume their *kapa* (bark cloth). Beginning in the late 1700s, sandalwood was indiscriminately cut down and exported to China to make incense and furniture. The trade ended around 1840 when the forests were depleted of 'iliahi.

In the level stretch before the saddle look for kōpiko, a native member of the coffee family. The small tree has leathery, oblong leaves with a light green midrib. Turn the leaf over to see a row of tiny holes (*piko* [navel]) on either side of the midrib. The kōpiko produces clusters of little white flowers and fleshy, orange fruits.

Take a well-deserved break on top of Pu'u Kaiwipo'o (the skull hill) and look at the panoramic view. To leeward are Pearl Harbor and the Wahiawā (place of noise) plain. In the distance is the Wai'anae (mullet water) Range with the prominent peaks of Pu'u Kaua (war hill) and Ka'ala (the fragrance), the highest point on O'ahu. *Mauka* is the imposing Ko'olau (windward) summit ridge. Along the ridge to the left is flat-topped 'Eleao (plant louse) and to the right, pointed Pu'u Keahi a Kahoe (hill of Kahoe's fire) with a small radar on top. Ahead the trail climbs toward a power-line tower.

On the final climb are two more native shrubs, pū'ahanui (kanawao) and ko'oko'olau. Pū'ahanui, a relative of hydrangea, has large, serrated, deeply creased leaves and clusters of delicate pink flowers. Early Hawaiians used the plants for medicinal purposes. The herb ko'oko'olau is related to the daisy and sunflower families. It has pointed, serrated leaves and flower heads with yellow petals. Early Hawaiians steeped the leaves to make a tea used as a tonic.

From the summit you can see Kāne'ohe (cutting husband) Bay from Kualoa (long back) to Mōkapu (taboo district) Points. In the bay are Mokoli'i (Chinaman's Hat) and Moku o Lo'e (Coconut) Islands. Along the shore are Kahalu'u (diving place) and He'eia fishponds. The pyramid peak on the left is Pu'u Ōhulehule (joining of waves hill).

Near the summit overlook is a native lapalapa tree. Its roundish leaves are arranged in groups of three and flutter in the slightest wind. Early Hawaiians used the bark, leaves, and purple fruit to make a blue black dye to decorate their kapa (bark cloth). The leaves also make a distinctive lei.

The 'Aiea Loop and Kalauao hikes also start from the same trailhead. Try the loop hike before taking the 'Aiea Ridge hike. That way you can find the key, unmarked junction with the ridge trail ahead of time. The Kalauao (multitude of clouds) hike descends to the valley of the same name on the left.

18 Kalauao

Type:	Valley
Length:	4-mile round trip
Elevation Gain:	700 feet
Danger:	Low
Suitable for:	Novice, Intermediate
Location:	Keaīwa Heiau State Recreation Area and 'Ewa Forest Reserve above 'Aiea
Topo Map:	Waipahu, Kāne'ohe
Access:	Open

Highlights
A steep descent from a popular trail leads to a lovely, uncrowded valley. Upstream are noisy rapids, quiet pools, and mountain apples. The hike ends at a delightful waterfall with a swimming hole.

Trailhead Directions
At Punchbowl St. get on Lunalilo Fwy (H-1) heading 'ewa (west).

Near Middle St. keep left on Rte 78 west (exit 19B, Moanalua Rd.) to 'Aiea.

While descending Red Hill, take the exit marked Hālawa-Stadium.

At the end of the long off-ramp continue straight on Ulunē St.

At the road end turn right on 'Aiea Heights Dr.

Pass 'Aiea High School on the left.

Climb gradually through 'Aiea Heights subdivision.

Reach the entrance to Keaīwa Heiau State Recreation Area.

Drive past the *heiau* and the camping area to the upper lot and

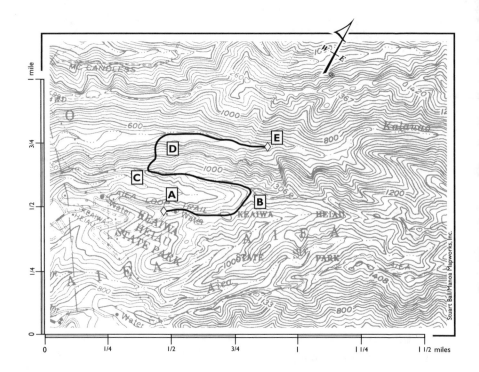

park there (elevation 1,080 feet) (map point A). At the trailhead are rest rooms and drinking water.

Bus: Route 11 to ʻAiea Heights Dr. and Kaʻamilo St. Walk 2.0
miles along ʻAiea Heights Dr. and through the recreation area to
the trailhead. Route 74 goes farther up ʻAiea Heights Dr., but it
only runs on weekday mornings and afternoons.

Route Description
At the back of the upper lot take the ʻAiea Loop Trail.
    Pass a small water tank on the right.
    Enter a grove of Sydney blue gum trees.
    Cross an open, eroded area. On the right is a view of Diamond
Head and Honolulu.
    Pass a power-line tower above and to the right.
    Almost immediately the trail curves to the right and then to
the left.

After that reverse S curve reach a junction (map point B). Turn left and down on a side trail. (The 'Aiea Loop Trail continues straight.)

Descend gradually along the side ridge through strawberry guava trees.

Walk under a power-line tower. In the distance to the right is the Wai'anae Range.

Continue the gradual descent through a narrow corridor of strawberry guavas. The trail is muddy in spots.

Pass a stand of paperbark trees.

Ironwood trees now line the route. Look for a few native koa trees and pūkiawe shrubs.

Enter a grove of eucalyptus trees on a wider trail.

As the trail levels out after an eroded spot, reach a junction marked by a mango tree on the right (map point C). Turn sharp right off the ridge on a narrow trail leading down into Kalauao Valley.

Pass several small ironwoods on the right.

Descend steeply through Christmas berry and strawberry guava trees. Watch your footing on the rocky, rooty trail. Watch for native lama and alahe'e trees.

Jog right and then left to avoid a rock face.

Resume the steep descent through mountain apple trees.

Reach a junction at Kalauao Stream (map point D). Turn right heading upstream under kukui and mountain apple trees. (To the left a less distinct trail leads downstream.) Memorize that junction for the return trip.

Cross the stream eight times. Highlights are as follows: After 1: a huge mango tree on the opposite bank. After 3, a sheer cliff on the right. At 6, the stream tumbles over a ledge.

After the eighth crossing reach a delightful waterfall with a good-sized pool (elevation 600 feet) (map point E). To get to the top of the waterfall, cross the stream and climb up the left side.

Notes

If you have already done the 'Aiea Loop hike, try this nearby more difficult variation. It is a challenging novice hike because of the steep, rough descent into Kalauao (multitude of clouds) Valley. The very pleasant walk by the stream to the waterfall, however, makes the scramble down and up worthwhile.

During dry weather the stream, waterfall, and pool disappear. To ensure flowing water, take this hike during the winter or after a heavy rain in summer. Watch your footing on the slippery stream crossings. If necessary, walk in the water rather than rock hopping. As usual with stream hikes, do not attempt the crossings if the water gets much above your knees.

On the side trail past the strawberry guavas, look for native pūkiawe shrubs and koa trees. Pūkiawe has tiny, rigid leaves and small white, pink, or red berries. Koa has sickle-shaped foliage and pale yellow flower clusters. Early Hawaiians made surfboards and outrigger canoe hulls out of the beautiful red brown wood. Today it is made into fine furniture.

On the steep trail down to the stream are some native lama and alaheʻe trees. Lama has oblong, pointed leaves that are dark green and leathery. Its fruits are green, then yellow, and finally bright red when fully ripe. Lama was sacred to Laka, goddess of the hula. Early Hawaiians used the hard, light-colored wood in temple construction and in hula performances.

Alaheʻe has shiny, oblong, dark green leaves. Its fragrant white flowers grow in clusters at the branch tips. Early Hawaiians fashioned the hard wood into farming tools, and hooks and spears for fishing.

In Kalauao Valley are groves of mountain apple (ʻōhiʻa ʻai). The trees have large, oblong, shiny leaves. In spring their purple flowers carpet the trail. The delicious pink or red fruit usually ripens in late July or early August. If none is in reach, shake the tree and try to catch the apples as they come down. The species is native to Malaysia and was brought over by early Hawaiians.

After the eighth crossing a gushing waterfall suddenly appears around a bend in the stream. Shady banyan and mango trees ring an inviting swimming hole. Take the plunge if you are so inclined. Remember to check the depth of the water before jumping from the ledges around the pool.

To make a loop hike, continue upstream from the top of the falls. After crossing the stream five more times, look for an obscure junction. Turn right there and climb a long, steep side ridge back to the 'Aiea Loop Trail. Turn right again to return to the recreation area.

The 'Aiea Loop and 'Aiea Ridge hikes also start from the same trailhead. Try the novice loop hike before taking the Kalauao or the ridge hike. That way you can find the key, unmarked junctions for both those hikes ahead of time.

19 Waimano Ridge

Type:	Graded ridge
Length:	15-mile round trip
Elevation Gain:	1,700 feet
Danger:	Low
Suitable for:	Intermediate, Expert
Location:	'Ewa Forest Reserve above Pearl City
Topo Map:	Waipahu, Kāne'ohe
Access:	Open

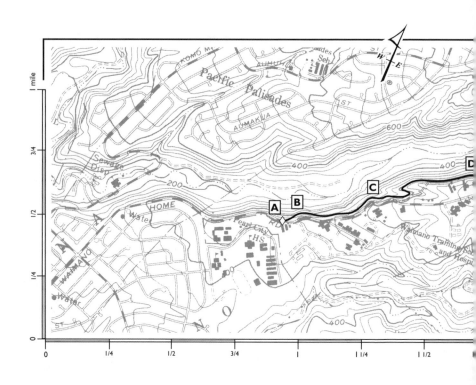

Highlights

This graded trail follows an abandoned irrigation ditch above Waimano Stream and then climbs gradually to the Koʻolau summit. Along the route are some delicious fruit and a good variety of native plants. At the top you look out to Kāneʻohe Bay on the windward side.

Trailhead Directions

At Punchbowl St. get on Lunalilo Fwy (H-1) heading ʻewa (west).
Near Middle St. keep left on Rte 78 west (exit 19B, Moanalua Rd.) to ʻAiea.
By Aloha Stadium bear right to rejoin H-1 to Pearl City.
Leave the freeway at exit 10, marked Pearl City–Waimalu.
Turn right on Moanalua Rd. at the end of the off-ramp.
As Moanalua Rd. ends, turn right on Waimano Home Rd.
The road narrows to two lanes.
Enter the grounds of Waimano Training School and Hospital.

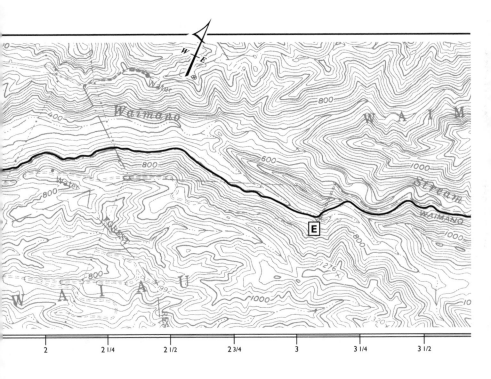

Look for a guard station ahead.

Park on the left in a dirt area just before the guard shack and across from the Pearl City Cultural Center (elevation 470 feet) (map point A).

Bus: Route 53 to the intersection of Waimano Home Rd. and Komo Mai Dr. Walk 1.0 mile up Waimano Home Rd. to the trailhead.

Route Description
Continue up Waimano Home Rd. on foot.

Bear left off the road by the hunter check-in mailbox near the guard shack.

Follow the path to the left of and next to a chain-link fence.

Shortly afterward reach a signed junction (map point B). Keep right, on the Upper Waimano Trail along the fence. (To the left the Lower Waimano Trail leads down into Waimano Valley.)

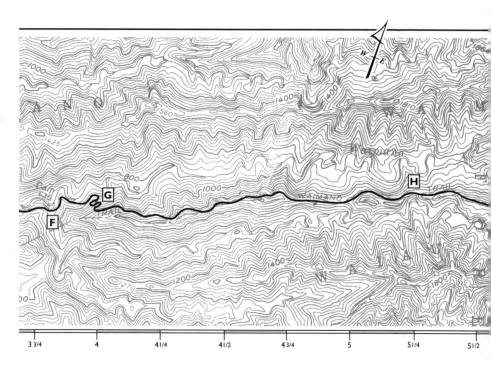

Parallel the fence and the road, passing several guard rails.

Across from a low white building turn left and down, leaving the road behind (map point C).

An abandoned irrigation ditch appears on the right.

Jump over a narrow concrete spillway.

Swing left into a side gully.

Cross over the top of an eroded side ridge. In the distance is a good view of the Wai'anae Range.

Contour along the side of Waimano Valley through strawberry guava and Christmas berry trees. Watch for an occasional native lama tree.

The ditch reappears on the right and then periodically disappears into short tunnels.

Reach a signed junction (map point D). Continue straight on the upper trail. (To the left the lower trail leads down to the floor of Waimano Valley.)

Negotiate two rock faces covered with slippery roots. Cables

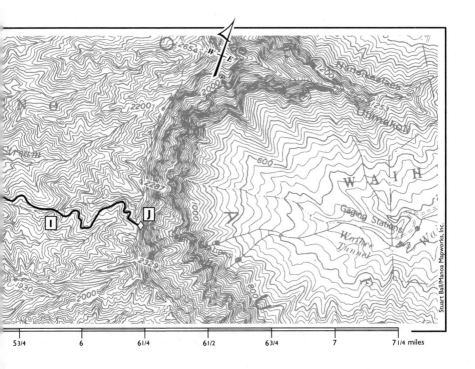

5 3/4   6   6 1/4   6 1/2   6 3/4   7   7 1/4 miles

are provided for assistance. You can use the short tunnels on the right to bypass both rock faces.

Pass several large mango trees.

Descend gradually to a tributary of Waimano Stream.

Just past a dead triple-trunked tree reach a signed junction (map point E). Turn left off the wide trail and cross the stream. (The wide trail climbs out of the valley back to Waimano Training School and Hospital.)

After crossing, turn right upstream.

Leave the stream behind and climb a low side ridge on the left with the help of two switchbacks.

Cross over the ridgeline at a grassy clearing with a covered picnic table. Nearby are some large koa and lama trees.

Contour along the left side of the ridge well above Waimano Stream. Look for mountain apple trees in this section.

Descend gradually to the stream through mountain apple groves and hau tangles. By the stream is the blocked intake for the irrigation ditch.

Almost immediately Waimano Stream forks (map point F). Cross the right fork and take the trail heading upstream along the right side of the left fork (got it?).

Climb steadily up the ridge, switchbacking four times (map point G). Tall ʻōhiʻa and palm trees line the route. As the trail levels off and turns a corner, look for several ʻiliahi (sandalwood) trees with their droopy leaves.

Resume contouring near the top of the ridge through native rain forest.

Reach the top of the ridge in a grove of Australian tea.

Leave the ridgeline and contour on its left side. The trail is lined with native naupaka kuahiwi shrubs.

After climbing a small hump, reach an obscure junction (map point H). Continue straight on the contour trail. (To the right a trail leads down to the right fork of Waimano Stream [crossed earlier] and a dilapidated cabin built by the Civilian Conservation Corps on the far bank.)

Climb gradually, working into and out of every side gulch.

Switchback once to gain the ridgeline and cross over to its right side (map point I).

Ascend steadily, weaving in and out of the side gullies just below the top of the ridge. Watch for native pū'ahanui (kanawao) shrubs and kōpiko trees along the trail.

Reach the Ko'olau summit in a saddle just to the right of a large landslide (elevation 2,160 feet) (map point J).

Notes

Don't be put off by the high mileage of this hike. The well-designed trail makes for steady, pleasant walking so the miles just seem to fly by. Soon you are in some wild country, and before you know it, you're at the summit. Leave time, though, to check out the native plants and to enjoy a delicious guava or mountain apple in season.

Built by the Civilian Conservation Corps in 1935, the Upper Waimano Trail is the best preserved of the Ko'olau ridge trails of that era. The footpath is graded, wide, and easy to follow, for the most part. Pay particular attention to the directions at the two stream crossings. Watch your step on the two rooty rock faces. From the stream to the final switchback, the trail may be somewhat overgrown with scratchy uluhe ferns and various introduced shrubs.

The route initially parallels an abandoned ditch once used by the Honolulu Plantation Company to irrigate sugarcane. Lining the trail are strawberry guava (waiawī 'ula'ula) trees whose tasty, dark red fruit usually ripen in August and September. Also along the path in this section are native lama trees. Their oblong, pointed leaves are dark green and leathery. The fruits are green, then yellow, and finally bright red when fully ripe. Lama was sacred to Laka, goddess of the hula. Early Hawaiians used the hard, light-colored wood in temple construction and in hula performances.

On the gradual descent to the stream and the ditch intake you pass through groves of mountain apple ('ōhi'a 'ai). The trees have large, oblong, shiny leaves. In spring their purple flowers carpet the trail. The delicious pink or red fruit usually ripens in late July or early August. If none is in reach, shake the tree and try to catch the apples as they come down. The species is native to Malaysia and was brought over by early Hawaiians.

After crossing Waimano (many waters) Stream, watch for the native shrub naupaka kuahiwi. It has light green, pointed leaves and half-flowers. Initially the naupaka along the trail has toothed leaves and white flowers. Closer to the summit, a slightly different variety appears with smoother leaf margins and purple streaks in the flowers.

Along the final stretch are two more native shrubs, pūʻahanui (kanawao) and kōpiko. A relative of the hydrangea, pūʻahanui has large, serrated, deeply creased leaves and clusters of delicate pink flowers. Kōpiko is a member of the coffee family and has leathery, oblong leaves with a light green midrib. Turn the leaf over to see a row of tiny holes (*piko* [navel]) on either side of the midrib. The kōpiko produces clusters of little white flowers and fleshy, orange fruits.

From the summit viewpoint you can look straight down into Waiheʻe (octopus liquid) Valley. In back is Kāneʻohe (cutting husband) Bay stretching to Mōkapu (taboo district) Point. By the bay is Kahaluʻu (diving place) fishpond and a wooded hill, known as Māʻeliʻeli (digging). Along the summit ridge to the right is the massive unnamed peak at the head of Waimalu (sheltered water) drainage. To the left past the landslide scar is the summit of ʻEleao (plant louse). In back of the lookout is a native ʻōhiʻa tree with clusters of salmon-colored flowers.

For a much shorter loop walk, take the Waimano Valley hike that starts from the same trailhead. For a longer, more challenging route, connect the Waimano Ridge and Mānana hikes. Go up Waimano, turn left along the Koʻolau summit ridge, and then go down Mānana. The 1-mile summit section is for experienced hikers only because the trail there is rough, narrow, overgrown, and frequently socked in.

Hanauma Bay and Koko Crater. (Photo by Jason Sunada.)

Mānoa Falls and pool. 'Aihualama-'Ōhi'a hike. (Photo by John Hoover.)

Second and third peaks. Olomana hike. (Photo by John Hoover.)

On the trail. Pu'u Kalena hike. (Photo by John Hoover.)

'Ōhi'a tree. Kānehoa-
Hāpapa hike. (Photo by
John Hoover.)

In the gulch. Ma'akua Gulch
hike. (Photo by Albert
Miller.)

Climbing the narrow dike. Pu'u Kalena hike. (Photo by John Hoover.)

Hiker in the mist. Pu'u Manamana hike. (Photo by John Hoover.)

Sheer ridge. Puʻu Manamana hike. (Photo by Jason Sunada.)

Up the waterfall. Kaʻau Crater hike. (Photo by John Hoover.)

Rainbow in Koʻiahi Gulch. ʻŌhikilolo hike. (Photo by Jason Sunada.)

Kolekole Pass: peaks of Puʻu Hāpapa, Puʻu Kānehoa, Puʻu Kaua, and Palikea. Puʻu Kalena hike. (Photo by John Hoover.)

Ridge route, Mākua Valley. ʻŌhikilolo hike. (Photo by John Hoover.)

Koʻolau cliffs, Kōnāhuanui in back. Kuliʻouʻou Ridge hike. (Photo by John Hoover.)

Kahana Valley. Kahana Valley hike. (Photo by John Hoover.)

Puʻu ʻŌhulehule. Schofield-Waikāne hike. (Photo by Albert Miller.)

20 Waimano Valley

Type:	Valley
Length:	2-mile loop
Elevation Gain:	400 feet
Danger:	Low
Suitable for:	Novice
Location:	'Ewa Forest Reserve above Pearl City
Topo Map:	Waipahu
Access:	Open

Highlights

This loop hike samples a short stretch of a peaceful, lovely valley. Smooth, reflective water alternates with shallow rapids in the stream there. The return route follows an abandoned irrigation ditch along the side of the valley.

Trailhead Directions

At Punchbowl St. get on Lunalilo Fwy (H-1) heading 'ewa (west).

Near Middle St. keep left on Rte 78 west (exit 19B, Moanalua Rd.) to 'Aiea.

By Aloha Stadium bear right to rejoin H-1 to Pearl City.

Leave the freeway at exit 10, marked Pearl City–Waimalu.

Turn right on Moanalua Rd. at the end of the off-ramp.

As Moanalua Rd. ends, turn right on Waimano Home Rd.

The road narrows to two lanes.

Enter the grounds of Waimano Training School and Hospital. Look for a guard station ahead.

Park on the left in a dirt area just before the guard shack and across from the Pearl City Cultural Center (elevation 470 feet) (map point A).

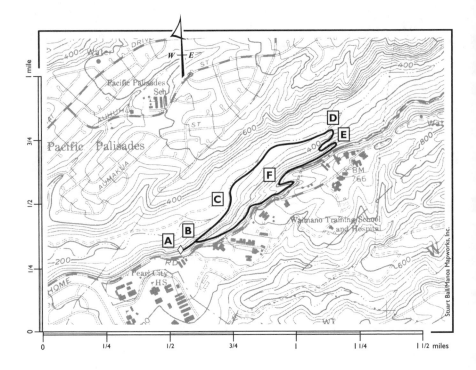

Bus: Route 53 to the intersection of Waimano Home Rd. and Komo Mai Dr. Walk 1.0 mile up Waimano Home Rd. to the trailhead.

Route Description

Continue up Waimano Home Rd. on foot.

Bear left off the road by the hunter check-in mailbox near the guard shack.

Follow the path to the left of and next to a chain-link fence.

Shortly afterward reach a signed junction (map point B). Bear left on the Lower Waimano Trail heading into the valley. (The trail along the fence is the upper trail, which is the return portion of the loop.)

Pass an old wooden signpost on the right.

Descend gradually down the side of the ridge. Lining the wide, grassy trail are strawberry guava and white-barked albizia trees. Look and listen for the white-rumped shama.

Walk under arching Christmas berry and Java plum trees.

Reach the valley floor (map point C). Keep right, heading upstream.

Pass a long hau grove on the left.

The trail edges close to Waimano Stream and parallels it. Watch your step on a short, rocky section near the water.

Bear right, away from the stream.

Climb gradually through a more open area with scattered albizia.

Shortly afterward reach a junction marked by two mango trees in a clearing (map point D). Turn right uphill on a wide trail. (The narrow trail straight ahead continues up the valley.)

As the trail narrows, work left initially and then straight up the side of the ridge.

Bear left and climb more gradually on two switchbacks.

Halfway up the ridge reach the junction with the Upper Waimano Trail (map point E). Turn sharp right on it. (To the left the trail goes all the way to the Ko'olau summit.)

An abandoned irrigation ditch comes in on the left and parallels the trail. Periodically the ditch disappears into short tunnels. The trail is narrow in spots and can be slippery when wet.

Contour through strawberry guava and Christmas berry trees. Watch for an occasional native lama tree.

Climb gradually through eucalyptus.

Swing left and cross over the top of an eroded side ridge (elevation 640 feet) (map point F). In the distance is a good view of the Wai'anae Range.

Descend into a side gully. The ditch reappears on the left.

Jump over a narrow concrete spillway.

Turn right along the fence by Waimano Home Rd.

Reach the junction with the lower trail (map point B) and, shortly afterward, the guard shack (map point A).

Notes

Waimano (many waters) Valley is the perfect hike for a sunny Sunday afternoon. Stroll into the valley and savor the lovely walk by the stream. The climb out is not difficult, but you'll know you've had some exercise!

This short loop is another good hike for beginners. For the most part, the trail is wide and well graded. Watch your footing, however, on the narrow spots by the ditch. Also, watch out for a few mosquitoes in the valley.

The first and last sections of the loop are lined with strawberry guava trees (waiawī 'ula'ula). They have glossy, dark green leaves and smooth brown bark. Their dark red fruit is delicious, with a taste reminiscent of strawberries. The guavas usually ripen in August and September. The strawberry guava is a native of Brazil but was introduced to Hawai'i from England in the 1800s.

On the descent into the valley look and listen for the white-rumped shama. It is black on top with a chestnut-colored breast and a long black-and-white tail. The shama has a variety of beautiful songs and often mimics other birds. A native of Malaysia, the shama has become widespread in introduced forests such as this one.

Along the stream are tangled groves of hau trees with large, heart-shaped leaves. Their flowers are bright yellow with a dark red center and resemble those of a hibiscus. Early Hawaiians used the wood for kites and canoe outriggers, the bark for sandals, and the sap as a laxative.

In the valley the unmarked junction with the return route uphill does not jump out at you. Look for the two mango trees, two small stumps, and scattered rocks. Beyond the junction the valley trail becomes more narrow and overgrown.

On the return contour section are native lama trees. Their oblong, pointed leaves are dark green and leathery. The fruits are green, then yellow, and finally bright red when fully ripe. Lama was sacred to Laka, goddess of the hula. Early Hawaiians used the hard, light-colored wood in temple construction and in hula performances.

For a much longer outing, take the Waimano Ridge hike that starts from the same trailhead. The entire hike is 15 miles round trip, but you can go as far as you want and then turn around.

21 Waimano Pool

Type:	Valley
Length:	3-mile round trip
Elevation Gain:	700 feet
Danger:	Low
Suitable for:	Novice, Intermediate
Location:	'Ewa Forest Reserve above Pacific Palisades
Topo Map:	Waipahu
Access:	Open

Highlights
This short, popular hike leads into lush Waimano Valley. Awaiting you along the stream are two deep swimming holes backed by a cascading waterfall. On the return, take your time climbing "cardiac hill."

Trailhead Directions
At Punchbowl St. get on Lunalilo Fwy (H-1) heading 'ewa (west).

Near Middle St. keep left on Rte 78 west (exit 19B, Moanalua Rd.) to 'Aiea.

By Aloha Stadium bear right to rejoin H-1 to Pearl City.

Leave the freeway at exit 10, marked Pearl City–Waimalu.

Turn right on Moanalua Rd. at the end of the off-ramp.

As Moanalua Rd. ends, turn right on Waimano Home Rd.

At the third traffic light and just before the road narrows to two lanes, turn left on Komo Mai Dr.

The road descends into Waimano Valley and then climbs the next ridge.

Drive through Pacific Palisades subdivision to the end of the road.

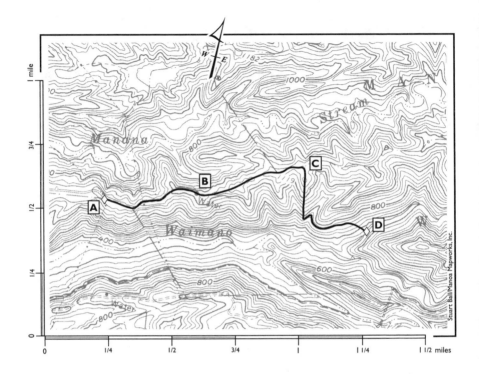

Park on the street just before the turnaround circle (elevation 960 feet) (map point A).

Bus: Route 53 to Komo Mai Dr. and ʻAuhuhu St. Walk 0.4 mile along Komo Mai Dr. to the trailhead.

Route Description

At the back of the circle walk through an opening in the fence next to a gate.

Proceed up the one-lane paved road. In the distance on the left is the Waiʻanae Range.

Reach a water tank at the road end (map point B).

Continue straight, on the Mānana Trail, through a eucalyptus forest.

Pass a utility tower on the left.

Stroll through a pleasant level section on top of the ridge.

The trail splits. Keep left, avoiding the grassy area on the right.

In a rooty clearing bear slightly left and down to continue on the main ridge.

Begin contouring to the right of a hump in the ridge (map point C).

Shortly afterward the trail forks by a metal stake. Keep right onto a side ridge leading down to Waimano Valley. (The left fork is the continuation of the Mānana Trail, which follows the main ridge all the way to the Koʻolau summit.)

The trail ascends briefly to a small grassy knoll (elevation 1,120 feet). In the distance is the Koʻolau Range.

Descend steeply along the eroded side ridge. Watch your step on the exposed roots and loose soil.

Partway down the ridge turn left in a strawberry guava grove.

Descend, steeply at times, across the side ridge into a small gulch. The trail is rough, narrow, and muddy.

Contour along the side of Waimano Valley through strawberry guava and kī (ti) plants.

Descend steadily, passing a small rock cliff.

Bear left and resume contouring. Ignore a side trail on the right.

Break out into the open briefly by native ʻōhiʻa trees. Below Waimano Stream splits in two.

Bear right and descend straight down toward the stream.

Reach the left fork of the stream at the lower pool (elevation 540 feet) (map point D). A narrow, slippery trail leads upstream to the upper pool at the base of a waterfall and to the top of the falls.

Notes

Waimano Pool is a popular outing because of its short length and its main attraction, two good-sized swimming holes. Take this hike in the wet season (November–April). After a good rain the stream keeps the pools full of cool, clear water. During summer the flow often slows to a trickle, leaving the pools shallow and stagnant. Whenever you go, be prepared to meet some pesky mosquitoes.

The initial route along the main ridge follows the well-groomed Mānana Trail. The remainder of the hike is over a rough, makeshift trail, which is often steep and usually muddy. The side ridge down to Waimano (many waters) Stream is informally and affectionately known as "cardiac hill." Watch your footing on the way down; take your time on the way up. Although suitable for novices, the complete hike may prove difficult for an out-of-shape beginner.

Along the main ridge and in the valley are strawberry guava trees (waiawī 'ula'ula). They have glossy, dark green leaves and smooth brown bark. Their dark red fruit is delicious, with a taste reminiscent of strawberries. The guavas usually ripen in August and September. Pickings may be slim along the trail, however, because of its popularity. The strawberry guava is a native of Brazil but was introduced to Hawai'i from England in the 1800s.

As the trail contours above the stream, look for kī (ti) plants. They have shiny leaves, 1–2 feet long, that are arranged spirally in a cluster at the tip of a slender stem. Early Polynesian voyagers introduced ti to Hawai'i. They used the leaves for house thatch, skirts, sandals, and raincoats. Food to be cooked in an *imu* (underground oven) was first wrapped in ti leaves. A popular sport with the commoners was *ho'ohe'e kī* or ti-leaf sledding. The sap from ti plants was used to stain canoes and surfboards.

In the brief clearing before the final descent are several native 'ōhi'a trees. They have oval leaves and clusters of delicate red flowers. Early Hawaiians used the flowers in *lei* (garlands) and the wood in outrigger canoes. The hard, durable wood was also carved into god images for *heiau* (religious sites).

The hike ends at two delightful swimming holes separated by a miniature cascade. In back of the upper pool is a larger waterfall. The lower pool offers easier access for a cooling dip. Nonswimmers can hike upstream to a breezy overlook at the top of the falls.

Overhanging the pools are some kukui trees. Their large, pale green leaves resemble those of the maple, with several distinct lobes. Early Polynesian voyagers introduced kukui into Hawai'i. They used the wood to make gunwales and seats for their outrigger canoes. The flowers and sap became medicines to treat a variety of ailments. Early Hawaiians strung the nuts together to make *lei hua* (seed or nut garlands). The oily kernels became house candles and torches for night spearfishing.

For a nearby ridge outing, try the Mānana hike that starts from the same trailhead. The route is suitable for everyone; go as far as you want and then turn around.

22 Mānana

Type:	Ungraded ridge
Length:	12-mile round trip
Elevation Gain:	1,700 feet
Danger:	Low
Suitable for:	Novice, Intermediate, Expert
Location:	'Ewa Forest Reserve above Pacific Palisades
Topo Map:	Waipahu, Kāne'ohe
Access:	Open

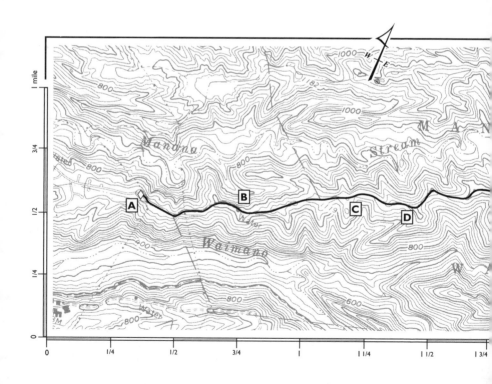

Highlights

This long, splendid ridge hike leads deep into the wild Ko‘olau Mountain Range. Along the way is an incredible variety of native dryland and rain forest plants. Lofty lookouts, en route and at the summit, provide stunning views of leeward and windward O‘ahu.

Trailhead Directions

At Punchbowl St. get on Lunalilo Fwy (H-1) heading ‘ewa (west).

Near Middle St. keep left on Rte 78 west (exit 19B, Moanalua Rd.) to ‘Aiea.

By Aloha Stadium bear right to rejoin H-1 to Pearl City.

Leave the freeway at exit 10, marked Pearl City–Waimalu.

Turn right on Moanalua Rd. at the end of the off-ramp.

As Moanalua Rd. ends, turn right on Waimano Home Rd.

At the third traffic light and just before the road narrows to two lanes, turn left on Komo Mai Dr.

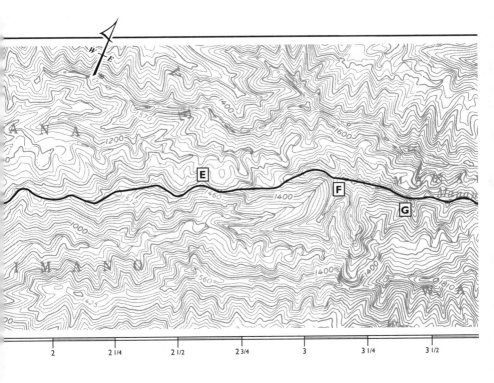

The road descends into Waimano Valley and then climbs the next ridge.

Drive through Pacific Palisades subdivision to the end of the road.

Park on the street just before the turnaround circle (elevation 960 feet) (map point A).

Bus: Route 53 to Komo Mai Dr. and ʻAuhuhu St. Walk 0.4 mile along Komo Mai Dr. to the trailhead.

Route Description

At the back of the circle walk through an opening in the fence next to a gate.

Proceed up the one-lane paved road.

Reach a water tank at the road end (map point B).

Continue straight, on the Mānana Trail, through a eucalyptus forest.

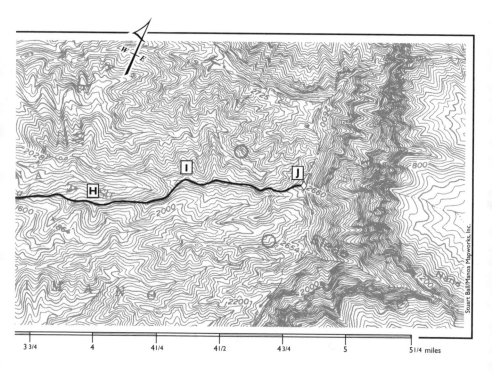

Pass a utility tower on the left.

Stroll through a pleasant level section on top of the ridge.

The trail splits. Keep left, avoiding the grassy area on the right.

In a rooty clearing bear slightly left and down to continue on the main ridge.

Begin contouring to the right of a hump in the ridge (map point C).

Shortly afterward the trail forks by a metal stake. Keep left around the hump on the main ridge. (The right fork leads down a side ridge into Waimano Valley and is described in the Waimano Pool hike.)

Descend briefly through an eroded section and then climb gradually through young brush box trees.

After another short descent the trail forks. Bear left and down (map point D).

Break out into the open. *Mauka* (inland) is a view of the entire ridge to be climbed.

Traverse a narrow, eroded stretch. Watch your footing, especially if the ground is wet.

The trail becomes a grassy avenue along the rolling ridge. Introduced pine and paperbark trees line the path. Look for the native trees koa and 'iliahi (sandalwood) and the native shrub naupaka kuahiwi.

On the left a side trail climbs to a small knob and then rejoins the main route.

Descend a short, steep, eroded section.

Pass a covered picnic table on the right.

The introduced trees end just past the table. Look for more 'iliahi near the trail.

Climb steeply to the first really distinct knob in the ridge (map point E).

Descend the next dip and ascend steeply to the next hump. The native vegetation gradually changes from dryland to rain forest. Along the route are 'ōhi'a and kōpiko trees and hāpu'u tree ferns.

Cross a short level section.

Climb very steeply to another knob, where a long side ridge comes in on the right (map point F).

The trail narrows and becomes rough and rooty.

Cross another level section, descend briefly, and then ascend a flat, cleared hill used occasionally as a helipad (map point G). There is a view in all directions. To leeward is Pearl Harbor and the Wai'anae Range. On the left is a native lapalapa tree with its fluttering leaves.

Traverse a long series of small but steep knobs in the ridge.

Cross a level muddy section.

Ascend steeply to a large hill with a small clearing on top (map point H). From there is a commanding view of the ridge ahead.

Swing left and climb steadily. The vegetation becomes stunted, and the wind picks up.

Curve right, toward the Ko'olau summit, as a long side ridge comes in on the left (map point I).

The main ridge narrows significantly.

Traverse a series of small humps. On the left are several native loulu palms.

The ridge broadens and levels briefly through low-lying sedge.

Cross a second series of humps on the narrow ridge.

Pass a waterfall chute down and on the right.

Climb steadily through increasing vegetation.

Reach the Ko'olau summit at a massive knob (elevation 2,660 feet) (map point J).

Notes

Mānana is the best of the Ko'olau (windward) ridge trails. The hike offers over 2 miles of the finest open ridge walking on the island. Along the route are some intriguing native plants and a chance at glimpsing some native birds. The windy finish, often in mist, is wild and wonderful. You feel as if you are on top of the world.

The Mānana Trail should appeal to all types of hikers. Novices can stroll to the picnic table. Intermediate hikers can continue to the helipad. Experts can head for the summit.

Although not graded, the trail is wide and clear to the picnic table. Watch your step, however, on the two eroded sections. Beyond the picnic table the route becomes rough, steep, narrow, and muddy, although rarely all at the same time. Between the helipad and the final climb, the trail may be overgrown with scratchy uluhe ferns and *Clidemia* shrubs.

On the initial trail section remember to keep left along the main ridge. Ignore the side trails leading down into Waimano (many waters) Valley on the right. Also, watch for mountain bikers, especially in the afternoon. Portions of the trail in this section are lined with strawberry guava (waiawī ʻulaʻula) trees whose tasty, dark red fruit usually ripens in August and September.

After leaving the introduced forest, the route winds through a lovely open stretch still recovering from a fire in 1972. Making a comeback are the native trees koa and ʻiliahi. Koa has sickle-shaped foliage and pale yellow flower clusters. Early Hawaiians made surfboards and outrigger canoe hulls out of the beautiful red brown wood. Today it is made into fine furniture.

Look for ʻiliahi, the sandalwood tree, just past the picnic table. Its small leaves are dull green and appear wilted. ʻIliahi is partially parasitic, with outgrowths on its roots that steal nutrients from nearby plants. Early Hawaiians ground the fragrant heart-wood into a powder to perfume their *kapa* (bark cloth). Beginning in the late 1700s, sandalwood was indiscriminately cut down and exported to China to make incense and furniture. The trade ended around 1840 when the forests were depleted of ʻiliahi.

Farther along the ridge is the native rain forest, dominated by ʻōhiʻa trees and hāpuʻu tree ferns. ʻŌhiʻa has oval leaves and clusters of delicate red flowers. Native birds, such as the ʻapapane, feed on the nectar and help in pollination. Early Hawaiians used the flowers in *lei* (garlands) and the wood in outrigger canoes. The hard, durable wood was also carved into god images for *heiau* (religious sites). Beneath the ʻōhiʻa are hāpuʻu tree ferns with delicate, sweeping fronds. Their trunks consist of roots tightly woven around a small central stem. The brown fiber covering the young fronds of hāpuʻu is called *pulu*.

At the helipad is a magnificent lapalapa tree. Its roundish leaves are arranged in groups of three and flutter in the slightest wind. Early Hawaiians used the bark, leaves, and purple fruit to make a blue black dye to decorate their *kapa*. The leaves also make a distinctive *lei*.

Beyond the helipad watch for 'elepaio, a small native bird. It is brown on top and white underneath with a black throat and a dark tail, usually cocked. The bird roams the forest understory catching insects on the fly or on vegetation. 'Elepaio are very curious, which is why you can sometimes see them. If you are very lucky, you may catch a glimpse of an 'apapane in the forest canopy. It has a red breast and head, black wings and tail, and a slightly curved black bill. In flight the 'apapane makes a whirring sound as it darts from tree to tree searching for insects and nectar.

On the final climb look for the native loulu palm, emerging out of the mist. It has rigid, fan-shaped fronds in a cluster at the top of a ringed trunk. Early Hawaiians used the fronds for thatch and plaited the blades of young fronds into fans and baskets.

As you near the top, listen for the Japanese bush warbler (uguisu), a bird often heard, but rarely seen. Its distinctive cry starts with a long whistle and then winds down in a series of notes. There seems to be at least one bush warbler at the top of every Ko'olau ridge trail.

The view from the summit lookout is exceptional, weather permitting. Ka'alaea (reddish earth) Valley lies 2,000 feet below. The windward coast stretches from Kualoa (long back) to Makapu'u (bulging eye) Points. In Kāne'ohe (cutting husband) Bay you can see three enclosed fishponds, Mōli'i (small section), Kahalu'u (diving place), and He'eia, from left to right. On the left are four windward valleys, Waiāhole, Waikāne, Hakipu'u (hill broken), and Ka'a'awa (the wrasse fish). Dominating those valleys is the massive peak Pu'u 'Ōhulehule (joining of waves hill). In the distance to the right is triple-peaked Olomana (forked hill).

For a shorter valley outing, take the Waimano Pool hike that starts from the same trailhead. For a longer, more challenging route connect the Mānana and Waimano Ridge hikes. Go up Mānana, turn right along the Ko'olau summit ridge, and then go down Waimano. The 1-mile summit section is for experienced hikers only because the trail there is rough, narrow, overgrown, and frequently socked in.

23 Pu'u Kaua

Type:	Ungraded ridge
Length:	3-mile round trip
Elevation Gain:	1,900 feet
Danger:	Low
Suitable for:	Intermediate
Location:	Honouliuli Preserve above Kunia
Topo Map:	Schofield Barracks
Access:	Conditional; open only to outdoor organizations with permission. Contact The Nature Conservancy, 923 Nu'uanu Ave., Honolulu, HI 96817 (phone 537-4508).

Highlights
Pu'u Kaua is the third highest peak on O'ahu. The short, steep climb to its summit passes through introduced forest and then a special section of native plants. En route you may see the Hawaiian land snail and the native bird 'elepaio.

Trailhead Directions
At Punchbowl St. get on Lunalilo Fwy (H-1) heading 'ewa (west).

Near Middle St. keep left on Rte 78 west (exit 19B, Moanalua Rd.) to 'Aiea.

By Aloha Stadium bear right to rejoin H-1 to Pearl City and on toward Wai'anae.

Take Kunia Rd. (exit 5B, Rte 750 north).

On the right pass Village Park and Royal Kunia subdivisions.

Look for the Hawaii Country Club on the right.

Just past the clubhouse the road dips slightly and then climbs.

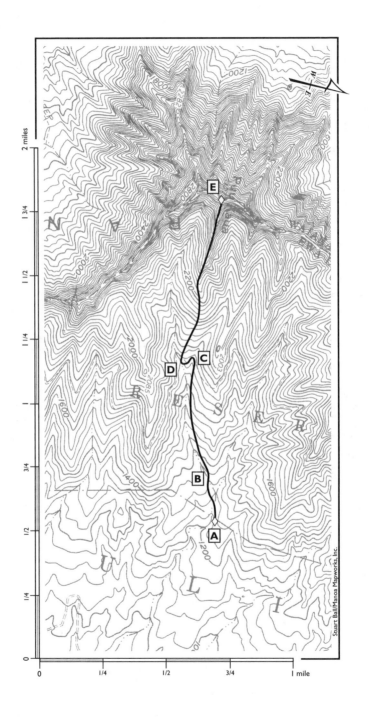

At the top of the rise and across from the boundary of the golf course, bear left on a dirt road paralleling the main highway. Reset your trip odometer (0.0 mile).

Almost immediately turn left by a raised water pipe through a gate on a dirt road heading into the pineapple fields.

Curve right and then descend gradually toward 'Ēkahanui Gulch.

Parallel the gulch, ascending gradually.

Another well-used dirt road comes in on the left (0.6 mile). Continue straight.

As the road tops out by two yellow posts and some irrigation pipes, turn left on a dirt road that descends briefly (0.9 mile).

Climb gradually along the edge of a pineapple field. The gulch remains on the left.

Park at the top of the field (1.6 miles) (elevation 1,240 feet) (map point A). Be sure to leave plenty of room for plantation vehicles to get by.

Bus: None, within reasonable walking distance of the trailhead.

Route Description

As the road begins to curve right around the top of the pineapple field, bear left on a trail through tall grass.

Descend gradually into 'Ēkahanui Gulch through a eucalyptus forest. Look for remnant coffee and macadamia nut trees.

Cross a dry streambed and turn left.

Wind through a series of blowdowns left by hurricane 'Iwa.

The trail roughly follows an overgrown dirt road that curves right to contour along the flank of the mountain.

Bear right, off the road, and cross a small streambed (map point B).

Turn right to rejoin the road, now more open and well defined.

Turn left straight uphill to bypass a clogged switchback on the road.

Turn left again to rejoin the road.

Climb steadily through plantings of Cook pines and tropical ash. The road becomes narrow and eroded.

As the road peters out, bear right up a short, steep section.

Reach the junction with the Honouliuli Contour Trail (map point C). Turn left on it. (To the right the contour trail leads to the Kānehoa-Hāpapa hike and Kolekole Pass.)

Descend briefly and cross a small streambed (map point D). Just after the crossing, reach a junction. Bear right and up on a makeshift trail. (To the left the contour trail, now indistinct, parallels the streambed and leads to Pālehua Rd.)

Climb steeply on the broad ridge through guava. The going is mostly straight up with an occasional attempt at a switchback. Look for the native bird 'elepaio.

The ridge narrows, and the incline lessens briefly. The guava gradually gives way to koa and Christmas berry trees. Watch for an occasional kōlea tree, a favorite habitat of the Hawaiian land snail.

Resume the steep ascent on the now partially open ridge.

Reach a small dip filled with 'ama'u ferns.

Negotiate a particularly steep, wet section through native vegetation. Between breaths look for 'ōhi'a and olomea trees and pū'ahanui (kanawao) shrubs.

Reach the top of Pu'u Kaua (elevation 3,127 feet) in a grassy area (map point E).

Notes

Pu'u Kaua (war hill) is the third highest peak on the island. The climb to its summit is short, steep, and very special. Along the ridge are unusual native plants and rare land snails. The hike is entirely within the Honouliuli (dark bay) Preserve of The Nature Conservancy.

During a heavy rain the approach road through the pineapple fields quickly becomes impassable for two-wheel-drive vehicles. If the road is muddy and slippery, leave your car off Kunia Rd. or park near the two yellow posts just before the road dips.

The initial route is somewhat obscure, with many turns and several junctions. Follow the route description closely. Surveyor's ribbon may mark the way, but don't count on it. The climb to the summit is very steep. Fortunately, the ridge is reasonably wide, but watch your step anyway.

Halfway up the ridge watch for the native tree kōlea. It has narrow, oval leaves growing at the branch tips. The leaves are bright pink when young, gradually turning dark green with age. Early Hawaiians used the light-colored wood in outrigger canoe construction and, as charcoal, to dye *kapa* (bark cloth). Also found along the trail is another variety, kōlea lau li'i. It resembles English boxwood, with many branches and small, rounded leaves.

Kōlea is a favorite habitat of endangered Hawaiian land snails. Look carefully for them on both sides of the leaves. The snails have white, spiral shells with brown rings and eat the mold on the leaves. Do not disturb the snails or allow them to fall to the ground. Years ago many valleys on O'ahu had their own species of snail. Now most are gone because of shell collecting, habitat loss, and predation from introduced snails and rats.

While climbing the ridge, look for the 'elepaio, a small native bird. It is brown on top and white underneath with a black throat and a dark tail, usually cocked. The bird roams the forest understory catching insects on the fly or on vegetation. 'Elepaio are very curious, which is why you can sometimes see them.

In the steep, wet section near the top are the native tree olomea and the shrub pū'ahanui (kanawao). Olomea has shiny leaves with serrated edges and red veins and stems. Pū'ahanui, a relative of hydrangea, has large, serrated, deeply creased leaves and clusters of delicate pink flowers. Early Hawaiians used the plants for medicinal purposes.

From the top you can see Lualualei and Wai'anae (mullet water) Valleys to leeward. To windward are the north shore, the Wahiawā (place of noise) plain, and, in the distance, Pearl Harbor and Diamond Head. In back is the Ko'olau (windward) Range stretching from Hale'iwa (house of the frigate bird) to Honolulu. To the north along the summit ridge are Kolekole (raw) Pass and flat-topped Ka'ala (the fragrance), the highest peak on the island.

24 Kānehoa-Hāpapa

Type:	Ungraded ridge
Length:	6-mile round trip
Elevation Gain:	1,500 feet
Danger:	Medium
Suitable for:	Intermediate, Expert
Location:	Schofield Barracks Forest Reserve and Honouliuli Preserve
Topo Map:	Schofield Barracks
Access:	Conditional; open only to outdoor organizations with permission. Contact The Nature Conservancy, 923 Nu'uanu Ave., Honolulu, HI 96817 (phone 537-4508) and Commander, U.S. Army Garrison, Hawai'i, Schofield Barracks, HI 96857 (attn: APVG-GWY-O).

Highlights
This spectacular hike follows the summit ridge of the Wai'anae Range. Starting from Kolekole Pass, the route traverses two peaks, Pu'u Kānehoa and Hāpapa. Along the sometimes narrow ridge are magnificent views of central O'ahu and the leeward coast.

Trailhead Directions
At Punchbowl St. get on Lunalilo Fwy (H-1) heading *'ewa* (west).

Near Middle St. keep left on Rte 78 west (exit 19B, Moanalua Rd.) to 'Aiea.

By Aloha Stadium bear right to rejoin H-1 to Pearl City.

Take H-2 freeway (exit 8A) to Wahiawā.

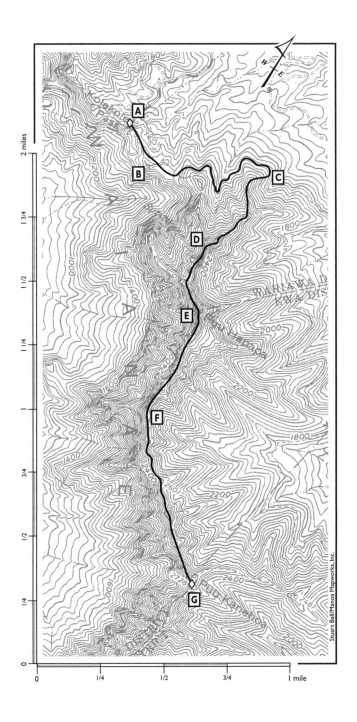

As the freeway ends, continue on Rte 99 north (Wilikina Dr.) bypassing Wahiawā.

At the second traffic light turn left on Kunia Rd.

At the next light turn right and enter Schofield Barracks through the Foote Gate.

Bear right on Devol Rd.

At the road end turn left on Waiʻanae Ave., which is one way.

Turn left again, on Heard Ave.

At the next intersection turn half right on Trimble Rd.

Pass Sergeant E. R. Smith Theater on the right.

The road widens to four lanes by the commissary.

Trimble Rd. then narrows to two lanes and becomes Kolekole Rd.

Ascend gradually toward Kolekole Pass.

Go through a series of S curves.

Look for a large sign on the left marked Kolekole Pass Rock. It's just before the guard station at the top of the pass.

Park in the dirt lot near the sign (elevation 1,640 feet) (map point A).

Bus: None, within reasonable walking distance of the trailhead.

Route Description
Take the trail leading to Pōhaku Hūpēloa (Kolekole Pass Rock).

Descend briefly and then climb steeply on wooden steps.

Reach Pōhaku Hūpēloa.

Descend the steps past the boulder and turn left on a dirt road.

Pass a communications tower on the right.

The road forks. Keep left uphill on a deeply rutted road.

The road forks again. This time keep right downhill.

Enter a lovely, small meadow. To the right are views of Lualualei Valley.

On the far left side of the meadow pick up the Honouliuli Contour Trail (map point B).

Climb gradually and then begin contouring through strawberry guava and Christmas berry trees.

Break out into the open briefly by an eroded hill. To the left is a view of Kolekole Pass.

Cross a small landslide on a narrow trail.

Descend gradually through a grove of paperbark trees.

Cross a rocky streambed in a gully.

Cross a second gully.

Contour under arching Christmas berry and silk oak trees.

Descend gradually along the side of a spur ridge.

As the trail crosses the ridge, turn right, up the ridge (map point C).

Ascend steeply through Christmas berry and then grass.

Reach a rock outcrop. A steep trail on the right leads back down to the contour trail. Continue climbing.

A side ridge with a trail comes in on the left.

Another side ridge with a steep trail comes in on the right.

Reach the Waiʻanae summit ridge (map point D) and turn left along it. (A faint trail to the right ends in a sheer precipice!)

Climb steadily under Christmas berry and native ʻōhiʻa trees.

Pass an eroded spot on the left with good views leeward.

Reach the broad summit of Hāpapa (elevation 2,883 feet) (map point E).

At its top enter the Honouliuli Preserve of The Nature Conservancy.

Descend steeply off Hāpapa. A short rock face must be negotiated without a cable.

Traverse a series of small knobs along the ridge. The last one has a magnificent 360-degree view.

Descend steeply off the knob with a view and cross another series of low humps in the ridge. Look for the native shrub koʻokoʻolau.

Climb a rocky knob that juts out from the ridge (map point F). Bypass its summit on the right.

Ascend very steeply to a second distinct hump and then drop steeply off its back side.

Bear right and down to avoid two large rock formations.

Climb over a third knob.

Traverse a rocky, narrow section. Go around to the right of the worst spot.

Reach the eroded summit of Puʻu Kānehoa (elevation 2,728 feet) (map point G). (To the left an overgrown trail leads down a long side ridge to a junction with the Honouliuli Contour Trail.)

Notes

Kānehoa-Hāpapa is another "wow" hike. Much of the route follows the highly scenic crest of the Wai'anae (mullet water) Range above Kolekole (raw) Pass. Along the summit ridge are two peaks to be climbed, Pu'u Kānehoa (companion of Kāne hill) and Hāpapa (rock stratum).

The summit section, however, is sometimes as narrow as the views are spectacular. Don't walk and sightsee at the same time. Watch your footing, particularly on the open stretches because the grass there can hide steep drop-offs. Take extra care on the narrow, rocky section just before Kānehoa.

The route initially passes Pōhaku Hūpēloa, an ancient Hawaiian stone. The 6-foot-high boulder has an unusual extension with a bowl-shaped depression. According to legend, Hūpēloa represents a female spirit who guards Kolekole Pass. Hawaiian martial arts warriors in her service used the area to practice their skills on unfortunate travelers. Another story mentions the boulder as a site for preparing dead chiefs for burial.

From the meadow just beyond the stone, you can look down into Lualualei Valley, used by the Navy for ammunition storage and radio communication. The peak jutting into the valley on the right is Pu'u Ka'īlio (dog hill). It consists of remnant lava from the summit caldera of the old Wai'anae volcano. The huge caldera was centered leeward of Kolekole Pass and extended almost 9 miles from Nānākuli (look at knee) to Mākaha (fierce) Valleys.

After leaving the meadow, the hike follows a short section of the Honouliuli (dark bay) Contour Trail. Constructed by the Civilian Conservation Corps in 1934–1935, the trail contours along the windward flank of the Wai'anae Range from Kolekole Pass to Pālehua Rd. The Pu'u Kaua (war hill) hike also uses a portion of the Honouliuli Contour Trail.

After reaching the Wai'anae summit, look for native 'ōhi'a trees. They have oval leaves and clusters of delicate red flowers. Early Hawaiians used the flowers in *lei* (garlands) and the wood in outrigger canoes. The hard, durable wood was also carved into god images for *heiau* (religious sites).

The views all along the summit ridge are breathtaking. To leeward are Lualualei and Wai'anae Valleys. To windward are the Wahiawā (place of noise) plain, Pearl Harbor, and, in the distance, Honolulu and Diamond Head. In back you can see the Ko'olau (windward) Range from the north shore to Nu'uanu (cool height) Pali.

Watch for the native herb ko'oko'olau, related to the daisy and sunflower families. It has pointed, serrated leaves and flower heads with yellow petals. Early Hawaiians steeped the leaves to make a tea used as a tonic.

The hike is described out and back. To make a loop, turn left down the side ridge at Pu'u Kānehoa. By a grove of evergreens turn left again on the Honouliuli Contour Trail. Follow the contour trail back to Kolekole Pass. The complete loop is for experienced hikers only because the return portion is overgrown and obscure in spots.

If you enjoyed Kānehoa-Hāpapa, tackle the Kalena (the lazy one) hike next. It starts on the other side of Kolekole Pass.

25 Kalena

Type:	Ungraded ridge
Length:	5-mile round trip
Elevation Gain:	2,100 feet
Danger:	High
Suitable for:	Expert
Location:	Schofield Barracks Forest Reserve
Topo Map:	Schofield Barracks
Access:	Conditional; open to individuals and outdoor organizations with written permission. Write Commander, U.S. Army Garrison, Hawai'i, Schofield Barracks, HI 96857 (attn: APVG-GWY-O).

Highlights

This short, steep hike climbs Kalena, the second highest peak on the island. Along the way are knife-edge ridges and intriguing native plants. From windy lookouts, en route and at the summit, are panoramic views of leeward and central O'ahu.

Trailhead Directions

At Punchbowl St. get on Lunalilo Fwy (H-1) heading 'ewa (west).

Near Middle St. keep left on Rte 78 west (exit 19B, Moanalua Rd.) to 'Aiea.

By Aloha Stadium bear right to rejoin H-1 to Pearl City.

Take H-2 freeway (exit 8A) to Wahiawā.

As the freeway ends, continue on Rte 99 north (Wilikina Dr.) bypassing Wahiawā.

At the second traffic light turn left on Kunia Rd.

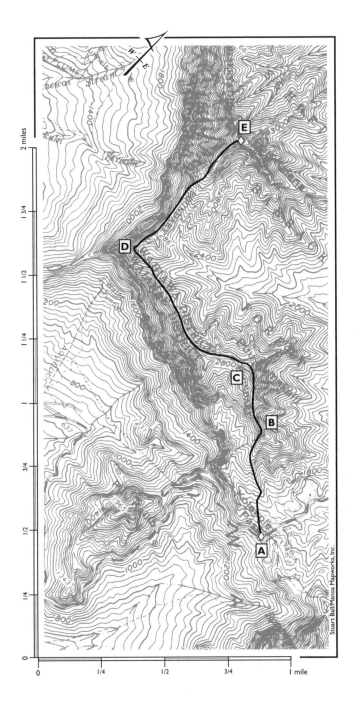

At the next light turn right and enter Schofield Barracks through the Foote Gate.

Bear right on Devol Rd.

At the road end turn left on Wai'anae Ave., which is one way.

Turn left again, on Heard Ave.

At the next intersection turn half right on Trimble Rd.

Pass Sergeant E. R. Smith Theater on the right.

The road widens to four lanes by the commissary.

Trimble Rd. then narrows to two lanes and becomes Kolekole Rd.

Ascend gradually toward Kolekole Pass.

Go through a series of S curves.

Look for a large sign on the left marked Kolekole Pass Rock. It's just before the guard station at the top of the pass.

Park in the dirt lot near the sign (elevation 1,640 feet) (map point A).

Bus: None, within reasonable walking distance of the trailhead.

Route Description

Take the dirt road across Kolekole Rd. from the parking lot.

Ascend steadily as the road curves right and then left.

At the road end walk through an enclosure with wooden railings.

Climb a steep, eroded section.

Pick up a distinct trail, which climbs straight up the ridge through Formosa koa trees.

Keep right briefly to bypass a small rock face.

The angle of ascent eases and then steepens.

Bear right, off the ridgeline, to avoid a larger rock face.

Reach a junction with the ridge coming in on the right. Turn left up it. (To the right a faint trail leads down to a quarry.) Memorize that junction for the return trip.

Almost immediately reach a rocky outcrop with a benchmark (map point B). Catch your breath and take in the panoramic view.

The ridge levels briefly through stunted Christmas berry trees.

Resume steep climbing over rock; bypass a narrow section to the left.

The ridge again levels momentarily.

Climb gradually on a narrow rock dike. Watch your footing; crawl if necessary.

Ascend more steeply, negotiating a small rock face.

Reach the top of Puʻu Kūmakaliʻi (map point C). From here you can see Kalena in front of flat-topped Kaʻala.

The ridge swings left and becomes relatively level.

Cross another narrow rock dike.

Climb a small rock face and then bear right past a knife-edge side ridge.

Descend gradually along the main ridge through a mixed forest of strawberry guava, Christmas berry, and native ʻōhiʻa. Look for the native herb koʻokoʻolau.

Go around to the right of a landslide.

In a flat area keep left on the main ridge.

Descend steeply to a saddle through guava and native koa trees.

Ascend a small dirt hump in the middle of the saddle.

Climb steeply on the eroded trail to reach a distinct peak (map point D). At its top look for native pūkiawe shrubs.

The main ridge swings right, toward Kalena.

Descend into a second saddle and ascend to another smaller peak.

Descend steadily and then begin the final climb to the summit of Kalena.

Climb very steeply through uluhe ferns and *Clidemia* shrubs.

The angle of ascent eases a bit through native vegetation. Along the trail are olomea and ʻōhiʻa ʻāhihi trees.

Cross a relatively level section.

Resume steep climbing. Look for the native shrubs kūkaemoa (alani) and pūʻahanui (kanawao).

Reach the summit of Kalena (elevation 3,504 feet) (map point E).

Notes

Kalena means the lazy one. The name sounds innocuous enough, but don't be fooled. Kalena is the second highest peak on Oʻahu. The short ascent to its summit is very steep and a bit scary.

Serious climbing begins right away, so the hike is for sure-footed experts only.

From start to finish the route is a scramble over loose rock and dirt. Watch your footing constantly. You must traverse two very narrow rock dikes (yikes!) with steep drop-offs on both sides. Use extreme caution, especially in high winds. If necessary, crawl along the top. It's not elegant, but it's a whole lot safer. On the final climb blackberry bushes may overgrow the trail. Wear gloves and long pants for protection against the thorns.

The views are panoramic right from the start. To leeward are Lualualei and Wai'anae (mullet water) Valleys. To windward are the Wahiawā (place of noise) plain, Pearl Harbor, and, in the distance, Honolulu and Diamond Head. In back you can see the Ko'olau (windward) Range. To the south are Kolekole (raw) Pass and the peaks of Hāpapa (rock stratum), Kānehoa, and Kaua (war hill) along the Wai'anae summit ridge.

From Pu'u Kūmakali'i (rising Pleiades hill) look down and leeward for Pu'u Ka'īlio (dog hill). It consists of remnant lava from the summit caldera of the old Wai'anae volcano. The huge caldera was centered leeward of Kolekole Pass and extended almost 9 miles from Nānākuli (look at knee) to Mākaha (fierce) Valleys.

The rocks you have been scrambling over are part of a dike complex in the northwest rift zone of the volcano. Rift zones are areas of structural weakness extending from the summit of a shield volcano. Rising molten rock or magma worked its way into cracks in the rift zone and solidified. The resulting dikes are sheetlike, vertical intrusions of hard, dense rock. Over the years streams have eroded the softer, surrounding material, leaving the dikes exposed.

After crossing the second dike, relax by looking for the native herb ko'oko'olau, related to the daisy and sunflower families. It has pointed, serrated leaves and flower heads with yellow petals. Early Hawaiians steeped the leaves to make a tea used as a tonic.

In the first saddle are native koa trees and pūkiawe shrubs. Koa has sickle-shaped foliage and pale yellow flower clusters. Early Hawaiians made surfboards and outrigger canoe hulls out of the beautiful red brown wood. Today it is made into fine furniture.

Pūkiawe has tiny, rigid leaves and small white, pink, or red berries.

On the final climb notice that a few trees, both native and introduced, have tags on them. The tags identify the trees as possible homes of the endangered Hawaiian land snail. Years ago many valleys on Oʻahu had their own species of snail. Now most are gone because of shell collecting, habitat loss, and predation from introduced snails. Do not disturb the trees or the tags.

Halfway up the final pyramid look for native ʻōhiʻa ʻāhihi trees. They have narrow, pointed leaves with red stems and midribs. Their delicate red flowers grow in clusters and are similar to those of the more common ʻōhiʻa, which you saw on the way up. ʻŌhiʻa ʻāhihi is found only in the Koʻolau and Waiʻanae Mountains on Oʻahu.

Just before the summit are native pūʻahanui (kanawao) and kūkaemoa (alani) shrubs. Pūʻahanui, a relative of hydrangea, has large, serrated, deeply creased leaves and clusters of delicate pink flowers. Early Hawaiians used the plants for medicinal purposes. Kūkaemoa (chicken dung) has curled, dark green leaves, which give off a slight anise odor. The fruits resemble miniature cauliflowers or chicken droppings.

At the top stretch out and take in the commanding views of leeward and central Oʻahu. Now you can see the rest of the summit ridge ascending to massive Kaʻala (the fragrance). To leeward is Kawiwi, a prominent triangular peak along Kamaileʻunu (the stripped maile) Ridge. The beautiful north shore makes an appearance to windward. At the summit is a native olomea tree. It has shiny leaves with serrated edges and red veins and stems.

If you liked Kalena, try the Kānehoa-Hāpapa hike. It starts on the opposite side of Kolekole Pass.

26 Schofield-Waikāne

Type:	Graded ridge
Length:	14-mile round trip
Elevation Gain:	1,200 feet
Danger:	Low
Suitable for:	Novice, Intermediate, Expert
Location:	'Ewa Forest Reserve above Wahiawā
Topo Map:	Hau'ula
Access:	Conditional; open to individuals and outdoor organizations with permission.

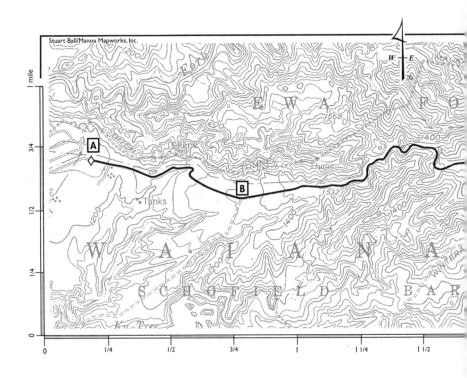

Write Commander, U.S. Army Garrison,
Hawai'i, Schofield Barracks, HI 96857
(attn: APVG-GWY-O).

Highlights

This rugged hike follows an old Army trail that traverses the
Ko'olau Range. The route pushes through some very wild and
remote country in central O'ahu. Along the way are awesome
overlooks, a variety of native plants, and, perhaps, some native
birds.

Trailhead Directions

At Punchbowl St. get on Lunalilo Fwy (H-1) heading 'ewa
(west).

Near Middle St. keep left on Rte 78 west (exit 19B, Moanalua
Rd.) to 'Aiea.

By Aloha Stadium bear right to rejoin H-1 to Pearl City.

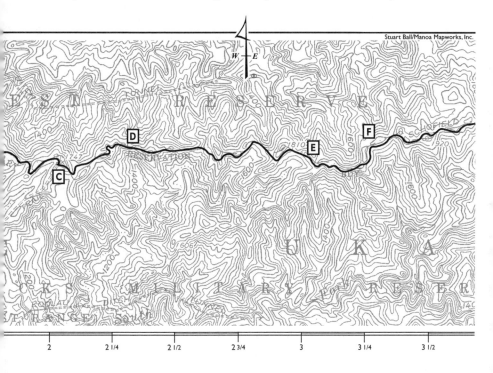

Take H-2 freeway (exit 8A) toward Wahiawā.

Get off H-2 at Wahiawā (exit 8, Rte 80 north).

At the end of the off-ramp merge into Kamehameha Hwy.

Cross Wilson Bridge and enter Wahiawā town.

At the third traffic light by a Shell service station turn right on California Ave.

The road narrows to two lanes.

Pass Leilehua High School on the right.

The road jogs right and then left.

Just after the second jog turn right through a gate into the East Range, an Army training area.

The paved road swings left to parallel California Ave.

Look for the Headquarters, Light Infantry Training Command on the right.

Park on the road near the headquarters building (elevation 1,240 feet) (map point A). Do not park in the lot.

Check in with the duty section at the headquarters.

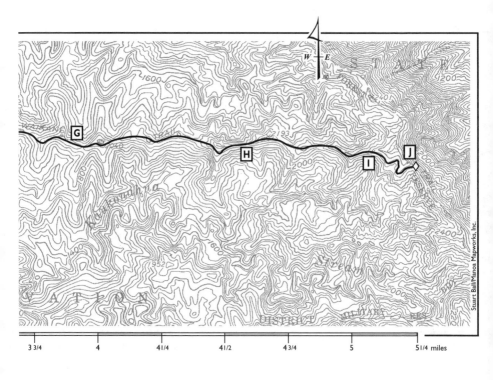

Bus: Route 62 to California Ave. and the entrance to the East Range. Walk 0.3 mile to the headquarters building.

Route Description

On foot, continue along the road through a gate.

The pavement ends, and the road narrows to one lane.

Pass a training area on the right.

Climb steadily on two switchbacks. Keep left on the main road at the junction by the second switchback.

Reach a major junction (map point B). Again, keep left toward the mountains. (The dirt road on the right heads down to the South Fork of Kaukonahua Stream and then exits the East Range by Wheeler Airfield.)

The road ascends steadily and then levels off.

Descend gradually and then resume climbing.

Walk another level stretch.

The road curves right and climbs past a small hump in the ridge.

Just past the hump reach a junction. Turn left on the Schofield-Waikāne Trail (map point C). (To the right the road heads down and back toward Wheeler Airfield.)

Descend briefly on a switchback.

Jump over a deep, but narrow, cut in the ridge.

Contour on the left and then on the right side of the ridge. Along the trail are the magnificent native rain forest trees koa and 'ōhi'a. Some of the 'ōhi'a trees have yellow flowers.

Reach a junction (map point D). Take the right fork heading up the ridge. (The left fork leads down to some good swimming holes along the North Fork of Kaukonahua Stream.)

Contour along the right side of the ridge.

Descend along the top of the ridge and then climb briefly on its left side.

Cross over to the right side of the ridge.

Climb steeply up a rock stairway.

The trail levels off on top of the ridge.

On the right pass two large side ridges forming a pocket valley (map point E). Look back to see the Wai'anae Range in the distance. To the right of Kolekole Pass are the summits of Kalena and Ka'ala.

Cross over to the left side of the ridge briefly and then switch once again to the right side. The trail becomes rough and narrow.

Pass two more side ridges on the right (map point F). In the valley formed by the ridges are 'ōhi'a trees with red, yellow, and orange flowers.

Continue contouring on the right side of the ridge for a long stretch. The trail gets really rough.

Pass another pair of side ridges (map point G).

Cross a relatively level section on top of the ridge. The vegetation is lower there because of the wind.

Climb steadily now following the crest of the ridge (map point H). The trail contours to the right twice and to the left once to skirt humps in the ridge. Look for native loulu palms and 'ōlapa trees with their fluttering leaves.

Begin the last contour section around the right side of a large peak along the summit ridge (map point I).

Step on some metal roofing, all that's left of an old cabin blown down in 1963.

On the right just before the top pass a small open area with good views of the Wai'anae Range.

Reach the Ko'olau summit (elevation 2,320 feet) (map point J) and the junction with the Ko'olau Summit Trail.

Notes

Schofield-Waikāne is a rugged ridge hike that penetrates deep into the central Ko'olau (windward) Range. The trail traverses country so wild that it's hard to believe you're on populous O'ahu. Remote overlooks en route and at the summit offer green views in all directions. Get an early start because of the high mileage and the rough, overgrown trail.

If the East Range gate is closed, follow the directions for the Wahiawā Hills hike. At the end of California Ave. take the trail paralleling the water tank fence to the headquarters building.

While checking in at infantry headquarters, ask about the condition of the dirt approach road. If the weather is dry, you may be able to drive as far as map point B. In a four-wheel-drive vehicle you may be able to get to the trailhead (map point C).

The U.S. Army built the Schofield-Waikāne Trail in the

1920s to connect Schofield Barracks with the windward side. The original path was wide, graded, and suitable for horses and mules. In the mid-1930s deteriorated sections of the trail were reconstructed by the Civilian Conservation Corps. Since then the trail has gradually fallen into disrepair. Although still graded, the treadway has many uneven and narrow spots because of slippage and erosion through the years. Overgrowing vegetation, particularly uluhe ferns, on the high side of the trail tends to force you downslope. Watch your footing constantly; expect to fall down a few times and get muddy and wet.

For the most part the trail winds through magnificent native rain forest dominated by 'ōhi'a and koa trees. 'Ōhi'a has oval leaves and clusters of delicate red, yellow, or orange flowers. Early Hawaiians used the flowers in *lei* (garlands) and the wood in outrigger canoes. The hard, durable wood was also carved into god images for *heiau* (religious sites). Koa has sickle-shaped foliage and pale yellow flower clusters. Early Hawaiians made surfboards and outrigger canoe hulls out of the beautiful red brown wood. Today it is made into fine furniture.

If you are very lucky, you may catch a glimpse of an 'apapane or 'i'iwi in the forest canopy. Both birds have a red breast and head, and black wings and tail. The 'i'iwi has a long, curved, salmon-colored bill for sipping 'ōhi'a nectar. The 'apapane has a slightly curved black bill. In flight the 'apapane makes a whirring sound as it darts from tree to tree searching for insects and nectar.

As the vegetation opens up, look for native loulu palms. They have rigid, fan-shaped fronds in a cluster at the top of a ringed trunk. Early Hawaiians used the fronds for thatch and plaited the blades of young fronds into fans and baskets.

Also along the open ridge are native 'ōlapa trees. Their leaves are opposite, oblong, and flutter in the slightest wind. In a special hula stance named after the tree, dancers mimic the exquisite movements of the leaves. Early Hawaiians used the bark, leaves, and purple fruit to make a blue black dye to decorate their *kapa* (bark cloth).

On the final stretch look closely for the native shrub 'ōhelo. It has rounded, toothed leaves and delicious red berries, about the size of blueberries. According to legend, 'ōhelo is sacred to Pele, goddess of fire. She changed her dead sister, Ka'ōhelo, into the shrub and named it after her.

Weather permitting, the view from the summit lookout is one of the best on the island. Directly below the *pali* (cliff) are five undeveloped valleys: from left to right, Punalu'u (coral dived for), Kahana (cutting), Ka'a'awa (the wrasse fish), Hakipu'u (hill broken), and Waikāne (Kāne's water). Pu'u 'Ōhulehule (joining of waves hill) is the impressive mountain dead ahead. To the right the Ko'olau Summit Trail hugs the *pali* and then works leeward behind Pu'u Ka'aumakua (the family god hill). You can also make out the continuation of the Schofield-Waikāne Trail as it descends the windward slopes into Waikāne Valley.

There are two attractive variations to the route as described. For a shorter, novice hike, take the side trail at map point D down to Kaukonahua (place his testicles) Stream. Walk up or downstream to find a swimming hole to your liking. Total distance round trip is about 6 miles. For a more challenging outing, connect the Schofield-Waikāne and Poamoho Ridge hikes. At the top of Schofield-Waikāne turn left on the Ko'olau Summit Trail and then go down Poamoho Ridge. The 2-mile summit section is for experienced hikers only because the trail there is rough, narrow, and frequently socked in.

27 Wahiawā Hills

Type:	Foothill
Length:	5-mile loop
Elevation Gain:	1,300 feet
Danger:	Low
Suitable for:	Intermediate
Location:	'Ewa Forest Reserve above Wahiawā
Topo Map:	Hau'ula
Access:	Conditional; open to individuals and outdoor organizations with written permission. Write Commander, U.S. Army Garrison, Hawai'i, Schofield Barracks, HI 96857 (attn: APVG-GWY-O).

Highlights

This intricate loop traverses the Ko'olau foothills above Wahiawā. In the process you cross two streams twice and climb and descend three ridges. The reward for all this meandering is a cooling dip in a delightful stream pool.

Trailhead Directions

At Punchbowl St. get on Lunalilo Fwy (H-1) heading 'ewa (west).

Near Middle St. keep left on Rte 78 west (exit 19B, Moanalua Rd.) to 'Aiea.

By Aloha Stadium bear right to rejoin H-1 to Pearl City.

Take H-2 freeway (exit 8A) toward Wahiawā.

Get off H-2 at Wahiawā (exit 8, Rte 80 north).

At the end of the off-ramp merge into Kamehameha Hwy.

Cross Wilson Bridge and enter Wahiawā town.

At the third traffic light by a Shell service station turn right on California Ave.

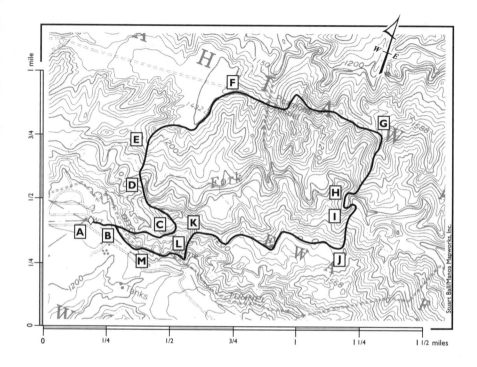

The road narrows to two lanes.

Pass Leilehua High School on the right.

The road jogs right and then left.

Drive to the end of California Ave. near two large, green water tanks.

Park there on the street (elevation 1,240 feet) (map point A).

Bus: Route 62 to the trailhead.

Route Description

Take the trail starting at the end of the pavement. On the right is a fence surrounding the water tanks.

Shortly afterward the trail splits; keep right.

Angle left away from the fence through a paperbark grove.

Walk through a clearing. Ignore side trails on the left and right.

Bear right along the edge of the main ridge.

Shortly afterward reach an obscure junction (map point B). Turn left and descend steeply down a side ridge. (The trail to the right is the return portion of the loop.)

As the ridge levels off, bear left off of it on a graded trail.

Descend gradually into a gully with a small stream.

Just below a tiny waterfall the trail forks. Turn left and cross the stream (map point C).

Climb the opposite bank on two short switchbacks. To the right is a huge fallen trunk.

Turn right past the trunk and ascend more gradually along the side of the gully above the stream.

Switchback to the left, leaving the stream behind.

Bear right and climb straight upslope.

Gain the ridgeline and turn left along it.

Reach a junction. Turn left on a side trail. (To the right the main trail crosses Kaukonahua Stream and intersects the loop between map points E and F.)

Descend gradually along the ridge.

Cross a narrow neck with the North Fork of Kaukonahua Stream on the right and the smaller stream just crossed on the left.

After climbing briefly, the ridge levels off. Turn right down a side ridge.

Two-thirds of the way down bear left off the side ridge and descend to Kaukonahua Stream.

Head downstream briefly and then turn right to cross the stream. The ford is wide and shallow with overhanging trees on the far side (map point D).

Scramble up the steep bank and then ascend gradually through the forest.

Climb steeply up a side ridge covered with uluhe ferns. To the left is a good view of the Wai'anae Range.

Near a grove of koa trees gain the main ridgeline (map point E) and turn right along it.

Join an overgrown dirt road.

Reach a junction with another dirt road. Cross it onto a trail.

Bear left across a flat area with eucalyptus.

Cross a line of rusty metal stakes.

Stroll through paperbark trees on the broad ridge. Keep to the right along its edge.

Break out into the open through a stretch of uluhe ferns. Look for native 'ōhi'a trees on the right.

Reach a junction with a dirt road near a stand of bamboo (map point F). Turn right on the road. (The trail across the road leads down to Poamoho Stream.)

After a brief descent the road ends. Continue along the ridge on a trail.

A side ridge comes in on the left. Keep right on the main ridge.

Work around a series of tree trunks uprooted by hurricane 'Iwa.

Another side ridge comes in on the right. Keep left.

In a grove of paperbark trees bear left to bypass a hump in the ridge.

Regain the ridgeline.

Shortly afterward the ridge levels and then climbs slightly to a breezy lookout (elevation 1,480 feet) (map point G). From there is a good view *mauka* (inland) toward the Ko'olau summit.

At the lookout turn right down a side ridge.

The ridge splits into two fingers. Take the right one.

Descend steeply toward the North Fork of Kaukonahua Stream. Along the trail is the native shrub pūkiawe.

Cross a narrow neck. The stream makes a sharp bend around the end of the ridge and so is visible on both sides.

Shortly afterward reach a junction. Turn right and descend to a long, deep, and inviting pool (map point H).

When you've had enough swimming and sunning, retrace your steps to the junction and turn right to continue along the finger ridge.

Bear left around the tip of the finger and descend to the stream.

Ford it just below another pool, somewhat smaller than the first (map point I).

Bear right and climb steeply up a side ridge. Look back for a view of Ka'ala, the flat-topped peak in the Wai'anae Range.

In a clearing reach the top of the main ridge (map point J) and turn right along it.

Follow the edge of the broad ridge through native 'ōhi'a and koa trees.

A side ridge comes in on the right. Keep left.

Enter a long stretch of eucalyptus forest. The ridge is a series of ups and downs. Look for the native shrub naupaka kuahiwi with its white half-flowers.

The ridge narrows and then flattens.

Angle left and down, off the ridge crest, through a paperbark grove (map point K).

Bear left down a side ridge.

Descend very steeply to a small stream (map point L).

Cross it and turn left upstream.

Turn sharp right and climb steeply up a side ridge.

As the ridge broadens, work to its right side.

Continue climbing along the right flank of the ridge.

Reach an abandoned irrigation ditch and turn right alongside it.

As the ditch goes into a tunnel, bear right around a bulge in the ridge.

The ditch reappears on the left.

At a spillway cross the ditch (map point M).

Bear left and switchback once.

Climb gradually up the side of the ridge above the ditch.

Pass a metal post on the right.

Almost immediately turn right just before reaching a dirt road in the East Range, an Army training area.

Cross an overgrown dirt road.

Keep right along the edge of the ridge.

Reach the original junction (map point B). Angle left through the paperbark forest toward the water tanks.

Emerge at the end of California Ave. (map point A).

Notes

The Wahiawā (place of noise) Hills hike is a true test of my ability to write clear directions and your ability to follow them. The complicated route twists and turns and climbs and descends constantly. As described, the hike is a clockwise loop. You can, of course, walk it in the opposite direction. However, the route is confusing enough without having to follow the narrative in reverse.

The hike was cobbled together from trails and roads of various difficulty. Watch your step on the slippery downhill sections at the beginning of the loop. The side ridges and the main ridge on the return may be overgrown with scratchy uluhe ferns. There are a few mosquitoes along the stream.

Much of the hike passes through stands of paperbark and eucalyptus trees planted in the 1930s and 1940s for reforestation. You can easily recognize paperbark by its spongy white bark. The eucalyptus along the trail comes in several varieties. Sydney blue gum has smooth blue gray bark and very narrow, pointed leaves. Swamp mahogany has spongy, reddish brown bark and slightly wider leaves. Ironbark has black or gray bark, heavily furrowed.

The hike twice fords Kaukonahua (place his testicles) Stream, the longest in the state at 33 miles. Near the second crossing are two inviting swimming holes above and below a sharp bend in the stream. Take a dip in the cool, clear water before climbing the hot, open ridge on the way back.

Kaukonahua Stream can rise suddenly during a heavy rainstorm. As always, do not cross if the water is much above your knees. If you are caught on the far side, wait until the stream goes down. The debris on the shrubs and trees lining the banks gives you a good idea of how high the water can get.

On the return portion of the loop native ʻōhiʻa and koa trees make a brief appearance. ʻŌhiʻa has oval leaves and clusters of delicate red flowers. Early Hawaiians used the flowers in *lei* (garlands) and the wood in outrigger canoes. The hard, durable wood was also carved into god images for *heiau* (religious sites). Koa has sickle-shaped foliage and pale yellow flower clusters. Early Hawaiians made surfboards and outrigger canoe hulls out of the beautiful red brown wood. Today it is made into fine furniture.

On the way back, look for the native shrub naupaka kuahiwi among the eucalyptus. Naupaka has toothed and pointed leaves and white half-flowers. The unusual appearance of the flowers has given rise to several unhappy legends. According to one, a Hawaiian maiden believed her lover unfaithful. In anger she tore all the naupaka flowers in half. She then asked him to find a whole flower to prove his love. He was, of course, unsuccessful and died of a broken heart.

For a much longer ridge outing, try the Schofield-Waikāne hike that starts from the same trailhead. You can access the trail through the East Range gate or at the end of California Ave.

28 Poamoho Ridge

Type:	Graded ridge
Length:	12-mile round trip (from forest boundary)
Elevation Gain:	1,100 feet
Danger:	Low
Suitable for:	Novice, Intermediate, Expert
Location:	Kawailoa and 'Ewa Forest Reserves above Helemano
Topo Map:	Hau'ula

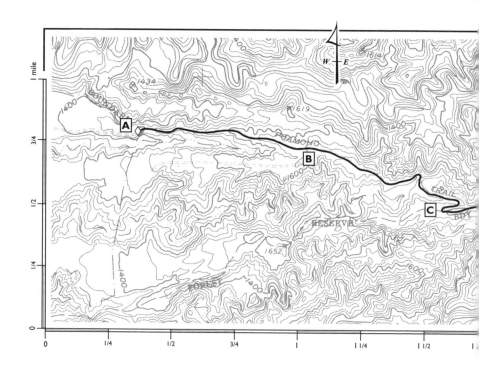

Access: Closed; for current status check website
                     at www.hgea.org/~lmasu/oindex.html

Highlights
This classic ridge hike follows a dirt road and a graded trail to the
Koʻolau summit. Along the route are native plants galore and,
perhaps, some native birds. From the windy lookout at the top is
one of the best views on the island.

Trailhead Directions
At Punchbowl St. get on Lunalilo Fwy (H-1) heading *ʻewa*
(west).
    Near Middle St. keep left on Rte 78 west (exit 19B, Moanalua
Rd.) to ʻAiea.

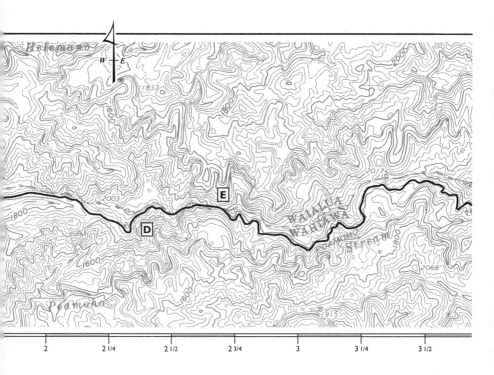

By Aloha Stadium bear right to rejoin H-1 to Pearl City. Take H-2 freeway (exit 8A) to Wahiawā.

As the freeway ends, continue on Rte 99 north (Wilikina Dr.) bypassing Wahiawā.

Pass Schofield Barracks on the left.

The road narrows to two lanes, dips, and then forks. Take the right fork to the north shore (Kamananui Rd., but still Rte 99 north).

At the road end turn left on Kamehameha Hwy (Rte 99).

Pass the Dole Pavilion and then Helemano Plantation on the right.

Just past a bus stop, turn right on the paved road that borders the plantation. Reset your trip odometer (0.0 mile).

As the pavement ends, continue straight on a well-traveled dirt road (0.2 mile).

The road parallels a line of utility poles through pineapple fields.

At a small concrete building turn right (1.1 miles) and circle

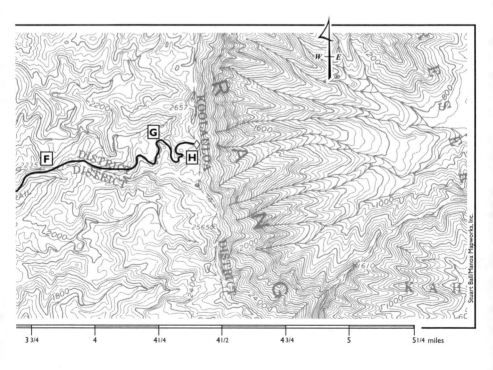

around Helemano Military Reservation. On the left is an uncultivated strip marking the reservation boundary.

In back of the reservation, turn right (1.8 miles), leaving the strip behind.

The road forks (2.1 miles). Bear left.

Descend briefly through a narrow swath of grass and scrub trees (2.6 miles).

Climb gradually to the top of the last pineapple field.

Reach the forest reserve boundary (3.9 miles) (elevation 1,460 feet) (map point A) and park there along the road.

If the road is dry and the weather looks good, continue through the forest to an open area on the right (4.8 miles) (map point B) and park there.

Bus: None, within reasonable walking distance of the trailhead.

Route Description

Continue along the dirt road on foot.

Descend briefly and then switchback twice to gain altitude gradually (map point C).

On the right pass a hiker/hunter check-in mailbox by a hunting area sign.

Reach the road end and the start of the Poamoho Ridge Trail (map point D). From an overlook there you can trace the ridge as it climbs to the Ko'olau summit.

Thread through a barrier to thwart dirt bikes.

Descend gradually along the right side of the ridge.

Cross over to the left side for a short distance and then switch to the right side again (map point E). Below are occasional views of Poamoho Stream.

Contour for a long stretch through strawberry guava and native koa and 'ōhi'a trees. Look for the native shrub naupaka kuahiwi on the high side of the trail.

As the ridge narrows, the trail follows the crest briefly and then switches to the left side of the ridge (map point F).

Cross over to the right side briefly and then resume contouring on the left side. Along the slick and deeply rutted trail are native manono trees and na'ena'e shrubs.

Work up a side gulch above a small stream (map point G). Look for native loulu palms and pū'ahanui (kanawao) shrubs.

After passing a grassy campsite on the right, descend briefly to the stream.

After fording it, turn left downstream and resume the gradual climb.

Cross over to the right side of the ridge.

Traverse a more open, windswept area.

Bear right to cross a grassy strip.

Reach the junction with the Ko'olau Summit Trail at the stone memorial to Geraldine Cline.

Keep the memorial on the left and ascend a small grassy hump to reach the Ko'olau summit (elevation 2,500 feet) (map point H).

Notes

The Poamoho Ridge hike winds through the rugged Ko'olau wilderness in central O'ahu. Although long, the route is not a marathon because of the tolerable condition of the road and the trail. Start early, though, to have plenty of time to enjoy the native plants and birds and the splendid view from the summit.

The condition of the dirt road from the forest reserve boundary to the trailhead varies from year to year. The conservative approach is to park your car at the reserve boundary. From there the hike is the full 12 miles. If the road and weather look good, drive another mile to the open area on the right for a 10-mile hike. Continue farther along the road only if you have a four-wheel-drive vehicle.

The Civilian Conservation Corps built the Poamoho Ridge Trail in 1935. Since then, periodic maintenance has kept the lower section wide and well graded for the most part. The upper section, however, is deeply rutted and very slippery. Watch your footing constantly; expect to fall down a few times and get muddy and wet. Novices and intermediates can go as far as they like and then turn around.

On the trail watch for the native shrub naupaka kuahiwi. It has light green, pointed leaves and half-flowers. Initially the naupaka along the trail has toothed leaves and white flowers.

Closer to the summit, a slightly different variety appears with smoother leaf margins and purple streaks in the flowers.

Throughout the hike listen for the Japanese bush warbler (Uguisu), a bird often heard, but rarely seen. Its distinctive cry starts with a long whistle and then winds down in a series of notes. The bush warbler is olive brown on top with a white breast and a long tail. If you are very lucky, you may catch a glimpse of a native 'apapane in the forest canopy. It has a red breast and head, black wings and tail, and a slightly curved black bill. In flight the 'apapane makes a whirring sound as it darts from tree to tree searching for insects and nectar.

On the upper section look for native na'ena'e shrubs and manono trees. Na'ena'e has narrow, shallowly toothed leaves grouped near the branch tips. Its purple green flower heads are displayed in cone-shaped clusters. Manono has thick, glossy, oblong leaves with purple stems, small yellow green flowers, and purple black fruits.

Along the small stream near the summit are native pū'ahanui (kanawao) shrubs and loulu palms. A relative of hydrangea, pū'ahanui (kanawao) has large, serrated, deeply creased leaves and clusters of delicate pink flowers. The shrub is a favorite habitat of the endangered Hawaiian land snail. Early Hawaiians used the plants for medicinal purposes. Loulu palms have rigid, fan-shaped fronds in a cluster at the top of a ringed trunk. Early Hawaiians used the fronds for thatch and plaited the blades of young fronds into fans and baskets.

At the Ko'olau (windward) summit is one of the great viewpoints on the island. You can look straight down into green Punalu'u (coral dived for) and Kahana (cutting) Valleys. Separating the two is the summit of Pu'u Piei. The pyramid peak on the right is Pu'u 'Ōhulehule (joining of waves hill). In front of it and partially hidden is Ka'a'awa Valley. Beyond, the windward coast stretches from Mōkapu (taboo district) to Makapu'u (bulging eye) Points. To leeward you can see the Wai'anae (mullet water) Range. From left to right along its summit ridge are Pu'u Kaua (war hill), Kolekole (raw) Pass, Kalena (the lazy one), and flat-topped Ka'ala (the fragrance), the highest mountain on O'ahu.

Below the viewpoint is the junction with the Koʻolau Summit Trail, an 18.5-mile footpath along the top of the Koʻolau Range for experienced hikers only. Turn right to reach the Poamoho Cabin, a half mile away, and the Schofield-Waikāne Trail. Turn left to get to Lāʻie Trail and the Pūpūkea (white shell) Summit hike. The mileage to each trail junction is listed on a plaque in the stone memorial to Geraldine Cline. A beloved member of the Hawaiian Trail and Mountain Club and the Sierra Club, she died tragically in an automobile accident.

WINDWARD SIDE

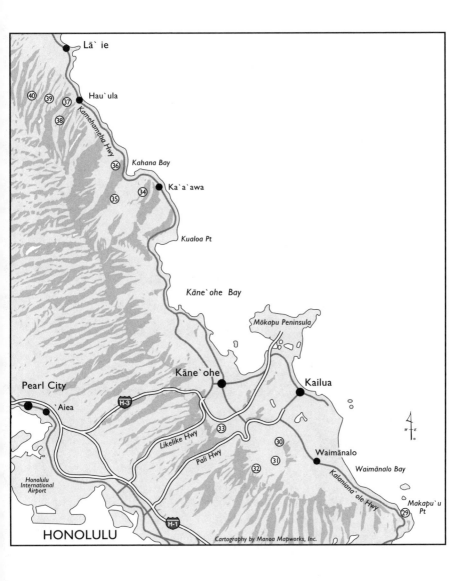

Lā`ie

Hau`ula

㊵ ㊴ ㊲

Kamehameha Hwy

㊳

Kahana Bay

㊱

Ka`a`awa ㉞

㉟ ㉞

Kualoa Pt

Kāne`ohe Bay

Mōkapu Peninsula

Kāne`ohe

Pearl City

`Aiea

Kailua

H-3

Likelike Hwy

㉝

Pali Hwy

㉚

Honolulu
International
Airport

㉜ ㉛

Waimānalo

Waimānalo Bay

Kalaniana`ole Hwy

Makapu`u
Pt ㉙

H-1

HONOLULU

Cartography by Manoa Mapworks, Inc.

29 Makapu'u Point

Type:	Ungraded ridge
Length:	3-mile loop
Elevation Gain:	600 feet
Danger:	Low
Suitable for:	Novice, Intermediate
Location:	Makapu'u Point State Wayside
Topo Map:	Koko Head
Access:	Open

Highlights
This short, scenic hike climbs the windswept cliffs above the easternmost point on the island. Along the way are remnant fortifications, a lighthouse, and some rock scrambling. From ocean overlooks you can often see humpback whales and colonies of seabirds.

Trailhead Directions
At Ward Ave. get on Lunalilo Fwy (H-1) Koko Head bound (east).

As the freeway ends, continue straight on Kalaniana'ole Hwy (Rte 72).

The highway narrows to two lanes just past Koko Marina Shopping Center in Hawai'i Kai.

Pass Hanauma Bay and Sandy Beach Parks on the right and Hawai'i Kai Golf Course on the left.

After the road swings left and begins to climb, look for a black gate across a one-lane paved road on the right. Park on the highway near the gate (elevation 60 feet) (map point A). Don't block it.

Bus: Route 22, 57, or 58 to Sea Life Park. Walk 0.5 mile along Kalaniana'ole Hwy to Makapu'u lookout.

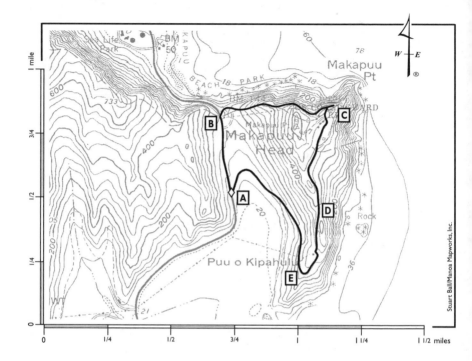

Route Description

Continue along Kalaniana'ole Hwy on foot.

As the road swings left and down, reach Makapu'u lookout (map point B). Turn right, along the edge of the cliff. There is no defined trail on the rock. Look for the low-lying native shrub 'ilima papa with its delicate yellow orange flowers.

Pass three walled-up observation bunkers.

Climb steadily along the cliff edge. As necessary, work right to avoid steep rock faces.

Pick up a makeshift trail in a relatively flat area.

The top of Makapu'u Point Lighthouse appears dead ahead.

Pass some pānini cactus on the right.

Climb steeply, roughly following a water pipe and a utility line.

Pass a huge cactus on the right.

Work left around the front of the cliff.

Pass a concrete water tank on the right.

Descend briefly to a road and turn left on it.

The road narrows to a path that climbs to a lookout (map point C).

From the lookout retrace your steps back to the road.

In a level area the road splits. Turn left and down. (The right fork becomes a rough trail that ascends to the top of Makapu'u Head [elevation 647 feet]).

Descend along the crest of a ridge past night-blooming cereus, pānini cactus, and koa haole trees.

Reach a junction with a gravel road. Continue straight on the main road. (The gravel road to the left leads past a red-roofed structure to the lighthouse at Makapu'u Point. The lighthouse, however, is strictly off-limits to the public.)

Just before a hump reach an unmarked junction (map point D). Continue straight on the paved road. (To the left an obscure trail marked with white paint descends steeply down the cliff to some tide pools and a double blowhole.)

On the left pass the small hump in the ridge.

The road leaves the ridgeline at Pu'u o Kīpahulu and curves right through scrub kiawe trees (map point E).

Go around a black gate. Along the coast to the left is a prominent rock formation known as Pele's chair.

The road swings left toward the highway.

Go around a second black gate and reach Kalaniana'ole Hwy (map point A).

Notes

Makapu'u (bulging eye) Point is a very popular hike with tourists and locals alike. Most people walk up and back on the paved road. If you are a novice hiker, that's exactly what you should do. More experienced hikers can try the loop route described here. It starts with a steep scramble up the edge of the Makapu'u cliffs and ends with the pleasant stroll down the paved road.

Take this hike during winter (November–April) when temperatures are cooler and the sun less intense. Migrating humpback whales are also on view then. Don't forget the two essentials for this hike, sunscreen and binoculars.

Near the start of the trail is the low-lying native shrub 'ilima papa. It has oblong, serrated leaves, about 1 inch long. The yellow orange flowers strung together make a regal *lei* (garland), in both ancient and modern Hawai'i.

On the climb up look out for the thorny pānini (prickly pear cactus). It has red or yellow flowers and a delicious, dark red, pear-shaped fruit. Wear gloves when handling the fruit because the skin has small bristles. Don Marin, a Spaniard and advisor to King Kamehameha I, introduced pānini from Mexico in the early 1800s.

From the *makai* (seaward) lookout is a magnificent view along the windward coast to Mōkapu (taboo district) Point. Below are Makapu'u Beach and Sealife Park. Beyond is the broad sweep of lovely Waimānalo (potable water) Bay. The two islands offshore, Mānana and Kāohikaipu (Mokuhope), are state seabird sanctuaries. On a clear day you can see the neighbor islands of Moloka'i and Maui across Kaiwi (the bone) Channel.

While at the lookout, scan the ocean for humpback whales. They migrate from the North Pacific to the Hawaiian Islands, arriving in October and leaving in May. The whales congregate off the leeward coast of Maui and occupy themselves calving, nursing, breeding, and generally horsing around.

From the lookout you can also see frigatebirds soaring overhead. Those large, mostly black seabirds have slender wings and a forked tail. Early Hawaiians called them 'iwa or thief because they often force other seabirds to drop their food, which the 'iwa then catch in midair.

The short side trip to the top of Makapu'u Head is well worthwhile. From the summit bunker you can see the Ko'olau (windward) Range gradually rising to a flat-topped mountain, Pu'u o Kona (hill of leeward). Standing alone is triple-peaked Olomana (forked hill), and beyond is Nu'uanu Pali (cool height cliff). On the leeward side are Koko Crater (Kohelepelepe) and Hanauma Bay, and in the distance, Diamond Head.

On the way down as the road heads *mauka* (inland), look left along the coast for a prominent rock formation resembling a chair. According to legend, Pele, the goddess of fire, rested there before leaving O'ahu for Maui and the Big Island. The Makapu'u area was also the site of Mālei, another ancient stone. It was a physical representation of the goddess Mālei who watched over the uhu (parrot fishes) of Makapu'u Point. Fishermen left offerings by the stone or sang to it to ensure a good catch. The stone disappeared many years ago and has never been found.

30 Olomana

Type:	Ungraded ridge
Length:	6-mile round trip
Elevation Gain:	1,600 feet
Danger:	High
Suitable for:	Intermediate, Expert
Location:	Windward side near Maunawili
Topo Map:	Mōkapu, Koko Head
Access:	Conditional; check in with the guard at the entrance to Luana Hills Country Club.

Highlights
Olomana is the craggy, commanding mountain windward of Nu'uanu Pali. The steep, narrow climb to its three peaks demands concentration, sure feet, and little fear of heights. From the summit is a panorama unsurpassed on O'ahu.

Trailhead Directions
At Punchbowl St. get on Pali Hwy (Rte 61 north) heading up Nu'uanu Valley.

Go under the Pali through the twin tunnels.

At the first traffic light (Castle junction) continue straight on Kalaniana'ole Hwy (still Rte 61).

At the third traffic light turn right on A'uloa Rd.

Shortly afterward the road forks. Keep left on Maunawili Rd.

Pass Maunawili Valley Neighborhood Park on the left. The park has rest rooms and drinking water.

As the road widens, enter Maunawili subdivision.

Park on the street just past the intersection with Maunawili Lp. (elevation 80 feet) (map point A).

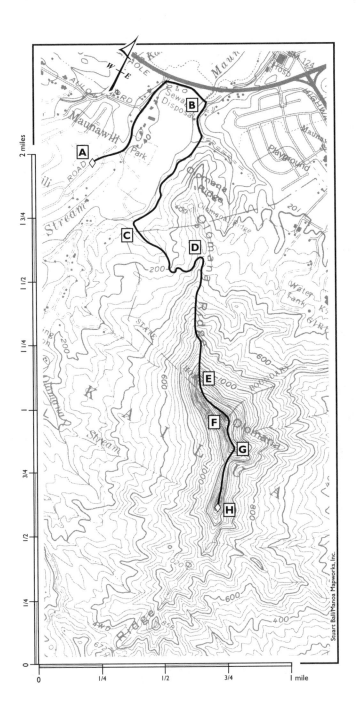

Bus: Routes 56 or 57 to Kalaniana'ole Hwy and A'uloa Rd. Turn left on an unnamed, paved road that parallels the highway and pick up the description below.

Route Description

Walk back to Kalaniana'ole Hwy.

Just before reaching it, turn right on an unnamed, paved road that parallels the highway.

After crossing Maunawili Stream on a bridge, turn right on the access road leading into Luana Hills Country Club (map point B).

Go through a gate and check in at the security station on the left.

Continue along the country club road.

As the road curves right and climbs, look for a grassy turnout on the left marked by two red metal No Parking posts.

Just past the second post, reach a signed junction (map point C). Turn left off the road, cross a narrow drainage ditch, and pick up the trail to Olomana. (Beyond the junction the road is closed to the general public.)

Ascend gradually along the right side of a gully.

Cross the gully near an abandoned pumping shack and keep left by a huge banyan tree.

Climb steadily up the side of Olomana Ridge through Christmas berry and strawberry guava trees. Laua'e ferns carpet the ground, and liliko'i (passion fruit) vines drape over the trees.

Gain the ridgeline at a small dip marked by a metal pipe and a utility pole (map point D). Turn right, up the ridge.

Cross an eroded spot and enter an ironwood grove. Look for the native shrub 'ākia in the open sections.

Gradually ascend the flank of the mountain through a corridor of Christmas berry and laua'e. Watch out for a rusty barbed-wire fence on the right.

Begin climbing more steeply on a rocky trail (map point E).

Keep right up a long rock face partially covered by vegetation. A series of cables and ropes provides some assistance.

Continue climbing very steeply. Underfoot are exposed rock dikes.

The angle of ascent decreases briefly (whew!).

Climb a short, but nearly vertical rock face with the aid of a cable.

The ridgeline contracts to a thin rock dike.

Bear right off the ridge to avoid an especially narrow section.

Reach the summit of Olomana at a rocky outcrop (elevation 1,643 feet) (map point F). Admire the panoramic views of the windward coast and the Koʻolau cliffs.

Descend steeply to a saddle and then climb briefly to the second peak, known as Pākuʻi (map point G). Among the grass and Christmas berry is the sprawling native shrub ʻūlei.

Just past the summit of the second peak, turn sharp right and down to continue along the main ridge to the third peak. The route no longer has fixed cables and should be attempted by agile, expert climbers only.

Descend precipitously to a saddle between the second and third peaks.

Begin climbing the very thin ridge of the third peak.

Inch left around a large dike section with a hole in it.

Scramble up a long, steep rock face.

Keep right around a large free-standing boulder.

Bear right off the ridgeline and climb the final rock face.

Reach the flat summit of the third peak, known as Ahiki (map point H).

Notes

Olomana is Oʻahu's version of the Matterhorn. The main peak is a steep-sided pyramid that looks unclimbable from a distance. Closer inspection, however, reveals the classic route up the northwest ridge. Although thousands of hikers have taken that climb over the years, treat this dangerous, alluring mountain with respect.

Olomana (forked hill) has three distinct peaks. The elongated, razor-thin third peak is called Ahiki, and the second, central peak, Pākuʻi. Both are named after *konohiki* (overseers) of the ancient fishponds of Kaʻelepulu (the moist blackness), now called Enchanted Lake, and Kawainui (the big water). The first and highest peak is named after the legendary giant Olomana.

Olomana was a fearsome, evil warrior, 12 yards high, who dominated the windward side. None dared challenge him, not even the chief of Oʻahu. One day the chief commanded Palila, a brash young soldier, to rid the island of the giant. Palila journeyed to Kaʻelepulu where he surprised Olomana by jumping up on his shoulder. The giant haughtily asked the boy soldier what he was doing up there and where he was from. Palila replied that he came from a temple on Kauaʻi noted for great warriors with supernatural powers. On hearing that, Olomana became afraid and begged for his life. Palila deftly struck the giant, cutting him in two. One part flew *makai* (seaward) and became Mahinui (great champion) mountain along the coast. The other part remained as the present peak of Olomana.

Much of the route up the mountain is a scramble over loose rock and dirt. The climb to the first and second peaks is an intermediate hike with medium danger. You must negotiate a narrow rock dike and a near-vertical rock face just below the first peak. Test all ropes and cables before using them. The descent from the second peak and the ascent to the third are for experienced, acrobatic hikers only. The rock is rotten, and the ridge plunges straight down on both sides. Take your time and be extraordinarily careful. There is no shame in turning back if you don't like what you see.

On the hike look for the native dryland shrub ʻākia in the open areas along Olomana Ridge. The shrub has dark branches jointed with white rings. Its leaves are bright green, oval, and pointed. Early Hawaiians pounded the leaves and bark and then dropped the mixture into tidal pools to poison fish. The red orange fruits were used in *lei* (garlands) and as a poison for criminals.

From the top of the first peak is an awesome 360-degree view. *Makai* is the windward coast from Kualoa (long back) to Mōkapu (taboo district) to Makapuʻu (bulging eye) Points. On a clear day you can see the islands of Molokaʻi and Maui across Kaiwi (the bone) Channel. *Mauka* (inland) is Maunawili (twisted mountain) Valley and the sheer, fluted cliffs of the Koʻolau (windward) Range. The massive peak to the left of Nuʻuanu Pali (cool height cliff) is Kōnāhuanui (large fat testicles), the highest point in the

Ko'olau Range. Try picking out the other major peaks on the summit ridge. From left to right are Pu'u o Kona (hill of leeward), Lanipō (dense), and Olympus (Awaawaloa). Beyond Kōnāhuanui is Lanihuli (turning royal chief) and Pu'u Keahi a Kahoe (hill of Kahoe's fire). In the distance is the steep pyramid of Pu'u 'Ōhulehule (joining of waves hill).

Between the first and second peaks is the sprawling native shrub 'ūlei. It has small, oblong leaves arranged in pairs; clusters of white, roselike flowers; and white fruit. Early Hawaiians ate the berries and used the tough wood for making digging sticks, fish spears, and 'ūkēkē (the musical bow).

From the second peak is a good view along the length of the mountain. Olomana is a remnant of the mile-high caldera of the old Ko'olau volcano. Filled with lava, the caldera stretched 7 miles from Waimānalo (potable water) to Kāne'ohe (cutting husband). When the volcano became dormant, streams gradually eroded the softer lava, leaving intrusions of hard, dense rock, known as dikes. Olomana remains because of its complex of narrow, vertical dikes over which you scramble carefully.

While resting on the third peak, look for small white nodules of opal in the dark lava. Over millions of years volcanic gases altered the composition of the rocks in the caldera. In the process excess silica collected in small cavities to form the white spheres, called amygdules.

31 Maunawili Falls

Type:	Valley
Length:	3-mile round trip
Elevation Gain:	400 feet
Danger:	Low
Suitable for:	Novice
Location:	Waimānalo Forest Reserve above Maunawili
Topo Map:	Koko Head, Honolulu
Access:	Open

Highlights
This short hike winds along Maunawili Stream past remnant coffee groves and taro terraces. From a ridge lookout you can see the Koʻolau Range and Kāneʻohe Bay. At the end is lovely Maunawili Falls, cascading into a deep swimming hole.

Trailhead Directions
At Punchbowl St. get on Pali Hwy (Rte 61 north) heading up Nuʻuanu Valley.

Go under the Pali through the twin tunnels.

At the first traffic light (Castle junction) continue straight on Kalanianaʻole Hwy (still Rte 61).

At the third traffic light turn right on Aʻuloa Rd.

Almost immediately the road forks. Keep left on Maunawili Rd. Drive through Maunawili subdivision.

The road narrows and winds through a forested area.

At the end of Maunawili Rd. turn right on Kelewina St.

Park on the street near that intersection (elevation 160 feet) (map point A).

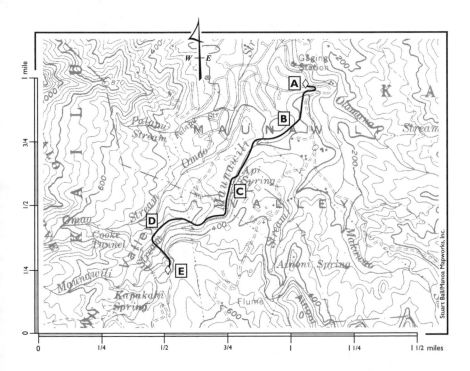

Bus: Route 70 to Maunawili Rd. and Aloha 'Oe Dr. Walk 0.3 mile along Maunawili Rd. to the trailhead.

Route Description

Walk back to the intersection and turn right on a one-lane private road.

Just before the road swings right, reach a signed junction. Turn right on the access trail to Maunawili Falls.

Climb some steps through a hau tangle.

Parallel the private road above Olomana Stream.

Climb gradually and cross over a side ridge under some power lines.

Descend to Maunawili Stream and ford it (map point B). Watch your footing on the slippery rocks.

Go through a break in a stone wall and turn left upstream through a coffee grove.

Follow the stream under a canopy of mango and monkeypod trees. Red ginger lines the trail.

Cross Maunawili Stream again and turn right upstream paralleling another stone wall.

Walk through a level section on a rocky trail. Overhead are mango, coffee, and kukui trees; underfoot are kukui nuts.

Jump over a small stream channel coming from 'Api Spring on the left.

Ford Maunawili Stream for the third time. At the crossing are 'ape plants with huge, heart-shaped leaves.

Shortly afterward reach the boundary of the Waimānalo Forest Reserve and the start of the official Maunawili Falls Trail (map point C).

Climb steadily above the stream. Look for purple Philippine ground orchids.

Gain the top of a side ridge (elevation 460 feet) and turn left uphill. *Mauka* (inland) are imposing views of the Ko'olau Range.

Ascend gradually along the ridge.

Just before an ironwood grove, reach a signed junction (map point D). Turn left off the ridge. (Straight ahead the Maunawili Falls Trail climbs to a junction with the Maunawili Trail.)

Descend steeply on plastic steps. Kī (ti) plants anchor the eroding slope.

Reach Maunawili Stream where it forks under a spreading mango tree. Cross the right fork.

Proceed up the right side of the left fork. Walk in the stream at first and then pick up a rocky, slippery trail.

Reach Maunawili Falls and swimming hole (map point E).

Notes

Volunteers under the direction of the Sierra Club Hawai'i Chapter completed this new access to Maunawili (twisted mountain) Falls in October 1996. Since then, the hike has proven very popular, especially on sunny weekend afternoons. The route is short, pleasant, and leads to a superb swimming hole. To avoid the crowds, go on a weekday or start early.

Before you begin hiking, several cautions are in order. The route initially follows a public right-of-way through private property; stay on the trail. The treadway is well built, but may be muddy and deteriorated in spots from the heavy traffic. Watch your footing while crossing the stream. If possible, wear tabis (Japanese reef walkers), which can grip wet, slippery rocks. As always, do not ford the stream if the water is much above your knees. Finally, don't feed the mosquitoes.

On the trail, look and listen for the white-rumped shama. It is black on top with a chestnut-colored breast and a long black-and-white tail. The shama has a variety of beautiful songs and often mimics other birds. A native of Malaysia, the shama has become widespread in introduced forests such as this one.

After the first stream crossing are groves of Arabian coffee trees. They have glossy, dark green leaves and white flowers. Their fruit is red, drying to black or brown. Coffee was introduced to Hawai'i in the early 1800s and was widely cultivated in valleys along streams. Coffee is still commercially grown on the Big Island, where it is sold as Kona coffee.

Before reaching 'Api Spring, the trail is covered with fallen nuts from kukui trees. Their large, pale green leaves resemble those of the maple, with several distinct lobes. Early Polynesian voyagers introduced kukui into Hawai'i. They used the wood to make gunwales and seats for their outrigger canoes. The flowers and sap became medicines to treat a variety of ailments. Early Hawaiians strung the nuts together to make *lei hua* (seed or nut garlands). The oily kernels became house candles and torches for night spearfishing.

Near the spring look for the 'ape plant with its huge, heart-shaped leaves. It is a close relative of *kalo* (taro), the staple food of early Hawaiians. The tubers of 'ape are inedible unless specially prepared by repeated washing and boiling. Early Hawaiians created patterns on gourd bowls using a dye made from crushed 'ape leaves.

From the short ridge section are impressive views. *Mauka* are the sheer, fluted cliffs of the Ko'olau (windward) Range. Kōnāhuanui (large fat testicles) (elevation 3,150 feet) is the massive peak above Nu'uanu (cool height) Pali. Along the summit ridge to the left is Mount Olympus (Awaawaloa). *Makai* (seaward) is triple-peaked Olomana (forked hill) and

Kāneʻohe (cutting husband) Bay, ending at Mōkapu (taboo district) Point.

After a steep descent back to the stream, you soon reach Maunawili Falls. At its base is the large, lower pool encircled by fern-covered cliffs. Up a slippery slope is a second, smaller pool where the waterfall splits in two. Enjoy a refreshing swim in the cool mountain water. If you plan to jump into the lower pool from the cliffs, be sure to check its depth first!

For a longer hike, continue up the ridge on the falls trail to the junction with the Maunawili Trail. Turn left or right and go as far as you want.

32 Maunawili

Type:	Foothill
Length:	10 miles one way
Elevation Gain:	600 feet
Danger:	Low
Suitable for:	Novice, Intermediate
Location:	Waimānalo Forest Reserve above Maunawili
Topo Map:	Koko Head, Honolulu
Access:	Open

Highlights
This popular hike snakes along the base of the sheer, fluted Koʻolau cliffs. Along the way are lush gulches, ridge lookouts, and a waterfall that smiles. The one-way route starts along Pali Hwy and ends up in Waimānalo.

Trailhead Directions
At Punchbowl St. get on Pali Hwy (Rte 61 north) heading up Nuʻuanu Valley.

Go under the Pali through the twin tunnels.

At a sharp left curve, called the hairpin turn, bear right on a short access road to a scenic viewpoint. Park in the narrow lot there by a rock wall (elevation 640 feet) (map point A).

Bus: Routes 56 or 57 to Pali Hwy and Kamehameha Hwy (Castle junction). Walk 0.8 mile back up Pali Hwy to the viewpoint at the hairpin turn.

To get to the Waimānalo trailhead, continue along Pali Hwy from the hairpin turn.

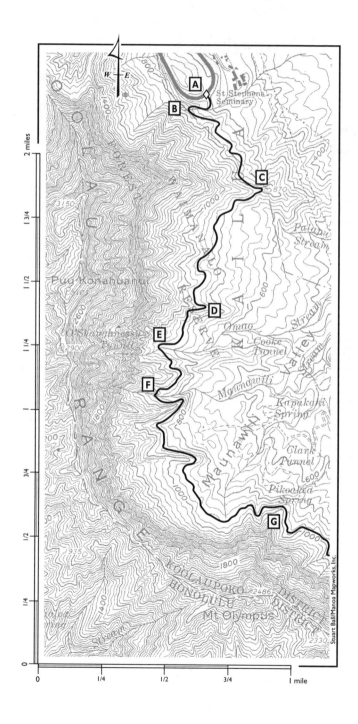

At the first traffic light (Castle junction), Pali Hwy becomes Kalaniana'ole Hwy (still Rte 61).

By Castle Memorial Hospital turn right on Rte 72 (still Kalaniana'ole Hwy) to Waimānalo.

The highway narrows to two lanes by Olomana Golf Course.

Take the second right on Kumuhau St.

At the road end turn right on Waikupanaha St. and cross a bridge.

Pass the intersection with Mahiku Pl.

Shortly afterward look for the signed trailhead on the right (elevation 140 feet) (map point M). It's through a gate just beyond a house on the left with a blue metal roof (no. 41-1020). Park on the street near the trailhead.

Bus: Route 57 to Kalaniana'ole Hwy and Kumuhau St. Walk 1.2 miles to the trailhead.

Route Description
Walk back up the access road.

Go through a gap in the guardrail on the left.

By a mango tree turn left on the connector trail heading into the forest.

Pass a water tank below and on the left.

Switchback twice past several mango trees.

By some plastic steps reach a signed junction with the Maunawili Trail (map point B). Turn left on it. (To the right the trail climbs to Old Pali Rd. and Nu'uanu Pali lookout.)

Pass a small water tank on the right.

Contour into and out of three gulches through guava (waiawī).

Cross over a prominent side ridge, known as Piliwale Ridge (map point C).

Break out into the open through native uluhe ferns and scattered 'ōhi'a trees. *Mauka* (inland) are spectacular views of the Ko'olau cliffs.

Enter another ravine and then emerge into the open again.

Work into and out of a series of shallow gulches and then two larger ones with rocky streambeds. Look for kukui trees lining the gulches.

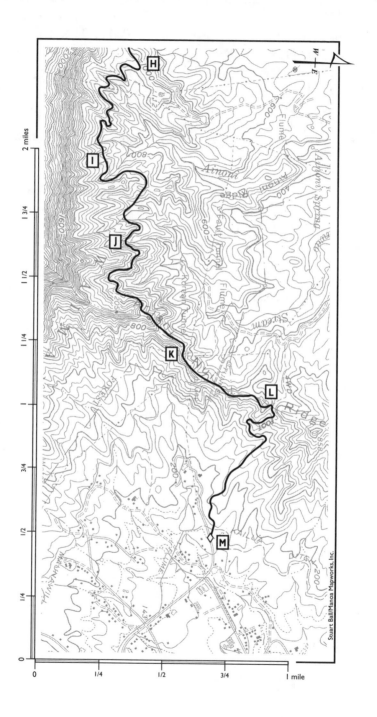

Cross over a broad side ridge with a stand of ironwood trees above and on the right.

Work into and out of another ravine and then cross over a narrow, open side ridge with good views *makai* (seaward) (map point D). In the cliffs ahead are four waterfall chutes.

Descend into a deep ravine on two switchbacks and then contour through a series of shallow gullies.

Enter a wide gulch with four waterfall chutes in back.

Cross a pair of rocky streambeds that join just below the trail. At the first one a faint side trail on the right leads to the bottom of a waterfall chute and the O'Shaughnessy Tunnel.

Cross intermittent 'Ōma'o Stream by some struggling bamboo (map point E). Another faint side trail leads upstream to Smiling Falls, named for the shape of the rock dike at its base.

Reach a signed junction. Continue straight on the Maunawili Trail. (To the left the Maunawili Falls Trail leads down a side ridge to the falls.)

Contour through a small ravine and then cross over an open side ridge with two ironwoods on the right. Listen for the distinctive call of the Japanese bush warbler.

Descend into a large gulch on two switchbacks.

Cross Maunawili Stream in a grove of mountain apple trees (map point F) and climb to the next side ridge and another good viewpoint.

Work into and out of two more gulches.

Wind through a long stretch of shallow ravines, some choked with hau trees. Along the trail are a few native naupaka kuahiwi shrubs.

Cross over a side ridge with a lone ironwood and several native koa trees (map point G).

Climb gradually through two narrow gulches.

Cross over a prominent side ridge with a power-line tower on top (map point H).

Work into and out of six long, deep gulches. Look for 'ōhi'a in the open sections and native māmaki trees in the ravines. In the fifth gulch are huge bird's-nest ferns.

Climb gradually to cross over another prominent side ridge with a small knob on the left.

Wind through four more gulches, which form the watershed of 'Ainoni Stream (map point I). The third one has a tiny waterfall. After the fourth gulch are a few native lama trees.

Descend along the side of 'Ainoni Ridge and then resume contouring in a paperbark grove.

Pass two waterfall chutes side by side in a deep ravine. On the next side ridge are several native alahe'e trees.

Work into and out of a large double gulch with a line of ironwoods and a small pool and waterfall (map point J). The trickle of water is a branch of Makawao Stream.

Descend gradually through three small gulches, two with weeping walls.

Reach a junction under some power lines (map point K). Continue straight through the clearing. (The dirt road to the left leads to Old Government Rd.)

Contour below Anianinui Ridge.

Gain the ridgeline and walk along its crest. To the right are views of Waimānalo town and the Ko'olau cliffs.

Descend gradually along the right side of the ridge. Along the trail are the low-lying native shrubs 'ūlei and 'ilima.

By a large mango tree reach a junction with Old Government Rd. (map point L). Turn right on the road. (To the left some boulders block vehicle access.)

Descend gradually on two switchbacks.

Reach a signed junction. Continue straight on the road. (To the left is the Maunawili Ditch Trail.)

Go through a gate and reach paved Waikupanaha St. (map point M).

Notes

Maunawili is the showpiece of the O'ahu trail system. Richard H. Davis of the Hawaiian Trail and Mountain Club scouted and flagged the proposed route. Volunteer crews under the direction of the Sierra Club, Hawai'i Chapter constructed 7.25 miles of trail between the summer of 1991 and the fall of 1993. The remaining 2 miles were completed in 1994 with the help of the Boy Scouts and the U.S. Marines. Starting from Pali Hwy, the trail now winds for almost 10 miles along the base of the Ko'olau cliffs to Waimānalo.

With its well-groomed and graded treadway, the Maunawili Trail is popular with hikers, runners, and mountain bikers. To avoid the crowds, start early or go during the week. Better yet, try the hike right after a heavy rainstorm when a waterfall suddenly appears out of every notch in the cliffs. Watch your footing in the slippery stream crossings, though.

Lining the gulches along the trail are kukui trees. Their large, pale green leaves resemble those of the maple, with several distinct lobes. Early Polynesian voyagers introduced kukui into Hawai'i. They used the wood to make gunwales and seats for their outrigger canoes. The flowers and sap became medicines to treat a variety of ailments. Early Hawaiians strung the nuts together to make *lei hua* (seed or nut garlands). The oily kernels became house candles and torches for night spearfishing.

The views from the open side ridges are breathtaking. *Makai* are Kailua (two seas) and Waimānalo (potable water) Bays with triple-peaked Olomana (forked hill) in front. *Mauka* loom the sheer, fluted Ko'olau (windward) cliffs from Makapu'u (bulging eye) Point to Kōnāhuanui (large fat testicles), the highest peak in the range. The aspect of the cliffs and Olomana constantly changes as you work around the Maunawili (twisted mountain) drainage.

Near the Maunawili Falls Trail junction listen for the Japanese bush warbler (uguisu), a bird often heard, but rarely seen. Its distinctive cry starts with a long whistle and then winds down in a series of notes. The bush warbler is olive brown on top with a white breast and a long tail.

After crossing Maunawili Stream, the trail enters a series of shallow ravines choked with tangled hau trees. They have large, heart-shaped leaves and bright yellow flowers with a dark red center, resembling those of a hibiscus. Early Hawaiians used the wood for kites and canoe outriggers, the bark for sandals, and the sap as a laxative. In the same area is the native shrub naupaka kuahiwi. It has light green, toothed leaves and white half-flowers.

After crossing the side ridge with a power-line tower, look for māmaki, a small native tree. It has leathery, light green leaves with toothed margins and prominent veins. Along the stems are the white, fleshy fruits. Early Hawaiians used the bark and sap in making *kapa* (bark cloth). They also steeped the leaves to prepare a tea as a tonic.

On the final descent along Anianinui Ridge are the sprawling native shrubs 'ūlei and 'ilima. 'Ūlei has small, oblong leaves arranged in pairs; clusters of white, roselike flowers; and white fruit. Early Hawaiians ate the berries and used the tough wood for making digging sticks, fish spears, and *'ūkēkē* (the musical bow). 'Ilima has oblong, serrated leaves, about 1 inch long. The yellow orange flowers strung together make a regal *lei* (garland), in both ancient and modern Hawai'i.

There are numerous variations to the one-way route as described. You can, of course, take the complete hike in the opposite direction. Most people, however, start from Pali Hwy, go as far as they want, and then turn around. You can also access the Maunawili hike from two other trailheads. From the Nu'uanu Pali (cool height cliff) lookout, follow the route description of the Likeke hike and then pick up the Maunawili Trail at the horseshoe curve of Old Pali Rd. From the Maunawili subdivision, follow the route description of the Maunawili Falls hike and then continue up the falls trail to its junction with the Maunawili Trail. Both those trailheads offer safer parking than the official ones. For a similar, but less crowded hike, try Likeke, which follows the foot of the Ko'olau cliffs toward Kāne'ohe (cutting husband).

33 Likeke (via Old Pali Road)

Type:	Foothill
Length:	7-mile round trip
Elevation Gain:	600 feet
Danger:	Low
Suitable for:	Novice, Intermediate
Location:	Kāneʻohe Forest Reserve below Nuʻuanu Pali
Topo Map:	Honolulu, Kāneʻohe
Access:	Open

Highlights
This hike takes the old road down from Nuʻuanu Pali to a cascade nestled below the Pali lookout. The route continues along the base of the Koʻolau cliffs, winding in and out of lush, dark gulches. Our destination is a pleasant windward overlook, unless you get sidetracked picking mountain apples and guava.

Trailhead Directions
At Punchbowl St. get on Pali Hwy (Rte 61 north) heading up Nuʻuanu Valley.
   Just before the tunnels turn right to the Pali lookout.
   Enter Nuʻuanu Pali State Park.
   Park in the lot (elevation 1,186 feet) (map point A).

Bus: Routes 56 or 57 to Pali Hwy and Kamehameha Hwy (Castle junction). Walk 0.8 mile back up Pali Hwy to the viewpoint at the hairpin turn and follow the route narrative for the Maunawili hike. At the signed junction turn right on the Maunawili Trail and climb to the horseshoe curve on the Old Pali Rd.

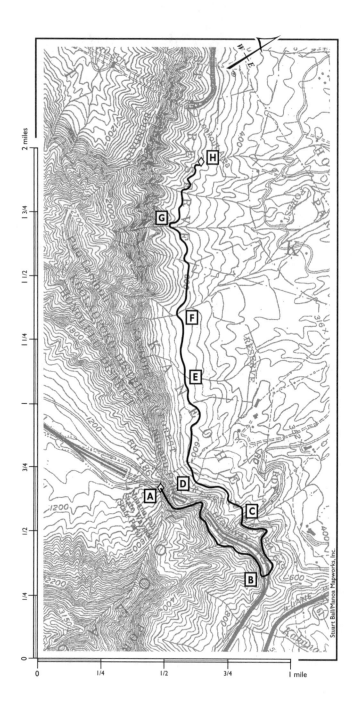

Route Description

Walk to the Pali lookout.

Turn right down the ramp to Old Pali Rd.

Go through a black gate.

Descend gradually along the paved road, which is lined with yellow ginger. Encroaching vegetation narrows the road to one lane in several spots.

Just before the road swings left in a horseshoe curve, reach a signed junction (map point B). Continue briefly along the road until it is blocked by Pali Hwy. (To the right is the start of the Maunawili Trail.)

Go around the end of the fence on the right and drop down below the main highway on some rickety wooden stairs.

Squeeze through a narrow passageway underneath the Kailua-bound lanes.

Go under the Honolulu-bound lanes on a much wider walkway.

Pick up Old Pali Rd. again, now much overgrown with grass and guava.

Descend gradually, working back toward Nuʻuanu Pali. Look and listen for the white-rumped shama.

Walk under three supports for the Honolulu-bound lanes of the highway.

The grass ends, and the pavement of the old road reappears. Look up for a view of two notches cut into the ridge above Nuʻuanu Pali by early Hawaiians.

Reach a junction with Aʻuloa Rd. Bear left on it.

Almost immediately look for a short concrete wall on the left before the road curves right.

Just past the wall and by a metal post, turn left up some stone steps, partially hidden by vegetation (map point C).

The steps become the Likeke Trail leading up the right side of a small gulch.

Climb the right side of the gulch on five short switchbacks.

Reach a four-way junction at the top of a side ridge. Continue straight across the ridge and then bear left down its other side.

Contour along the side of the ridge on a sometimes narrow trail. In the gulch on the right are some kukui trees.

The trail eventually widens and descends through a grove of white-barked albizia trees.

In a clearing bear right and down on an old grassy road.

Reach a junction. Turn left off the road onto a trail. (To road leads down to Kīʻonaʻole Rd.)

Pass several large mango trees.

Descend gradually and then climb briefly through a series of hau groves.

Pass a wet fern grotto and a low concrete structure.

Cross a small stream and turn left upstream.

Almost immediately reach a waterfall with a shallow pool at its base (elevation 680 feet) (map point D).

Descend beside a small gully filled with hau tangles.

Break out into the open through grass. Look *mauka* (inland) and up for a view of the Pali lookout.

Pass two groves of magnificent mango trees on the right. Near the second grove is a stand of mountain apple trees.

Cross a small, steep gulch lined with coffee trees and kī (ti) plants.

Cross a larger gulch, dark with guava (waiawī) trees (map point E).

By a mango tree descend into a deep gulch (map point F). Work up the gulch briefly and then climb out on one switchback.

By another mango tree descend into a narrow gulch and cross the streambed. Walk down the gulch for a short distance through ʻawapuhi (shampoo ginger) and then climb out.

Pass a viewpoint in a grove of hala trees.

Work into and out of a gulch with a tiny pool and a kukui grove.

Descend into a large gulch on one switchback and cross the stream below a small waterfall. Walk down the gulch briefly and then climb out between two mango trees (map point G).

Enter a hala grove and then traverse an open section with good views *makai* (seaward). Look for remnant native ʻōhiʻa trees and naupaka kuahiwi shrubs with their white half-flowers.

Cross a small gulch with hau tangles.

Contour through an open mixed forest. Purple Philippine ground and bamboo orchids line the trail.

Descend into a large gulch on one switchback through 'awa-puhi and then climb out.

Cross a wide, rocky streambed in a grove of mountain apple trees.

Cross a small streambed near a stand of bamboo and then turn left uphill through 'awapuhi.

Descend steeply into a deep gulch filled with mountain apple trees. Work up the gulch, first on one side of the streambed and then on the other.

Contour through a stretch of hala trees and uluhe ferns.

Reach a pleasant overlook under a shady hala tree (map point H). After the overlook the Likeke Trail crosses one more gulch and then climbs to a closed-off parking lot on Likelike Hwy near the Wilson Tunnel.

Notes

Likeke is a two-part hike. The novice segment follows the Old Pali Rd. and a short section of the Likeke Trail to a small water-fall. More experienced hikers can then continue along the base of the Ko'olau (windward) cliffs. The trail was built by Richard H. Davis of the Hawaiian Trail and Mountain Club. Likeke is Hawaiian for Richard.

The view at the Nu'uanu Pali (cool height cliff) lookout is world renowned. The windward coast stretches from Kāne'ohe (cutting husband) to Kailua (two seas) Bays. In the distance to the right is triple-peaked Olomana (forked hill). From the old road, look back along the summit ridge to see the peak of Lanihuli (turning royal chief). Towering above you and fre-quently in the clouds is Kōnāhuanui (large fat testicles) (eleva-tion 3,150 feet), the highest peak in the Ko'olau Range.

The Old Pali Rd. was constructed in 1897 and opened to vehi-cle traffic a year later. It maintains a grade of 8 percent along its 1.7-mile length. The road switchbacks once through a tight bend known as the horseshoe curve. Imagine what an adventure it was to drive a small car on this narrow, windy, winding road!

Past the horseshoe curve, watch for the white-rumped shama. It is black on top with a chestnut-colored breast and a long black-and-white tail. The shama has a variety of beautiful songs and often mimics other birds. A native of Malaysia, the shama has become widespread in introduced forests, such as this one.

After walking under the supports for the Pali Hwy, look for two notches in the flat ridge above and to the left of the Pali lookout. They are early Hawaiian observation posts carved out of natural depressions. Nearby are windbreaks and throwing stones.

In the side gulches along the trail to the waterfall are kukui trees. Their large, pale green leaves resemble those of the maple, with several distinct lobes. Early Polynesian voyagers introduced kukui into Hawai'i. They used the wood to make gunwales and seats for their outrigger canoes. The flowers and sap became medicines to treat a variety of ailments. Early Hawaiians strung the nuts together to make *lei hua* (seed or nut garlands). The oily kernels became house candles and torches for night spearfishing.

Stop for a break by the small cascade below Nu'uanu Pali. The sound of the water splashing on the rocks is exceedingly pleasant. Around the shallow pool are colorful impatiens and sundappled kukui leaves. Just down the trail you can gaze straight up at the Pali lookout.

Past the waterfall the Likeke Trail is occasionally hard to follow. Remember that it contours along the base of the Ko'olau cliffs at roughly the same elevation. The trail sometimes goes up or down a gulch or ridge, but not for long. Do not be diverted by side trails heading *mauka* or *makai*.

Along the trail are several stands of mountain apple trees ('ōhi'a 'ai). They have dark, oblong, shiny leaves. In spring their purple flowers carpet the trail. The delicious pink or red fruit usually ripens in late July or early August. If none is in reach, shake the tree and try to catch the apples as they come down. The species is native to Malaysia and was brought over by early Hawaiians.

Before reaching the final overlook, look for a grove of hala trees. They have distinctive prop roots that help support the heavy clusters of leaves and fruit on the ends of the branches. Early Hawaiians braided the long, pointed leaves, called *lau hala*, into baskets, fans, floor mats, and sails.

The hike ends at an overlook under a shady hala tree. From

there you can see Kāneʻohe Bay from Mōkapu (taboo district) to Kualoa (long back) Points. Hoʻomaluhia Botanical Garden lies *makai* of the H-3 freeway. *Mauka* are the near-vertical cliffs of the Koʻolau Range.

For a similar, more popular hike, take the Maunawili Trail that starts at the horseshoe curve on the Old Pali Rd. The Maunawili Trail contours along the base of the Koʻolau cliffs in the opposite direction toward Waimānalo (potable water).

34 Pu'u Manamana

Type:	Ungraded ridge
Length:	4-mile loop
Elevation Gain:	2,100 feet
Danger:	High
Suitable for:	Expert
Location:	Kahana Valley State Park
Topo Map:	Kahana
Access:	Open

Highlights
This challenging hike loops around the steep, knife-edge ridges above Kahana Valley. The dangerous route demands sure feet, agile hands, and a cool head. In between the narrow spots are stunning views, a good variety of native plants, and several early Hawaiian sites.

Trailhead Directions
At Punchbowl St. get on Lunalilo Fwy (H-1) heading 'ewa (west).

Take Likelike Hwy (exit 20A, Rte 63 north) up Kalihi Valley through the Wilson Tunnel.

The highway forks. Keep right for Kahekili Hwy (Rte 83 west).

Kahekili becomes Kamehameha Hwy (still Rte 83), which continues up the windward coast.

Drive through the villages of Kahalu'u and Waiāhole to Ka'a'awa.

Pass Swanzy Beach Park on the right and the Crouching Lion Inn on the left. There are rest rooms and drinking water at the park.

The road curves left to go around Kahana Bay.

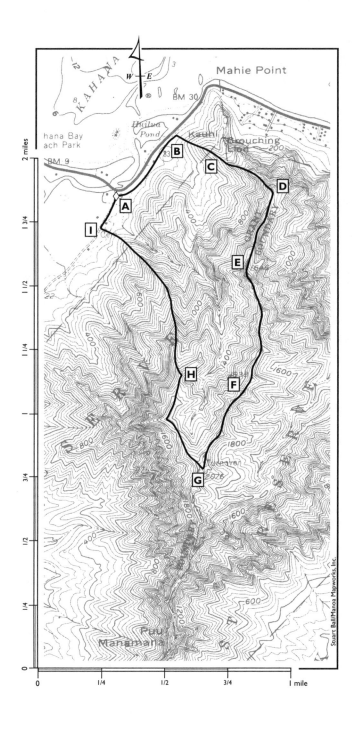

Park on the right shoulder just before the road swings right and crosses Kahana Stream (map point A). The spot is near a bus stop and a rock with a missing plaque.

Bus: Route 55 to the trailhead.

Route Description

Walk back along Kamehameha Hwy toward the Crouching Lion Inn.

Pass a short guardrail on the right with a Rte 83 sign near it.

At the first utility pole past the guard rail, turn right into the forest on an indistinct trail (map point B). Across the road is a line of ironwood trees and Huilua fishpond.

Climb straight up the slope through kī (ti) plants.

As the slope levels off, bear left through tangled Christmas berry trees.

Ascend gradually through a patch of ti plants. Nearby is Pu'u Makāne *heiau* (religious site).

Bear right into another Christmas berry tangle.

Work left, climbing steadily on the trail, now well defined.

Keep right past a wooden sign to the *heiau*.

Switchback right and then left across a rocky outcrop.

Swing right and begin climbing straight up the ridge.

Break out into the open in a grassy area. Look for the low-lying native shrub 'ūlei.

The ridge levels off briefly by the site of a fish lookout (map point C). The rock formation to the left is Kauhi'īmakaokalani, better known as the Crouching Lion.

Resume serious climbing up Pu'u o Māhie Ridge. Along the trail are the native shrubs 'ākia and akoko.

Cross a narrow, rocky neck.

Ascend very steeply past several rock faces. There are two cables for assistance.

Reach the main ridgeline and a stunning view of Kahana Bay and the windward coast (map point D). Turn right up the ridge heading *mauka* (inland).

Enter a small Christmas berry grove and then cross two eroded spots.

Climb steadily, mostly over rock, to a pointed peak. There is a cable in the worst spot.

After a level section go right, around a rock face, with the aid of another cable.

Descend a steep rock face with the help of a cable.

Ascend steadily, first over rock, and then through native lama trees.

Pass a small overlook on the right with views into Kahana Valley (map point E).

Descend steeply and then negotiate another rock face with the aid of a cable.

The ridge levels off somewhat and then resumes steep climbing. Don't let your guard down in this section. The vegetation provides some security, but the ridge is still very narrow, and the trail is rocky and rooty. There are cables in the tricky spots.

As the ridge finally widens, enter native forest dominated here by 'ōhi'a trees, woody 'ie'ie vines, and scratchy uluhe ferns.

Climb briefly to a knob on the ridge.

Descend and then climb steeply to a second knob.

Reach an obscure junction at the top of a third knob (map point F). Continue straight along the main ridge. (To the left a makeshift trail descends a side ridge into Makaua [Hidden] Valley.)

Descend briefly and then climb moderately to a broad knob. Watch for native manono and kōpiko trees.

Descend and then climb to a smaller knob.

Traverse a muddy level section. The ridge is quite broad here, and the trail works from side to side following the easiest route. Look for native pū'ahanui (kanawao) shrubs.

Pass a small open space with a nice updraft from the back of Makaua Valley.

Climb moderately toward a broad knob called Turnover.

Along its top reach a junction (map point G). Continue straight along the main ridge. (The trail to the right and down is the return portion of the loop.)

Shortly afterward reach a small clearing with a benchmark and the remains of a triangulation marker (elevation 2,027 feet). Nearby is a native 'ōhi'a tree with yellow blossoms.

From the clearing backtrack to the junction and turn left down the side ridge.

Descend, steeply at first, and then more gradually along the ridge. Keep to its left side.

Cross a wet level section interspersed with several muddy dips. Climb briefly to a small knob (map point H).

Resume the descent as the ridge begins to narrow.

Cross a short level section.

Descend very steeply on the ever-narrowing ridge under lama trees. Watch your footing on the rocky, rooty trail.

The ridge becomes razor thin. Short stretches are carpeted with moss.

The ridge finally widens through uluhe ferns, but the descent remains steep.

Descend a narrow rocky section. Look for the native herb ko'oko'olau and the shrub pūkiawe.

Go left around a rock outcrop with the help of a cable.

Descend steeply through a hala grove.

Follow the main path down through a small graveyard.

Reach Trout Farm Rd. by an old Mormon chapel (map point I). Turn right on the paved road.

Reach Kamehameha Hwy directly across from the bus stop (map point A).

Notes

Pu'u Manamana is one of the most dangerous hikes on the island. The route is for experienced hikers only because it becomes difficult right away and then gets worse. Start early because this short loop takes longer than you think. Frequently the clouds roll in from the ocean and blanket the ridge in swirling mist and rain, making the going slow and slippery.

The rock faces and narrow sections along the *makai* (seaward) portion of the main ridge are legendary. Watch your footing constantly on the bare roots, loose dirt, and crumbly rock. Test all cables before using them. There is no shame in turning back if you don't like what you see.

The return route down a wooded side ridge is just as narrow and steep. You drop 2,000 feet in a little over a mile. Hang on to tree trunks and exposed roots to control your descent. Before and after the Turnover clearing, the trail may be overgrown with *Clidemia* shrubs and scratchy uluhe ferns.

Before starting the climb, take a quick look at Huilua (twice joined), a fishpond fed by natural springs as well as the ocean. In earlier times the brackish water was perfect for raising ʻamaʻama (mullet) and awa (milkfish). According to legend, the pond was built by the Menehune, an elusive race of small people who worked only at night. Above the pond along the trail is the site of Puʻu Makāne *heiau,* a small temple devoted to fishing and farming.

Along Puʻu o Māhie (hill of pleasure) Ridge above the *heiau* is the rock formation Kauhiʻīmakaokalani (the watchtower of heaven). According to legend, the *malihini* (newcomer) demigod Kauhi was stationed permanently in the cliff above Kahana Bay. One day he spied Hiʻiaka, the beautiful sister of Pele, goddess of fire. The bored Kauhi longed to join Hiʻiaka on her travels around the island chain. She, however, had no time for Kauhi and so told him to stay. With all his might he heaved his body into a crouching position on all fours. That was the limit of his strength, however, and so Kauhi remains there to this day. The rock formation is more recently and widely known as the Crouching Lion.

Past the lion look for the native shrubs ʻākia and ʻakoko. ʻĀkia has oval, pointed, bright green leaves. Its dark branches are jointed with white rings. Early Hawaiians pounded the leaves and bark and then dropped the mixture into tidal pools to poison fish. The red orange fruits were used in *lei* (garlands) and as a poison for criminals. ʻAkoko has oval, darker green leaves with rounded ends. At the tips of the jointed branches are red seed capsules. Early Hawaiians used the milky sap as a stain for their canoe hulls.

Along the drier *makai* portion of the main ridge are native lama trees. Their oblong, pointed leaves are dark green and leathery. The fruits are green, then yellow, and finally bright red when fully ripe. Lama was sacred to Laka, goddess of the hula. Early Hawaiians used the hard, light-colored wood in temple construction and in hula performances.

Look for native manono and kōpiko trees in the wet *mauka* section of the ridge. Manono has thick, glossy, oblong leaves with purple stems, small yellow green flowers, and purple black fruits. A native member of the coffee family, kōpiko has leathery, oblong leaves with a light green midrib. Turn the leaf over to see a row of tiny holes (*piko* [navel]) on either side of the midrib. The kōpiko produces clusters of little white flowers and fleshy, orange fruits.

All along the main ridge are magnificent views. *Makai* the windward coast stretches from Lā'ie to Mōkapu (taboo district) to Makapu'u (bulging eye) Points. The massive peak across Kahana (cutting) Valley is Pu'u Piei. From the Turnover clearing you can see Ka'a'awa Valley on the left and Punalu'u (coral dived for) Valley on the right. Ahead along the ridge are Pu'u Manamana and Pu'u 'Ōhulehule (joining of waves hill). In back of Kahana Valley is the long Ko'olau (windward) summit ridge.

Before reaching Turnover, watch for the native shrub pū'ahanui (kanawao), a relative of hydrangea. It has large, serrated, deeply creased leaves and clusters of delicate pink flowers. Early Hawaiians used the plants for medicinal purposes.

After the hair-raising descent, the small graveyard in the valley is always a welcome sight. Several people buried there fell victim to a huge tsunami (on-shore wave) that swept inland from the bay on 1 April 1946. Just beyond the graveyard is an old Mormon chapel.

35 Kahana Valley

Type:	Valley
Length:	6-mile double loop
Elevation Gain:	400 feet
Danger:	Low
Suitable for:	Novice, Intermediate
Location:	Kahana Valley State Park
Topo Map:	Kahana, Hau'ula
Access:	Open

Highlights
This double-loop hike meanders around a vast, undeveloped windward valley. The intricate route has numerous junctions and stream crossings. Along the stream are deep, inviting pools and groves of mountain apple.

Trailhead Directions
At Punchbowl St. get on Lunalilo Fwy (H-1) heading 'ewa (west).

Take Likelike Hwy (exit 20A, Rte 63 north) up Kalihi Valley through the Wilson Tunnel.

The highway forks. Keep right for Kahekili Hwy (Rte 83 west).

Kahekili becomes Kamehameha Hwy (still Rte 83), which continues up the windward coast.

Drive through the villages of Kahalu'u and Waiāhole to Ka'a'awa.

Pass the Crouching Lion Inn on the left.

The road curves left to go around Kahana Bay.

Cross Kahana Stream on two bridges.

By a large palm grove turn left into Kahana Valley State Park.

Pass the green Orientation Center on the right. It has rest

rooms and drinking water. A shelf by the front door contains park brochures and trail maps.

Drive another 0.5 mile into the valley on the paved road.

Park in a cleared area on the right just before a locked gate (elevation 20 feet) (map point A).

Bus: Route 55 to the entrance of Kahana Valley State Park. Walk 0.6 mile along the park access road to the first locked gate.

Route Description

Continue along the paved access road on foot.

Pass houses on both sides of the road.

Go around a second locked gate. The road narrows to one lane.

Climb steadily through introduced forest. Puʻu Piei is the sharp peak on the ridge to the right.

Reach a junction marked by a hunting area sign (map point

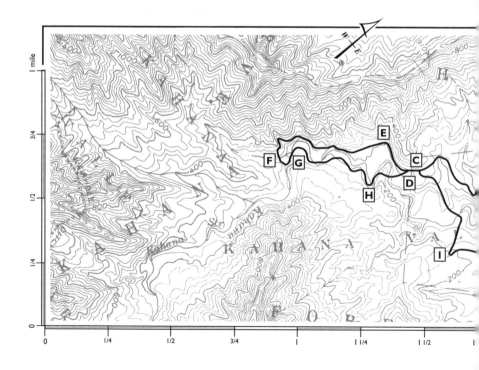

B). Turn left and down on a dirt road. (The paved road curves right and up through a locked gate.)

Almost immediately reach a signed junction. Turn right onto the Nakoa Trail. (The dirt road descends to Kahana Stream and is the return portion of the hike.)

Contour along the side of the valley through hala groves and hau tangles. Look for an occasional hāpuʻu tree fern and some mountain apple trees in this long section. In the openings you can see Puʻu Manamana and Puʻu ʻŌhulehule on the ridge to the left.

In a stand of kukui trees jog left and down into a gully to avoid a landslide.

Turn right and climb up the gully.

Bear left out of the gully and resume contouring in a grove of hala.

Work into and out of a side gulch with an intermittent stream.

Descend briefly and ford a small stream in a second gulch.

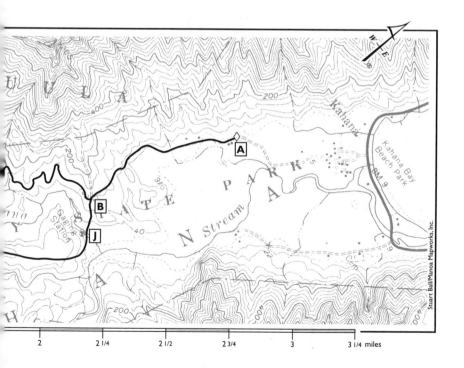

Descend into a third gulch on one switchback and cross another stream.

Pass a rusted triangular tank trap on the right.

Shortly afterward reach a four-way junction in a clearing surrounded by hala trees (map point C). Continue straight across. (To the left the Nakoa Trail descends to Kahana Stream and is the return portion of the hike. To the right a trail leads to a water tank and the paved access road.)

Pass several observation bunkers hidden in the trees on the left.

Shortly afterward reach a fork (map point D). Take the right fork. (The left fork leads down to Kahana Stream and is the return portion of the hike.)

Contour above Kahana Stream under magnificent albizia trees.

Cross a side stream on a slippery rock surface. Just before the crossing is a grove of mountain apples.

Cross a second side stream by two mango trees.

Reach an obscure junction in a flat area with scattered ginger (map point E). Continue straight on the trail into the valley. (To the left a trail provides a shortcut to Kahana Stream.)

Cross several side streams in groves of mountain apple. The trail is narrow and rough in spots.

Reach another obscure junction by a large side stream (elevation 360 feet) (map point F). Swing left and parallel the side stream. (To the right is the upper trail, which crosses the side stream and continues to the back of the valley.)

Cross the side stream and leave it behind.

Reach Kahana Stream and turn left downstream.

Ford the main stream just after it bends to the left, forming a lovely pool (map point G). The side stream that you crossed earlier comes in on the left.

Continue downstream, hugging the right bank.

The stream splits. One of the channels may be dry.

Ford the stream to the left bank.

Cross the stream to the right bank by two large albizia trees with white-flecked trunks.

Pass a large mango tree with exposed roots on the left bank of the stream.

Ford the stream to the left bank just before it turns sharp left (map point H). Nearby is a large mango tree and another deep, inviting pool.

Continue downstream briefly and reach an obscure junction. Turn right and cross Kahana Stream to the right bank. (To the left a short trail leads back to map point E on the contour trail.)

The stream splits briefly. Traverse the island in between and then return to the right side.

Reach a large mango tree and a lovely pool.

Ford the stream there to the left bank and enter a bamboo grove.

Ascend through the grove, leaving the stream behind.

Work left and then straight up the slope on a narrow, rutted trail.

Reach the familiar junction with the contour trail (map point D). Keep right.

Reach the four-way junction again (map point C). This time turn right downhill on the continuation of the Nakoa Trail.

Descend steadily along a terrace through hala.

Enter a hau grove.

Shortly afterward ford Kahana Stream and turn right upstream.

Ascend steadily on a terrace just below the ridgeline.

Reach a signed junction at the ridge line (map point I). Turn sharp left down the ridge.

Descend gradually down the flat ridge through hala.

Break out into the open briefly. The peak on the ridge to the left is Pu'u Piei.

Veer right, off the ridgeline onto a terrace.

The trail curves left to reach Kahana Stream by a gauging station (map point J).

Ford the stream for the last time on a small dam. Watch your footing because the concrete is very slippery. At the dam is a large swimming hole popular with valley residents.

Climb gradually on an eroded dirt road.

Cross a small *'auwai* (ditch) for irrigating *lo'i* (*kalo* or taro terraces).

Reach the familiar junction by the hunting area sign (map point B). This time turn right on the paved access road to reach your car.

Notes
This hike is an intriguing double loop in a largely undeveloped valley on the windward side. The initial stretch leaves something to be desired, but the stream loop is perhaps the most beautiful valley walk on the island. The water rushing by is cool and clear, and the pools are deep and inviting. There are few things better in life than spending a sunny afternoon by Kahana Stream.

Kahana (cutting) Valley is a unique state park, established to foster and spread native Hawaiian culture. About thirty families live in the lower section of the valley. They are helping to restore some of the ancient sites, such as Huilua (twice joined) fishpond and *lo'i* (irrigated terraces for growing *kalo* [taro]). Years ago, the *ahupua'a* (land division) of Kahana supported a thriving community based on ocean fishing, taro farming, and fish raising.

The trails in this wet valley are invariably muddy, sometimes overgrown, and occasionally obscure. Watch your footing while crossing the stream. If possible, change to tabis (Japanese reef walkers) for better traction on the slippery rocks. As always, do not ford the stream if the water is much above your knees.

Unfortunately, this magnificent valley harbors a large mosquito population. Local mosquitoes are usually laid back, but not so in Kahana. Bring insect repellent or cover up or keep moving. For lunch, pick a sunny pool with a breeze, and you won't be constantly bothered.

On the first section of the Nakoa Trail are groves of tangled hau trees. They have large, heart-shaped leaves. Their flowers are bright yellow with a dark red center and resemble those of a hibiscus. Early Hawaiians used the wood for kites and canoe outriggers, the bark for sandals, and the sap as a laxative.

Also common in the valley is the hala tree. It has distinctive prop roots that help support the heavy clusters of leaves and fruit on the ends of the branches. Early Hawaiians braided the long, pointed leaves, called *lau hala,* into baskets, fans, floor mats, and sails.

The wet side gulches are lined with kukui trees. Their large, pale green leaves resemble those of the maple, with several distinct lobes. Early Polynesian voyagers introduced kukui into Hawai'i. They used the wood to make gunwales and seats for their outrigger canoes. The flowers and sap became medicines to treat a variety of ailments. Early Hawaiians strung the nuts together to make *lei hua* (seed or nut garlands). The oily kernels became house candles and torches for night spearfishing.

On the second loop look for mountain apple trees ('ōhi'a 'ai) along the contour trail. They have dark, oblong, shiny leaves. In spring their purple flowers carpet the trail. The delicious pink or red fruit usually ripens in late July or early August. If none is in reach, shake the tree and try to catch the apples as they come down. The species is native to Malaysia and was brought over by early Hawaiians.

The walk along the stream is very pleasant, but the trail there may be obscure in spots. Follow the directions closely. Surveyors ribbon of various colors may mark the correct route but don't count on it. If you do lose the trail, continue walking downstream until you pick it up again. Watch for the bamboo grove on the left bank where the trail leaves the stream for good.

There are several variations to the route as described. You can, of course, do one or both loops in the opposite direction. However, the hike is complicated enough without having to read the narrative in reverse. For a short novice outing, walk only the first loop, on the Nakoa Trail. Be sure to visit the lovely pool near the bamboo by keeping left and down at the junction with the contour trail (map point D). Total distance for the first loop is about 5 miles. To shorten the second loop, turn left off the contour trail at map point E to reach the deep pool by the mango tree near map point H.

For a more difficult hike in the valley, take the upper trail that leaves from the second loop and ends at the intake of Waiāhole Ditch. Across the intake is the start (end) of the Waiāhole Ditch Trail, which contours around the back of Kahana, Waikāne, and Waiāhole Valleys.

36 Pu'u Piei

Type:	Ungraded ridge
Length:	3-mile round trip
Elevation Gain:	1,700 feet
Danger:	Medium
Suitable for:	Intermediate
Location:	Kahana Valley State Park
Topo Map:	Kahana
Access:	Open

Highlights
Pu'u Piei is the broad peak overlooking Kahana Bay and Valley. This rugged climb to its summit is short, but very steep. A brief side trip leads to an early Hawaiian fish shrine and lookout.

Trailhead Directions
At Punchbowl St. get on Lunalilo Fwy (H-1) heading 'ewa (west).

Take Likelike Hwy (exit 20A, Rte 63 north) up Kalihi Valley through the Wilson Tunnel.

The highway forks. Keep right for Kahekili Hwy (Rte 83 west).

Kahekili becomes Kamehameha Hwy (still Rte 83), which continues up the windward coast.

Drive through the villages of Kahalu'u and Waiāhole to Ka'a'awa.

Pass the Crouching Lion Inn on the left.

The road curves left to go around Kahana Bay.

Cross Kahana Stream on two bridges.

By a large palm grove turn left into Kahana Valley State Park.

Park in the lot in front of the green Orientation Center on the right (map point A). It has rest rooms and drinking water.

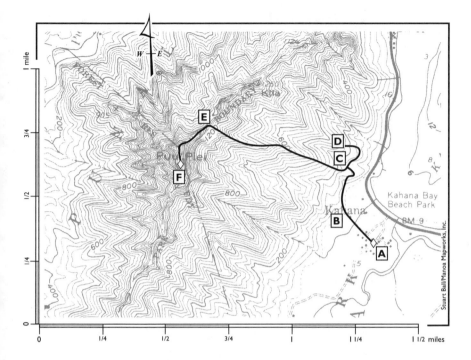

A shelf by the front door contains park brochures and trail maps.

Bus: Route 55 to the entrance of Kahana Valley State Park. Walk 0.1 mile along the park access road to the Orientation Center.

Route Description
Take the gravel road on the right just before the Orientation Center. Ignore private driveways on both sides.

The road becomes dirt after the last house.

Pass a banana grove on the left.

At the far edge of the grove and just past utility pole no. 3, turn left on a trail into the forest (map point B).

The trail gradually angles away from the road through tangled hau groves. Signs identify some of the native plants.

Climb up the side of a ridge. On the right are wooden handrails.

The trail swings left and descends into a gully.

At a rocky streambed reach a junction (map point C). For now keep right and cross the streambed. (The wide path on the left is the route to Pu'u Piei.)

Climb briefly to Kapa'ele'ele Ko'a, an ancient fish shrine.

After contouring for a short distance, reach another junction. Turn left upslope. (The trail to the right leads down to Kamehameha Hwy.) Look for 'ūlei, a low-lying native shrub.

By a stand of ironwoods reach Keaniani Kilo, a fish lookout (map point D). From there is a good view of Kahana Bay and Huilua fishpond.

Retrace your steps past the fish shrine to the junction by the streambed (map point C). This time continue straight on the wide, but less-traveled path uphill.

Shortly afterward the trail turns right and ascends gradually along the left edge of the ridge. Ignore side trails on the right. Look for the small native tree 'ākia.

At an eroded spot turn right toward the Piei cliffs and begin serious climbing.

Almost immediately the ridge narrows briefly by another eroded section.

Climb steadily through grass and scattered octopus (umbrella) trees. Generally keep to the right side of the broad ridge.

Pass another eroded section on the right.

Cross a small, bare patch backed by hala trees.

As the ridge narrows, climb steeply through hau, hala, and 'ākia trees.

The angle of ascent decreases briefly in a hala grove (whew!). Take a break.

As the top nears, the climbing becomes very steep and rocky. Roots and tree trunks provide some security.

Ascend several especially steep sections with the aid of cables.

Reach the top of the Piei ridge with its magnificent view of Kahana Valley (map point E). While catching your breath, look for the native herb ko'oko'olau.

Turn left along the very narrow ridge.

Climb over a small hump. There are cables on the worst sections.

Reach the broad summit of Pu'u Piei (elevation 1,740 feet) (map point F). Vegetation blocks most of the views there.

Notes

Pu'u Piei is for hikers who love to scramble. The route ascends 1,700 feet in a little over a mile. Now that's serious climbing! On the way up or down be sure to visit the early Hawaiian fish shrine and lookout.

This hike is made up of two very different trails. The improved route to the fish lookout is well graded and groomed. The trail up the ridge, on the other hand, is steep, unimproved, and may be overgrown. Watch your footing on the loose rock and dirt. Be very careful on the narrow and often slippery stretch just below the ridge top. Test all cables before using them.

The route initially follows the old rail bed of the Ko'olau Line. In the late 1800s and early 1900s its steam engines hauled sugar-cane grown in Kahana Valley to the mill up the coast at Kahuku (the projection). With a one-engine roundhouse Kahana was the southern terminus of the line. Step lively through this section to escape the hordes of mosquitoes.

The short side trip to the fish shrine, Kapa'ele'ele (black bark cloth) Ko'a, is well worthwhile. Early Hawaiians made offerings there to ensure a good catch of akule (bigeye scad) in the bay below. The rectangular *ko'a* was enclosed on three sides by large stones. The *makai* side facing the bay was left open. Stay on the trail to avoid disturbing the already deteriorated site.

Between the fish shrine and the lookout is the sprawling native shrub 'ūlei. It has small, oblong leaves arranged in pairs; clusters of white, roselike flowers; and white fruit. Early Hawaiians ate the berries and used the tough wood for making digging sticks, fish spears, and *'ūkēkē* (the musical bow).

Keaniani (the mirror) Kilo is a pleasant spot for a break, especially after climbing the ridge. The shady lookout offers an unobstructed view of Kahana Bay. In earlier times a *kilo i'a* (fish watcher) at the lookout would spot a school of akule and quick-ly hoist a flag of white *kapa* to signal fishermen waiting on the beach. They would then encircle the fish with nets and pull the catch to shore.

While climbing up the ridge, look for the small native tree 'ākia. It has dark branches jointed with white rings. Its leaves are bright green, oval, and pointed. Early Hawaiians pounded the leaves and bark and then dropped the mixture into tidal pools to poison fish. The red orange fruits were used in *lei* (garlands) and as a poison for criminals.

From the top of the Piei Ridge are breathtaking views of Kahana (cutting) Bay and Valley. Across the U-shaped bay is Huilua (twice joined) fishpond. The prominent peak toward the back of the valley is Pu'u 'Ōhulehule (joining of waves hill). Behind it are the sheer, fluted flanks of the Ko'olau (windward) Range. On the other side of the ridge you can see Punalu'u (coral dived for) Valley and the windward coast to Lā'ie Point.

On top of the ridge is the native herb ko'oko'olau, related to the daisy and sunflower families. It has pointed, serrated leaves and flower heads with yellow petals. Early Hawaiians steeped the leaves to make a tea used as a tonic.

37 Hau'ula-Papali

Type:	Foothill
Length:	7-mile double loop
Elevation Gain:	700 feet (Hau'ula), 800 feet (Papali)
Danger:	Low
Suitable for:	Novice, Intermediate
Location:	Hau'ula Forest Reserve above Hau'ula
Topo Map:	Hau'ula
Access:	Open

Highlights

This intricate double loop traverses the foothills of the windward Ko'olau Range. From secluded viewpoints you look down into deep, narrow gulches. Along the way are groves of stately Cook pines and some remnant native vegetation.

Trailhead Directions

At Punchbowl St. get on Lunalilo Fwy (H-1) heading 'ewa (west).

Take Likelike Hwy (exit 20A, Rte 63 north) up Kalihi Valley through the Wilson Tunnel.

The highway forks. Keep right for Kahekili Hwy (Rte 83 west).

Kahekili becomes Kamehameha Hwy (still Rte 83), which continues up the windward coast.

Drive through the villages of Ka'a'awa and Punalu'u to Hau'ula.

Pass a fire station on the left and cross a bridge.

Look for Hau'ula Beach Park on the right. At the park are rest rooms and drinking water.

Park on Kamehameha Hwy at the far end of the beach park near Hau'ula Congregational Church (map point A).

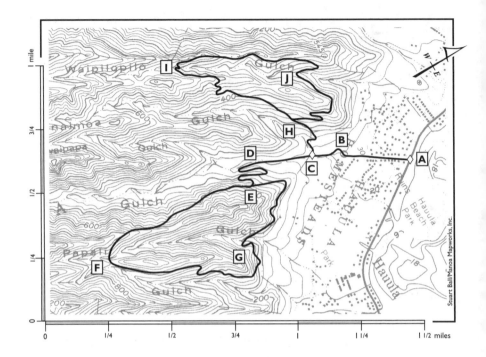

Bus: Route 55 to Kamehameha Hwy and Hau'ula Homestead Rd.

Route Description

Continue along Kamehameha Hwy on foot.

At the first intersection turn left on Hau'ula Homestead Rd.

As the road curves left, proceed straight on Ma'akua Rd.

As the pavement ends, pass a private driveway on the left.

The road forks by a utility pole (map point B). Take the left fork and go around a chain across the road.

The road crosses a streambed and swings right.

Shortly afterward reach a signed junction (map point C). Keep left on the dirt road. (To the right is the Hau'ula Loop Trail, which is described later on.)

The road straightens out briefly by a concrete retaining wall.

Just before the road curves right, reach a second signed junction (map point D). Bear left and down off the road onto the Papali–Ma'akua Ridge Trail. (To the right the road leads to the Ma'akua Gulch Trail.)

Almost immediately cross Ma'akua Stream and climb the embankment on the far side.

Work right and then left through a hau grove.

Climb gradually up the side of Ma'akua Gulch on eight switchbacks. At the sixth one is a good view of Hau'ula town and the ocean.

At the eighth switchback the trail splits, becoming a loop (map point E). Turn sharp right and start the loop in a counterclockwise direction.

Ascend steadily up the side of the gulch heading *mauka* (inland) through a mixed introduced forest. You can look deep into Ma'akua Gulch through breaks in the trees. Watch for tasty banana lilikoi.

Reach the ridgeline and stroll along it under shady Formosa koa trees.

Bear left off the ridge (elevation 800 feet) and descend gradually into Papali Gulch. Look for the native shrub naupaka kuahiwi and purple Philippine ground orchids in this section.

Cross the stream (map point F) by a stand of kukui trees and turn left downstream.

Climb gradually out of the gulch.

Gain the ridgeline briefly near some Cook pines.

Switch to the right side of the ridge and descend part way into Punaiki Gulch on a series of switchbacks.

Contour around the front of the ridge. There are good views of Hau'ula town and the ocean.

Descend once again into Papali Gulch and cross the rocky streambed (map point G).

Climb out of the gulch on switchbacks.

Contour along the front of the next ridge.

A cliff overhangs the trail on the left.

Reach the end of the loop (map point E). Bear right and down.

Retrace your steps to the dirt road and its junction with the Hau'ula Loop Trail (map point C).

Turn left off the road onto the trail.

Follow Hānaimoa Stream briefly and then cross it.

Ascend through ironwoods on two long switchbacks. At the first switchback look for noni with its large, shiny leaves.

The trail splits, becoming a loop (map point H). This time keep left and start the loop in a clockwise direction.

Climb *mauka* up the side of Hānaimoa Gulch on several switchbacks.

Reach the ridgeline and cross over it.

Descend gradually into Waipilopilo Gulch.

Cross the stream there (map point I) and climb out of the gulch.

Reach the ridgeline (elevation 680 feet) and turn right heading *makai* (toward the ocean). Below on the left are the sheer walls of Kaipapa'u Gulch. Look for a few native 'ōhi'a trees and pūkiawe shrubs along the trail.

Descend steadily along the top of the ridge. Steps are provided at a steep, eroded section.

Bear right off the ridgeline through a grove of Cook pines. The ground is covered with lau'ae ferns.

Descend into Waipilopilo Gulch once again (map point J) and then climb out of it.

Contour around the front of the ridge through Cook pines and ironwoods. Through a break in the trees you can see down the windward coast to Māhie Point on the far side of Kahana Bay.

Reach the end of the loop (map point H) and turn left.

Retrace your steps back to the dirt road (map point C).

Turn left on it to return to the highway (map point A).

Notes

The Hau'ula-Papali hike is perfect for beginners. The two loops are short, mostly shady, and surprisingly scenic. Along the trail are some easily identified native and introduced plants. Although in the same general area, each loop is different, so try them both.

The route narrative describes the Papali (small cliff) loop first in a counterclockwise direction and then the Hau'ula (red hau tree) loop in a clockwise direction. You can, of course, do just one or both loops in either order or direction. The Hau'ula loop is somewhat easier and more popular than Papali. Neither loop is crowded, however, probably because of their distance from Honolulu.

The trails making up the loops are wide, well graded, and easy to follow, for the most part. Watch your step, however, while crossing the rocky streambeds in the gulches. The Papali loop may be overgrown in spots with introduced shrubs.

An inexpensive interpretive pamphlet, Hau'ula Loop Trail: Field Site Guide, is available from Moanalua Gardens Foundation. If possible, pick one up at the foundation office before starting the Hau'ula loop. The address is in Appendix 2.

On the trail, look and listen for the white-rumped shama. It is black on top with a chestnut-colored breast and a long black-and-white tail. The shama has a variety of beautiful songs and often mimics other birds. A native of Malaysia, the shama has become widespread in introduced forests such as this one.

On the descent to Papali Gulch is the native shrub naupaka kuahiwi. It has light green, toothed leaves and white half-flowers. The unusual appearance of the flowers has given rise to several unhappy legends. According to one, a Hawaiian maiden believed her lover unfaithful. In anger she tore all the naupaka flowers in half. She then asked him to find a whole flower to prove his love. He was, of course, unsuccessful and died of a broken heart.

In Papali Gulch look for a stand of kukui trees. Their large, pale green leaves resemble those of the maple, with several distinct lobes. Early Polynesian voyagers introduced kukui into Hawai'i. They used the wood to make gunwales and seats for their outrigger canoes. The flowers and sap became medicines to treat a variety of ailments. Early Hawaiians strung the nuts together to make lei hua (seed or nut garlands). The oily kernels became house candles and torches for night spearfishing.

Above Kaipapa'u (shallow sea) Gulch on the Hau'ula loop are a few 'ōhi'a, the dominant tree in the native rain forest. They have oval leaves and clusters of delicate red flowers. Early Hawaiians used the flowers in lei and the wood in outrigger canoes. The hard, durable wood was also carved into god images for heiau (religious sites).

On the return leg of the Hau'ula loop you pass through a forest of tall Cook pines. They have overlapping, scalelike leaves about 1/4 inch long, rather than true needles. The pines were planted in the 1930s for reforestation. Discovered by Captain James Cook, they are native to New Caledonia (Isle of Pines) in the South Pacific between Fiji and Australia.

For a totally different experience, try the Ma'akua Gulch hike. It starts at the same trailhead, but involves rock hopping up a stream in a narrow canyon.

38 Ma'akua Gulch

Type:	Valley
Length:	6-mile round trip
Elevation Gain:	900 feet
Danger:	Medium
Suitable for:	Intermediate
Location:	Hau'ula Forest Reserve above Hau'ula
Topo Map:	Hau'ula
Access:	Closed: for current status check website at www.hgea.org/~lmasu/oindex.html

Highlights
This hike explores a deep and narrow windward gulch. Along the winding route are multiple stream crossings and groves of mountain apple. At the end is a delightful waterfall and swimming hole surrounded by towering cliffs.

Trailhead Directions
At Punchbowl St. get on Lunalilo Fwy (H-1) heading *'ewa* (west).

Take Likelike Hwy (exit 20A, Rte 63 north) up Kalihi Valley through the Wilson Tunnel.

The highway forks. Keep right for Kahekili Hwy (Rte 83 west).

Kahekili becomes Kamehameha Hwy (still Rte 83), which continues up the windward coast.

Drive through the villages of Ka'a'awa and Punalu'u to Hau'ula. Pass a fire station on the left and cross a bridge.

Look for Hau'ula Beach Park on the right. At the park are rest rooms and drinking water.

Park on Kamehameha Hwy at the far end of the beach park near Hau'ula Congregational Church (map point A).

Bus: Route 55 to Kamehameha Hwy and Hau'ula Homestead Rd.

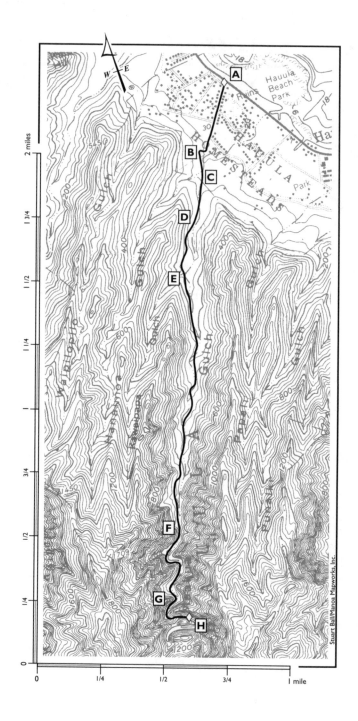

Route Description

Continue along Kamehameha Hwy on foot.

At the first intersection turn left on Hau'ula Homestead Rd.

As the road curves left, proceed straight on Ma'akua Rd.

As the pavement ends, pass a private driveway on the left.

The road forks by a utility pole (map point B). Take the left fork and go around a chain across the road.

The road crosses a streambed and swings right.

Shortly afterward reach a signed junction (map point C). Keep left on the dirt road. (To the right is the Hau'ula Loop Trail.)

The road straightens out briefly by a concrete retaining wall.

Just before the road curves right, reach a second signed junction (map point D). Continue straight on the road. (To the left is the Papali–Ma'akua Ridge Trail.)

Climb gradually above Ma'akua Stream on the road.

Pass a water pumping station on the right.

As the road, now paved, switchbacks to the right, continue straight, through a gap between a stone wall and a concrete retaining wall.

Pick up the Ma'akua Gulch Trail.

Descend briefly through tangled hau trees.

In a grove of ironwoods cross Kawaipapa Stream, which comes in from the right (map point E).

Descend gradually to Ma'akua Stream through mixed forest. Look for noni with its large, shiny leaves.

Ford Ma'akua Stream in a stand of hala trees.

Shortly afterward cross the stream a second time through a hau tangle.

After the third ford, parallel the stream briefly under kukui trees.

Beyond the fourth crossing the trail becomes rocky, rooty, and usually muddy. Walk through groves of mountain apple for the next ten crossings. Above the mountain apple are kukui and an occasional mango tree.

At the sixth ford the streambed splits in two. After crossing, jog left and then right upstream.

The trail briefly follows a rocky gully after the eighth crossing.

At the eleventh ford, the valley walls begin to close in. Walk in the streambed for a short distance before crossing to the opposite bank.

Walk in the streambed for a longer stretch at the fourteenth crossing.

At the fifteenth ford, a small side stream comes in on the right (map point F). If you have tabis (Japanese reef walkers), put them on here.

Beyond the fifteenth crossing the stream becomes the trail more often than not. Look for short trail sections on the inside bends of the stream. Notice the vertical rock dikes jutting into the gulch.

Wind past a waterfall chute, carved out of the near-vertical cliffs on the right (map point G).

Pass a lone loulu palm near a large boulder in the stream.

Pass a second, larger waterfall chute on the left.

Shortly afterward reach a point where the gulch narrows to 5 feet across (elevation 860 feet) (map point H).

Wade or swim through the narrows to reach a circular pool with a small waterfall. There the slippery cliffs block further progress upstream.

Notes

This spectacular hike is a walk on the narrow side. Ma'akua Gulch is not wide to begin with, and it just keeps getting narrower. Toward the back the stream bends around towering rock dikes. Near-vertical waterfall chutes scour the cliffs. At the end you can touch the walls on either side with your outstretched arms.

July and early August are the best months to take this hike. The mountain apples are in season then. Also, the midday sun is high enough to reach the pool at the end of the hike. Without the sun, the back of the gulch becomes a cold, damp hollow.

Before you start the hike, a few cautions are in order. Watch your footing on the slippery rocks in the streambed. Don't hesitate to get your boots wet if the rock hopping becomes dicey. Around the fifteenth crossing switch to tabis (Japanese reef walkers), if possible. Their fuzzy bottom provides secure footing for the final stretch in the stream. You can, of course, wear tabis for the whole hike if the bottom of your feet can take the pounding.

Ma'akua Stream is subject to flash flooding during very heavy rains. If the water suddenly rises much above your knees, head for the nearest high ground and wait there for the stream to go down. It is far better to be stranded for half a day than to get swept away.

The trail is usually rocky and rooty, sometimes muddy, and occasionally obscure. Each bank at a stream crossing may be marked with surveyor's ribbon of various colors, but don't count on it. If you lose the trail, keep walking upstream until you find the route again. The lower portion of the gulch is the home of some very persistent mosquitoes.

At the first few stream crossings are groves of tangled hau trees. They have large, heart-shaped leaves. Their flowers are bright yellow with a dark red center and resemble those of a hibiscus. Early Hawaiians used the wood for kites and canoe outriggers, the bark for sandals, and the sap as a laxative.

After the third ford, kukui trees form much of the forest canopy. Their large, pale green leaves resemble those of the maple, with several distinct lobes. Early Polynesian voyagers introduced kukui into Hawai'i. They used the wood to make gunwales and seats for their outrigger canoes. The flowers and sap became medicines to treat a variety of ailments. Early Hawaiians strung the nuts together to make *lei hua* (seed or nut garlands). The oily kernels became house candles and torches for night spearfishing.

Underneath the kukui are dense stands of mountain apple trees ('ōhi'a 'ai). They have dark, oblong, shiny leaves. In spring their purple flowers carpet the trail. The delicious pink or red fruit usually ripens in late July or early August. If none is in reach, shake the tree and try to catch the apples as they come down. The species is native to Malaysia and was brought over by early Hawaiians.

After the fifteenth ford, the stream trail winds around steep, narrow side ridges jutting into the gulch. Look at the exposed rock where the ridge meets the stream. The rock is part of a dike complex in the northwest rift zone of the old Ko'olau (windward) volcano. Rift zones are areas of structural weakness extending from the summit of a shield volcano. Rising molten rock or magma worked its way into cracks in the rift zone and solidified. The resulting dikes are sheetlike, vertical intrusions of hard, dense rock. Over the years the stream has eroded the softer, surrounding material, leaving the parallel dikes exposed.

The hike ends at a lovely waterfall with a deep, dark pool. To get to it, you must wade or swim through a short narrows. Before taking the plunge, look up and around at the close confines. Above, a blue ribbon of sky is all that separates the sheer, fern-covered canyon walls. The only egress is the sparkling ribbon of water soon lost from sight around a bend.

If you don't like rock hopping and cold swimming, try the Hau'ula-Papali hike that starts from the same trailhead. From the Papali loop you can look down into Ma'akua Gulch.

39 Koloa Gulch

Type:	Valley
Length:	8-mile round trip
Elevation Gain:	1,300 feet
Danger:	Medium
Suitable for:	Intermediate
Location:	Kahuku Forest Reserve above Lāʻie
Topo Map:	Kahuku, Hauʻula
Access:	Conditional; open to individuals and outdoor organizations with permission. Contact Hawaii Reserves, Inc., 55-510 Kamehameha Hwy, Lāʻie, HI 96762 (phone 293-9201).

Highlights

This deceptive hike starts purposefully up a hot, open ridge and then descends lazily into a cool, narrow gulch. The meandering path has abundant stream crossings and mountain apple groves. Awaiting you at the end is an inviting pool with a split-level waterfall.

Trailhead Directions

At Punchbowl St. get on Lunalilo Fwy (H-1) heading ʻewa (west).

Take Likelike Hwy (exit 20A, Rte 63 north) up Kalihi Valley through the Wilson Tunnel.

The highway forks. Keep right for Kahekili Hwy (Rte 83 west).

Kahekili Hwy becomes Kamehameha Hwy (still Rte 83), which continues up the windward coast.

Drive through Kaʻaʻawa and Punaluʻu to Hauʻula.

Pass Hauʻula Beach Park on the right and Hauʻula Shopping Center on the left.

On the right look for Kokololio Beach Park with its long rock wall. Turn right into the lot there and park at the far end (map point A). The beach park has rest rooms and drinking water.

Bus: Route 55 to Kokololio Beach Park.

Route Description

Continue along Kamehameha Hwy on foot.

Pass mile marker 20 and cross a small culvert marked by yellow poles.

Almost immediately turn left on a dirt road across from house number 55-147 (map point B).

Another dirt road comes in on the right through a gate. Continue straight, along a short row of ironwood trees.

As the road curves left to a house, bear right on a less-traveled dirt road with a chain across it.

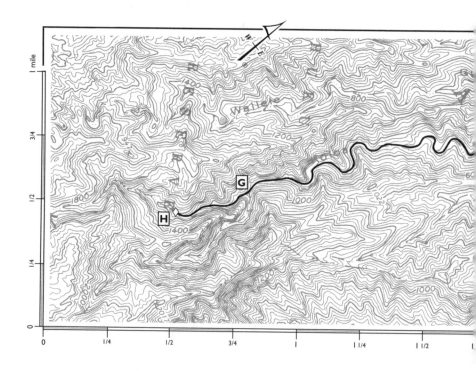

On the right pass a stone monument with a flagpole. It honors Jonathan Taylor, a Boy Scout killed by a flash flood in 1994.

Go through a metal gate in a fence.

The road narrows to a trail, which is choked with grass.

Ascend gradually following a gully on the left.

Reach an obscure junction by some ironwood trees (map point C). Turn right, between two rows of ironwoods. (The trail to the left enters 'A'akaki'i Gulch.)

Keep left along the edge of a grassy field.

Near a collapsed shack turn sharp left upslope through a grove of ironwoods (map point D).

Climb steeply to the ridgeline and bear left up it.

Ascend steadily through scattered ironwoods. Enjoy the wind sighing through their branches. Along the ridge are native 'ūlei and 'ākia shrubs.

Pass an eroded spot. Look back for views of the Polynesian Cultural Center and Lā'ie Point.

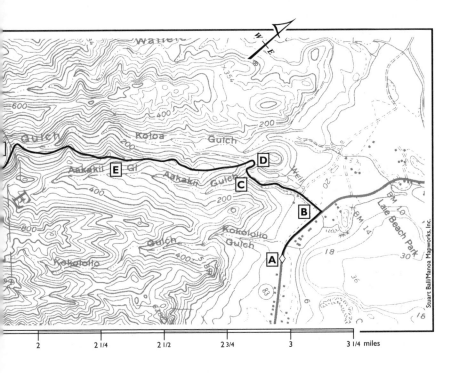

Descend briefly and then climb again across a narrow, eroded neck flanked by several scrawny ironwoods.

Bear to the left to go around a bare knob.

Just after a level, grassy section reach a junction (map point E). Bear right off the ridge through a tunnel of guava (waiawī). (The less-used trail to the left continues up the ridge.)

Descend into Koloa Gulch, gradually at first, and then more steeply. Look for native lama trees among the guava.

Reach Koloa Stream (map point F) and cross it. Bear left, heading upstream. The trail becomes rocky, rooty, and sometimes muddy.

Cross the stream twenty-two more times. Highlights are as follows: After 4: a stand of yellow ginger. After 5: some coffee trees. After 7: a grove of hala trees. After 8: an old house site under huge mango trees, and a mountain apple grove. At 9: the remains of a concrete dam. At 15: twin streambeds with a tiny island in between. After 17 and 18: kukui trees and more mountain apples. After 22: bird's-nest ferns.

After the twenty-third crossing, work around to the right of some fallen trunks and huge boulders in the stream. Nestled among them is a small pool with a miniature waterfall.

The trail becomes rough and obscure. Walk in the streambed as necessary.

The stream briefly splits and then rejoins. Keep to the right. Pass a small pool and a huge boulder on the right.

Edge around a massive rock dike jutting into the stream on the right.

Just past another dike forming a cliff on the left, reach a major fork in the stream (map point G). Again, keep to the right.

As the gulch narrows significantly, pass two waterfall chutes and a landslide.

Reach a circular, limpid pool backed by vertical cliffs and a small waterfall, which blocks further progress (elevation 1,120 feet) (map point H). Above and to the right is a larger waterfall.

Notes

Koloa Gulch penetrates deep into the heart of the windward Koʻolau Range. The hike starts up an open ridge and ends in a deep, narrow ravine. In the process you ford Koloa (native duck) Stream over twenty-three times. The reward for all that rock hopping is a lovely pool and waterfall nestled near the back of the gulch.

July and early August are the best months to take this hike. The mountain apples are in season then. Also, the midday sun is high enough to reach the pool at the end of the hike. Without the sun, the back of the gulch is a damp and chilly spot.

Before you start the hike, a few cautions are in order. Watch your footing on the slippery rocks in the streambed. Don't hesitate to get your boots wet if the rock hopping becomes dicey. Around the twenty-third crossing switch to tabis (Japanese reef walkers) if possible. Their fuzzy bottom provides secure footing for the final stretch in the stream. You can, of course, wear tabis for the whole hike if the bottom of your feet can take the pounding.

The trail along the stream is usually rocky and rooty, sometimes muddy, and occasionally obscure. Each bank at a stream crossing may be marked with surveyor's ribbon of various colors, but don't count on it. If you lose the trail, keep walking upstream until you find the route again. The lower portion of the gulch is the home of some very persistent mosquitoes.

The stone monument at the start of the hike is a stark reminder of the major hazard in the gulch—flash flooding. During a very heavy rainstorm, Koloa Stream can rise suddenly with little warning. If that happens, head for the nearest high ground and wait there for the stream to go down. It is far better to be stranded for half a day than to get swept away.

On the ridge portion of the hike look for the native dryland shrub 'ākia. It has dark branches jointed with white rings. Its leaves are bright green, oval, and pointed. Early Hawaiians pounded the leaves and bark and then dropped the mixture into tidal pools to poison fish. The red orange fruits were used in *lei* (garlands) and as a poison for criminals.

After the seventh stream crossing is a grove of hala trees. They have distinctive prop roots that help support the heavy clusters of leaves and fruit on the ends of the branches. Early Hawaiians braided the long, pointed leaves, called *lau hala*, into baskets, fans, floor mats, and sails.

After the eighth ford is an old house site with *loʻi* (terraces) for growing *kalo* (taro) nearby. Beyond the site is a dense stand of mountain apple (ʻōhiʻa ʻai) trees with dark, oblong, shiny leaves. In spring their purple flowers carpet the trail. The delicious pink or red fruit usually ripens in late July or early August. If none is in reach, shake the tree and try to catch the apples as they come down. The species is native to Malaysia and was brought over by early Hawaiians.

After the twenty-third crossing, the stream trail winds around steep, narrow side ridges jutting into the gulch. Look at the exposed rock where the ridge meets the stream. The rock is part of a dike complex in the northwest rift zone of the old Koʻolau (windward) volcano. Rift zones are areas of structural weakness extending from the summit of a shield volcano. Rising molten rock or magma worked its way into cracks in the rift zone and solidified. The resulting dikes are sheetlike, vertical intrusions of hard, dense rock. Over the years the stream has eroded the softer surrounding material, leaving the parallel dikes exposed.

The hike ends at a small, but inviting pool backed by a waterfall. Take a cool, refreshing dip; you've earned it after all that rock hopping. From the pool look around the corner to see a larger waterfall, one level up.

For a slightly longer outing, go left where the stream splits near the end of the hike. Like the right fork, the left fork also leads to a pool and a waterfall.

40 Lā'ie

Type:	Graded ridge
Length:	12-mile round trip
Elevation Gain:	2,200 feet
Danger:	Low
Suitable for:	Intermediate, Expert
Location:	Kahuku Forest Reserve above Lā'ie
Topo Map:	Kahuku, Hau'ula
Access:	Conditional; open to individuals and outdoor organizations with permission. Contact Hawaii Reserves, Inc., 55-510 Kamehameha Hwy, Lā'ie, HI 96762 (phone 293-9201).

Highlights
This hike follows a hot dirt road and then a rugged ridge trail to the Ko'olau summit. On the way up is a cool swimming hole with waterfalls above and below. At the top are superb views of both sides of the island.

Trailhead Directions
At Punchbowl St. get on Lunalilo Fwy (H-1) heading 'ewa (west).

Take Likelike Hwy (exit 20A, Rte 63 north) up Kalihi Valley through the Wilson Tunnel.

The highway forks. Keep right for Kahekili Hwy (Rte 83 west).

Kahekili Hwy becomes Kamehameha Hwy (still Rte 83), which continues up the windward coast.

Drive through the villages of Ka'a'awa, Punalu'u, and Hau'ula to Lā'ie.

Pass the Polynesian Cultural Center and Lā'ie Shopping Center on the left.

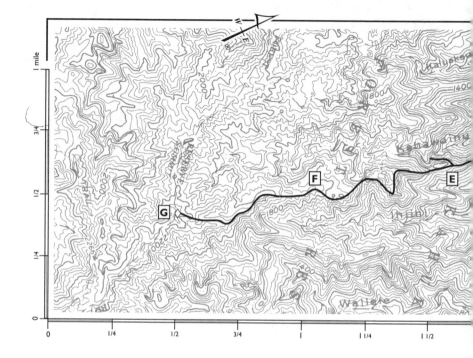

Turn left on Naniloa Lp. It is the fourth left after the entrance road to the Mormon Temple. The loop has a grass median strip.

Enter a small traffic circle and exit at the second right on Poʻohaili St.

Park on the grass to the left by Lāʻie Field (map point A).

Bus: Route 55 to Kamehameha Hwy and Naniloa Lp. Walk 0.2 mile along Naniloa Lp. and Poʻohaili St. to Lāʻie Field.

Route Description

Continue along Poʻohaili St. on foot.

After passing the last house, go through a yellow gate.

As the paved road curves left through another gate, reach a junction. Bear right on a dirt road paralleling a utility line (map point B).

Pass several taro fields on the left and a green pump shack on the right.

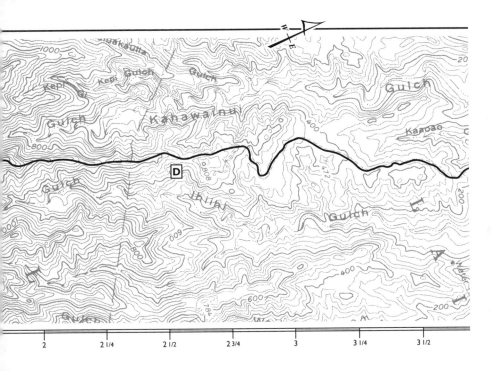

A side road comes in on the left. Continue straight on the main road across a small concrete bridge.

Reach a signed junction (map point C). Turn left and up on a side road through a yellow gate. (The main road swings right.)

At the next fork bear left, again uphill. (The right fork leads to an open dirt area.)

Climb steadily along the broad ridge for a long stretch. Ironwoods and other introduced trees provide some shade. Ignore several less-traveled roads coming in on the left.

Pass a wooden gate post attached to a barbed wire fence.

The road curves right to follow the fence line and then curves left away from it.

Shortly afterward reach another junction. Take the right, more eroded fork.

At an open, flat area keep right uphill on a very eroded section of the road.

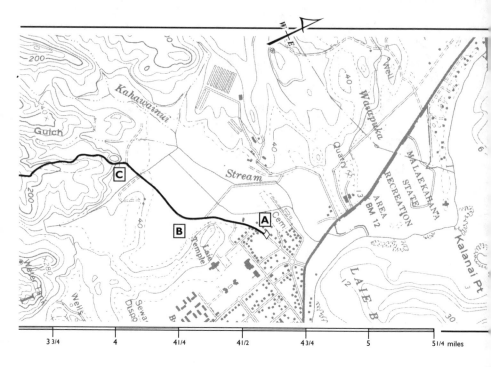

The road narrows to a trail and is flanked by uluhe ferns and strawberry guava trees.

Reach a grove of Cook pines and the start of the Lā'ie Trail (map point D). Look *makai* (seaward) for a good view of Lā'ie town and Point.

Walk through the pine grove and then descend briefly.

Climb gradually along the left side of the ridge through a long corridor of strawberry guavas.

After the guavas finally switch to uluhe ferns, reach a junction (map point E). Keep left toward the summit on the Lā'ie Trail. (To the right and up a low embankment is a short side trail that descends steeply to a small pool and two waterfalls along Kahawainui Stream.)

Ascend gradually in and out of small side gulches. The trail becomes rough and narrow in spots. The guavas gradually give way to native vegetation. Look for native 'ōhi'a, lama, and kōpiko trees and naupaka kuahiwi shrubs.

Pass an open stretch with a steep cliff on the right and a sharp drop-off on the left.

Bear left and down into a gully to cross a large landslide blocking the original trail.

Climb out of the gully and continue the gradual ascent along the left side of the ridge. Downslope on the left are native loulu palms and lapalapa trees with their fluttering leaves.

Reach the ridgeline and cross over to the right side of the ridge (map point F). A small clearing there makes a good rest stop before the final push to the summit.

Work up the side of Kahawainui Gulch toward its end at the summit ridge. Along the very muddy trail are native ʻōlapa trees and more loulu palms.

Just before the top the trail splits. Take the left fork.

Almost immediately reach the junction with the Koʻolau Summit Trail, marked by a Lāʻie sign. Cross the Summit Trail and climb the low mound on the right to get to a viewpoint of both sides of the island (elevation 2,240 feet) (map point G). Behind the viewpoint are native alani and pūʻahuani (kanawao) shrubs.

Notes

Lāʻie (ʻieʻie leaf) is three hikes in one. First comes a hot climb on a dry dirt road. Next follows a pleasant stroll in a cool corridor of Cook pines and strawberry guava trees. Finally there is the rough wet slog through native forest to reach the Koʻolau (windward) summit.

Start early to avoid the hot sun on the approach road. The road and the trail to the pool junction are usually in good condition. Although still graded, the trail above the pool has some rough sections because of erosion and landslides. The treadway may also be overgrown with bristly uluhe ferns and *Clidemia* shrubs. Watch your footing constantly; expect to slip a few times and get muddy and wet. The trail was originally built by the Civilian Conservation Corps in 1935.

At the start of the Lāʻie Trail is a cool, shady grove of Cook pines planted by Territorial Forestry in 1929. Take a water break there and admire the grand view of the windward coast. Behind

Lā'ie town a small peninsula, called Laniloa (tall majesty), juts into the ocean. According to legend, the peninsula was a *mo'o* or serpent in ancient times. The *mo'o* often reared up and killed Hawaiian people passing by. One day the demigod Kana and his brother Nīheu set out to destroy the serpent. After a long-drawn-out battle, the two succeeded in slaying the monster. Kana cut the head of the *mo'o* into five pieces and threw them in the ocean. The pieces became five small islands, which you can still see today. Kīhewamoku islet is offshore of Kahuku town. *Makai* of Mālaekahana are Moku'auia (island to one side), better known as Goat Island, and Pulemoku (broken prayer). Close to Laniloa are Kukuiho'olua (oven-baked candlenut), and Mokuālai (island standing in the way). All five islands are now state seabird sanctuaries.

Beyond the pines, strawberry guava trees (waiawī 'ula'ula) line the trail. They have glossy, dark green leaves and smooth brown bark. Their dark red fruit is delicious, with a taste reminiscent of strawberries. The guavas usually ripen in August and September. The strawberry guava is a native of Brazil but was introduced to Hawai'i from England in the 1800s.

The swimming hole along Kahawainui Stream is small, but refreshing after the hot climb. Intermediate hikers can make the pool their goal. Summit hikers can stop there on the way back. The makeshift trail down to the pool is steep, narrow, and slippery; take it slowly.

After crossing the landslide gully, look for native loulu palms and lapalapa trees. The palms have rigid, fan-shaped fronds in a cluster at the top of a ringed trunk. Early Hawaiians used the fronds for thatch and plaited the blades of young fronds into fans and baskets. Lapalapa has roundish leaves that are arranged in groups of three and flutter in the slightest wind. Early Hawaiians used the bark, leaves, and purple fruit to make a blue black dye to decorate their *kapa* (bark cloth). The leaves also make a distinctive *lei* (garland).

From the viewpoint at the Ko'olau summit you can see Kahuku (the projection) and Lā'ie towns to windward. To leeward are the Wahiawā (place of noise) plain and the Wai'anae (mullet water) Range. Along its crest, from left to right, are Pu'u

Kaua (war hill), Kolekole (raw) Pass, flat-topped Kaʻala (the fragrance), and Kaʻena (the heat) Point. All around is the convoluted topography of the northern Koʻolau Range.

On the leeward side of the viewpoint, look for the native shrub pūʻahanui (kanawao), a relative of hydrangea. It has large, serrated, deeply creased leaves and clusters of delicate pink flowers. Early Hawaiians used the plants for medicinal purposes.

Below the viewpoint is the junction with the Koʻolau Summit Trail, an 18.5-mile footpath along the top of the Koʻolau Range. Turn right to reach Pūpūkea Road. See the Pūpūkea Summit hike for a partial description of that segment. Turn left to get to the Poamoho Ridge and Schofield-Waikāne Trails. The Summit Trail is for experienced hikers only because it is overgrown, obscure, and frequently socked in.

NORTH SHORE

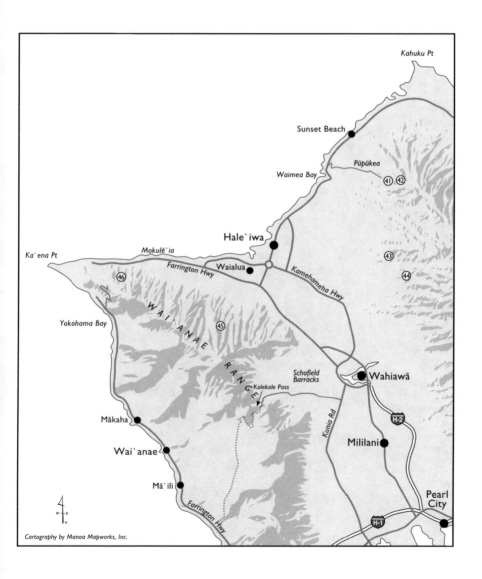

41 Kaunala

Type:	Foothill
Length:	6-mile loop
Elevation Gain:	500 feet
Danger:	Low
Suitable for:	Novice, Intermediate
Location:	Pūpūkea Paumalū Forest Reserve above Pūpūkea
Topo Map:	Waimea, Kahuku
Access:	Conditional; open on weekends and Federal and State holidays only.

Highlights

This meandering loop hike winds through the lush gulches of the Ko'olau foothills above Pūpūkea. On the return leg are some beautiful views of the north shore.

Trailhead Directions

At Punchbowl St. get on Lunalilo Fwy (H-1) heading 'ewa (west).

Near Middle St. keep left on Rte 78 west (exit 19B, Moanalua Rd.) to 'Aiea.

By Aloha Stadium bear right to rejoin H-1 to Pearl City.

Take H-2 freeway (exit 8A) to Wahiawā.

As the freeway ends, continue on Rte 99 north (Wilikina Dr.) bypassing Wahiawā.

Pass Schofield Barracks on the left.

The road narrows to two lanes, dips, and then forks. Take the right fork to Hale'iwa (Kamananui Rd., but still Rte 99 north).

At the road end turn left on Kamehameha Hwy (Rte 99).

Pass Dole Plantation on the right.

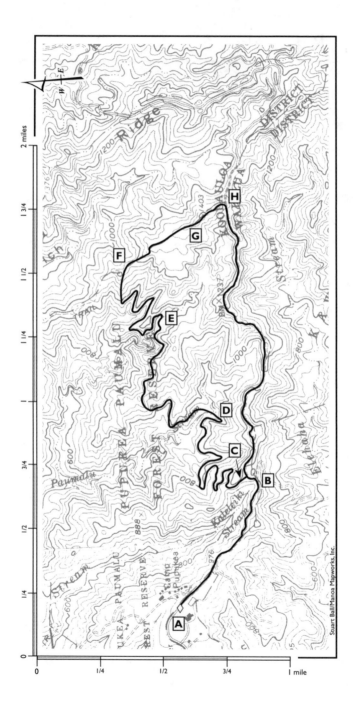

Before entering Haleʻiwa, reach an intersection. Keep right on Joseph P. Leong Hwy, better known as Haleʻiwa Bypass (Rte 83). (To the left Kamehameha Hwy continues into Haleʻiwa town.)

The bypass becomes Kamehameha Hwy (still Rte 83).

Go around Waimea Bay, passing Waimea Falls Park on the right.

At the first major intersection after the bay turn right on Pūpūkea Rd. by Foodland Supermarket.

Switchback once up a small *pali* (cliff).

Drive to the end of the paved road at Camp Pūpūkea (elevation 960 feet) (map point A). Park off the road near the entrance to the Boy Scout camp. Leave plenty of room for vehicles exiting the camp and the farm across the street.

Bus: None, within reasonable walking distance of the trailhead.

Route Description

Proceed along the dirt road past the Boy Scout camp.

Go around a locked gate and enter Kahuku Range, an Army training area.

On the right pass an abandoned cattle loading ramp in a stand of ironwoods.

Reach a junction (map point B). Keep left on the main road. (The dirt road to the right through the locked McCormack Gate is Paʻalaʻa Uka Pūpūkea Rd.)

Shortly afterward reach a signed junction at the edge of a grove of paperbark trees (map point C). Turn left on the wide Kaunala Trail. (The dirt road curves to the right and is the return portion of the loop.)

The path splits almost immediately. Take the left fork. (The right fork goes up a hill.)

Contour around the hill, which is covered with paperbark trees.

Descend gradually on four switchbacks through a eucalyptus forest. Ignore trails going straight down the side ridges.

Cross over a side ridge and begin to contour into and out of several gulches.

The first one is long and narrow.

Descend into the second gulch on two short switchbacks (map point D). At the bottom are kukui trees, kī (ti) plants, and tiny Paumalū Stream.

Cross over a side ridge in a paperbark grove.

Work into and out of a large gulch with a stream (map point E).

After crossing a small stream in the next gulch, climb gradually to an open area covered with uluhe fern. In front are the rolling ridges of Paumalū. In back are several native ʻiliahi (sandalwood) trees. Listen for the distinctive call of the Japanese bush warbler.

Ascend the right side of a side ridge through koa and strawberry guava trees.

Contour briefly and then switchback once.

Reach a signed junction with a dirt road in a grove of paperbark trees (map point F). Turn right on the road. (To the left it leads down to Camp Paumalū, a Girl Scout camp.) Kaunala Trail extended continues across the road.

Climb steadily on top of a wide ridge past native ʻōhiʻa and koa trees. Keep to the main road.

Reach a flat, cleared area (elevation 1,403 feet) (map point G). From there is a good view of the Waiʻanae Range and the north shore.

Descend steeply, but briefly and then go around a locked gate.

Almost immediately reach a junction with the original dirt road near a stand of Cook pines (map point H). Turn right on it. (To the left the road is the route of the Pūpūkea Summit hike.)

Descend gradually along an up-and-down ridge.

Reach the familiar junction with the Kaunala Trail at the far edge of the paperbark grove (map point C).

Retrace your steps to the Boy Scout camp (map point A).

Notes

Kaunala (the plaiting) is a pleasant valley-ridge combination above Pūpūkea (white shell) along the north shore. The trail section contours in and out of lush gulches through mostly introduced forest. The return portion follows a ridge-top road through the Kahuku training area of the U.S. Army.

The hike route is generally wide and well graded, with gradual elevation changes. The Kaunala Trail may be muddy and mosquitoey in the gulches. Watch out for mountain bikers on the dirt roads.

Lining the gulches of the Kaunala Trail are kī (ti) plants. They have shiny leaves, 1–2 feet long, that are arranged spirally in a cluster at the tip of a slender stem. Early Polynesian voyagers introduced ti to Hawai'i. They used the leaves for house thatch, skirts, sandals, and raincoats. Food to be cooked in an *imu* (underground oven) was first wrapped in ti leaves. A popular sport with the commoners was *ho'ohe'e kī* or ti-leaf sledding. The sap from ti plants was used to stain canoes and surfboards.

After crossing the stream in the large gulch, listen for the Japanese bush warbler (uguisu), a bird often heard, but rarely seen. Its distinctive cry starts with a long whistle and then winds down in a series of notes. The bush warbler is olive brown on top with a white breast and a long tail.

Behind the clearing on the last side ridge are a few native 'iliahi (sandalwood) trees. Their small leaves are dull green and appear wilted. 'Iliahi is partially parasitic, with outgrowths on its roots that steal nutrients from nearby plants. Early Hawaiians ground the fragrant heartwood into a powder to perfume their *kapa* (bark cloth). Beginning in the late 1700s, sandalwood was indiscriminately cut down and exported to China to make incense and furniture. The trade ended around 1840 when the forests were depleted of 'iliahi.

On the return look for native koa and 'ōhi'a trees along the dirt road. Koa has sickle-shaped foliage and pale yellow flower clusters. Early Hawaiians made surfboards and outrigger canoe hulls out of the beautiful red brown wood. Today it is made into fine furniture. 'Ōhi'a has oval leaves and clusters of delicate red flowers. Early Hawaiians used the flowers in *lei* (garlands) and the wood in outrigger canoes. The hard, durable wood was also carved into god images for *heiau* (religious sites).

From the cleared area along the road are fine views of the north shore, Ka'ena (the heat) Point, and the Wai'anae (mullet water) Range. Its main peaks are Pu'u Kaua (war hill), Hāpapa (rock stratum), Kalena (the lazy one), and flat-topped Ka'ala (the fragrance) from left to right. Kolekole (raw) Pass separates Hāpapa and Kalena.

For a longer hike, take the rough Kaunala extension, which starts across the road at the end of the official Kaunala Trail. After contouring through more gulches, the extension eventually reaches the main dirt road. Turn right on the road to return to the Boy Scout camp. The first left on the way back is the start of the Koʻolau (windward) Summit Trail, which is described in the Pūpūkea Summit hike. Access to Kaunala extended or the Summit Trail requires written permission from the U.S. Army. See the Pūpūkea Summit hike for the address.

42 Pūpūkea Summit

Type:	Graded ridge
Length:	9-mile round trip
Elevation Gain:	900 feet
Danger:	Low
Suitable for:	Novice, Intermediate
Location:	Pūpūkea Paumalū and Kahuku Forest Reserves above Pūpūkea
Topo Map:	Waimea, Kahuku
Access:	Conditional; open to individuals and outdoor organizations with permission. Write Commander, U.S. Army Garrison, Hawai'i, Schofield Barracks, HI 96857 (attn: APVG-GWY-O).

Highlights
This hike follows a short, tame section of the wild and woolly Ko'olau Summit Trail. Along the way are intriguing native plants and convoluted topography. Our destination is a remote, secluded lookout over the windward coast.

Trailhead Directions
At Punchbowl St. get on Lunalilo Fwy (H-1) heading 'ewa (west).

Near Middle St. keep left on Rte 78 west (exit 19B, Moanalua Rd.) to 'Aiea.

By Aloha Stadium bear right to rejoin H-1 to Pearl City.

Take H-2 freeway (exit 8A) to Wahiawā.

As the freeway ends, continue on Rte 99 north (Wilikina Dr.) bypassing Wahiawā.

Pass Schofield Barracks on the left.

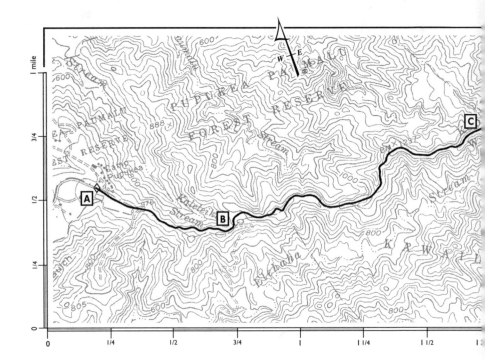

The road narrows to two lanes, dips, and then forks. Take the right fork to Haleʻiwa (Kamananui Rd., but still Rte 99 north).

At the road end turn left on Kamehameha Hwy (Rte 99).

Pass Dole Plantation on the right.

Before entering Haleʻiwa, reach an intersection. Keep right on Joseph P. Leong Hwy, better known as Haleʻiwa Bypass (Rte 83). (To the left Kamehameha Hwy continues into Haleʻiwa town.)

The bypass becomes Kamehameha Hwy (still Rte 83).

Go around Waimea Bay, passing Waimea Falls Park on the right.

At the first major intersection after the bay turn right on Pūpūkea Rd. by Foodland Supermarket.

Switchback once up a small *pali* (cliff).

Drive to the end of the paved road at Camp Pūpūkea (elevation 960 feet) (map point A). Park off the road near the entrance

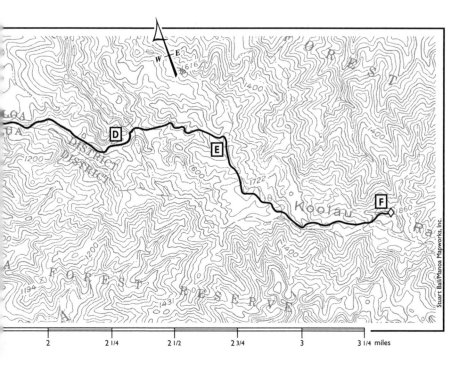

Stuart Ball/Manoa Mapworks, Inc.

to the Boy Scout camp. Leave plenty of room for vehicles exiting the camp and the farm across the street.

Bus: None, within reasonable walking distance of the trailhead.

Route Description

Proceed along the dirt road past the Boy Scout camp.

Go around a locked gate and enter Kahuku Range, an Army training area.

On the right pass an abandoned cattle loading ramp in a stand of ironwoods.

Reach a junction. Keep left on the main road. (The dirt road to the right through the locked McCormack Gate is Pa'ala'a Uka Pūpūkea Rd.)

Shortly afterward reach a signed junction at the edge of a grove of paperbark trees (map point B). Continue straight on the dirt road. (To the left the Kaunala Trail contours below the ridge.)

Climb along the up-and-down ridge through mostly introduced forest. Look for an occasional kukui or native koa tree downslope.

Reach another junction by some Cook pines (map point C). Continue straight on the main road. (The road to the left is the return portion of the Kaunala loop.)

Just after that junction walk through a locked gate and descend briefly.

Resume the gradual climb along the ridge, now lined with white-barked albizia and ironwood trees.

The road descends gradually and then curves left.

As the road begins to climb again, reach a junction with another dirt road in a grove of albizia trees (map point D). Turn right on the side road, which is the Koʻolau Summit Trail.

The dirt road soon deteriorates and then narrows to a trail by the last albizia tree.

Climb gradually along the right side of the ridge below its top. On the hillside to the right are some native loulu palms.

Cross the ridgeline and contour along the left (windward) side of the ridge. Along the trail are native ʻōhiʻa trees and naupaka kuahiwi shrubs.

Reach signed Black Junction (map point E). For now, turn left on the side trail leading to a windward lookout. (The Summit Trail continues to the right.)

Backtrack to Black Junction and turn left on the Summit Trail.

Keep left in a paperbark grove.

Switch to the right (leeward) side of the ridge. In the distance are the Waiʻanae Range and Kaʻena Point.

Walk through an open section with views to windward and leeward.

Switch to the left side of the ridge through strawberry guava trees.

On the left pass an intermittent stream in a dense stand of rose apple.

Swing right and then left through a flat, grassy, wet area.

Ascend steadily on the right side of the ridge around a large hill.

Reach a junction on the leeward side of the hill. Turn left and up on a rough side trail. (To the right the Koʻolau Summit Trail contours around the hill.)

Climb steeply up the side of the hill through native vegetation. Look for hāpuʻu tree ferns and kōpiko trees.

Reach the top of the hill at a small lookout with a benchmark (elevation 1,860 feet) (map point F).

Notes

The Pūpūkea (white shell) Summit hike follows a relatively benign stretch of the Koʻolau Summit Trail, the most rugged and least-used footpath on Oʻahu. In the early 1920s the U.S. Army built the initial section to Black Junction and called it the Pūpūkea-Kahuku Trail. Between 1934 and 1936 the Civilian Conservation Corps (CCC) rebuilt the Army section and extended the trail along the crest of the Koʻolau (windward) Range. When the CCC was finished, the new Summit Trail stretched 18.5 miles from Black Junction to the end of the Kīpapa (placed prone) Trail above Mililani (beloved place of chiefs).

Unfortunately, the trail has received little maintenance since its initial construction. Although still graded, the treadway is often uneven because of slippage and erosion through the years. Sections of the trail may be overgrown with strawberry guava (waiawī ulaʻula) and scratchy uluhe ferns. Watch your footing constantly. Try not to fall into one of the legendary mud holes!

After the long walk on the approach road, the Summit Trail is actually a welcome sight. The graded route gradually winds upward through the convoluted topography of the northern Koʻolau Range. The scrub forest along the way consists mostly of native ʻōhiʻa trees. They have oval leaves and clusters of delicate red flowers. Early Hawaiians used the flowers in lei (garlands) and the wood in outrigger canoes. The hard, durable wood was also carved into god images for heiau (religious sites).

Among the ʻōhiʻa are a few native loulu palms. They have

rigid, fan-shaped fronds in a cluster at the top of a ringed trunk. Early Hawaiians used the fronds for thatch and plaited the blades of young fronds into fans and baskets.

Also along the initial trail section is the native shrub naupaka kuahiwi. It has toothed and pointed leaves and white half-flowers. The unusual appearance of the flowers has given rise to several unhappy legends. According to one, a Hawaiian maiden believed her lover unfaithful. In anger she tore all the naupaka flowers in half. She then asked him to find a whole flower to prove his love. He was, of course, unsuccessful and died of a broken heart.

At Black Junction take the short side trip down to the lovely windward lookout. The grassy, windswept area has some old landing mats and foxholes once used by the Army in training. From the lookout you can see Kahuku (the projection) and Lāʻie (the ʻieʻie leaf), backed by Lāʻie Point. Offshore, between the two towns, is Mokuʻauia (island to one side), better known as Goat Island, a state seabird sanctuary.

From the lookout retrace your steps to the main trail and continue the gradual ascent toward a prominent hill on the summit ridge. At the base of the hill leave the Summit Trail once again and climb steadily to a second lookout. On the way up keep your eyes out for kōpiko, a native member of the coffee family. It has leathery, oblong leaves with a light green midrib. Turn the leaf over to see a row of tiny holes (*piko* [navel]) on either side of the midrib. The kōpiko produces clusters of little white flowers and fleshy, orange fruits.

The second lookout has a benchmark and more windward views. From there the side trail proceeds along the top of the hill, passes the obscure junction with the abandoned Kahuku Trail and then descends to rejoin the main route. It continues along the Koʻolau crest to the junction with the Lāʻie Trail. That segment may be overgrown with strawberry guavas and uluhe ferns.

For a shorter outing, try the Kaunala (the plaiting) loop that starts from the same trailhead. Unlike Pūpūkea Summit, Kaunala does not require a permit from the Army.

43 Kawainui

Type:	Valley
Length:	6-mile round trip
Elevation Gain:	800 feet
Danger:	Low
Suitable for:	Novice, Intermediate
Location:	Kawailoa Forest Reserve above Hale'iwa
Topo Map:	Hau'ula
Access:	Conditional; open only to outdoor organizations with permission. Contact Bishop Estate, 567 S. King St., Honolulu, HI 96813 and Commander, U.S. Army Garrison, Hawai'i, Schofield Barracks, HI 96857 (attn: APVG-GWY-O).

Highlights

This lovely hike follows an irrigation ditch up a rushing mountain stream. Along the way are placid pools and delicious mountain apple and strawberry guava. Our goal is an idyllic swimming hole, perhaps the best on the island.

Trailhead Directions

At Punchbowl St. get on Lunalilo Fwy (H-1) heading 'ewa (west).

Near Middle St. keep left on Rte 78 west (exit 19B, Moanalua Rd.) to 'Aiea.

By Aloha Stadium bear right to rejoin H-1 to Pearl City.

Take H-2 freeway (exit 8A) to Wahiawā.

As the freeway ends, continue on Rte 99 north (Wilikina Dr.) bypassing Wahiawā.

Pass Schofield Barracks on the left.

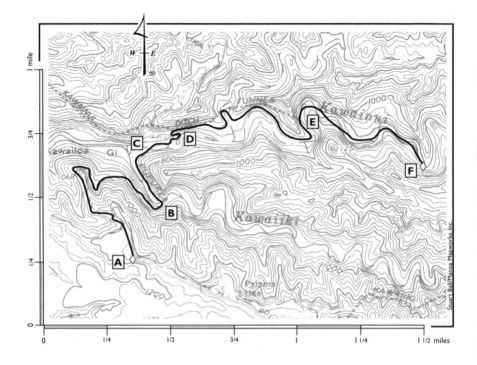

The road narrows to two lanes, dips, and then forks. Take the right fork to the north shore (Kamananui Rd., but still Rte 99 north).

At the road end turn left on Kamehameha Hwy (Rte 99).

Pass Dole Plantation on the right.

Before entering Hale'iwa, reach an intersection. Keep right on Joseph P. Leong Hwy, better known as Hale'iwa Bypass (Rte 83). (To the left Kamehameha Hwy continues into Hale'iwa town.)

Take the first right after the intersection on Emerson Rd.

Turn right at the stop sign.

As the pavement ends, go through a locked gate.

Almost immediately turn sharp right on a paved road and go through another locked gate.

Take the first left on paved 'Ōpae'ula Rd. and reset your trip odometer (0.0 mile).

Ascend gradually through cropland.

The road forks (1.5 miles). Keep right on the paved main road paralleling 'Ōpae'ula Gulch.

The road narrows, and the pavement deteriorates. Ignore side roads to the left.

As the pavement ends, go through a third locked gate (2.5 miles).

The road forks again (4.4 miles). Keep left on the main road.

'Ōpae'ula Rd. ends at a reservoir (5.2 miles). Continue straight on a military road, called Pa'ala'a Uka Pūpūkea.

Pass 'Ōpae'ula Lodge on the right in a grove of eucalyptus trees (5.3 miles).

At the top of the fields descend briefly into a small gulch and turn sharp left (6.7 miles). A rough side road leads to the trail-heads of the 'Ōpae'ula and Kawai Iki hikes.

Climb out of the gulch and pass Pālama Uka Camp on the right (6.9 miles).

As the road swings right and begins to descend, turn left into a grassy lot and park there (7.3 miles) (elevation 1,240 feet) (map point A).

Bus: None, within reasonable walking distance of the trailhead.

Route Description
Continue down the military road on foot.

Descend the side of the ridge into Kawai Iki Gulch. Along the way are koa and albizia trees.

The road curves left and crosses Kawai Iki Stream on a concrete culvert (map point B).

Parallel the stream on the left.

Leaving the stream behind, the road bears right into Kawainui Gulch.

Cross Kawainui Stream on a concrete culvert (map point C). Just downstream is an old bridge.

As the road turns sharp left to leave the gulch, bear right on a trail (map point D).

Climb an embankment and then turn right heading upstream through Christmas berry trees.

Climb again, this time on two switchbacks. Between the two on the right is a short access tunnel to the Kawainui Ditch.

Contour along the side of the gulch well above the stream through Christmas berry and strawberry guava trees.

Cross a small side stream. In the side gulch are kukui trees and kī (ti) plants.

Walk through a grove of mountain apple trees overlaid by kukui; underfoot are kukui nuts.

Descend to Kawainui Stream past native ʻōhiʻa trees (map point E). The improved trail ends here at a stone dam. The ditch intake is just upstream in the cliff on the left.

Cross the stream on the dam and bear left on an ungraded trail.

Cross the stream ten more times. Highlights are as follows: Between 1 and 2: another mountain apple grove. Between 3 and 4: a short, steep descent and a hau grove. Just after 4: a large pool on the left. Between 5 and 6: a long hau grove. After 7: walk in a dry channel. Just after 9: a small, kidney-shaped pool.

Reach a lovely, round pool ringed with kukui trees (elevation 800 feet) (map point F).

Notes

Kawainui means the big water. The stream is well named, with its rushing rapids and deep pools. The trail up the gulch passes by swimming holes that on any other hike would be the main attraction. Unless you are a water baby, however, save yourself for the last pool, which may be the best on the island.

The drive to the trailhead is long and a bit rough. The last few miles are over a dirt military road, called Paʻalaʻa Uka Pūpūkea. Although rutted in spots, the road is passable for two-wheel-drive vehicles under dry conditions. Paʻalaʻa Uka Pūpūkea Rd., formerly known as Drum Dr., winds through the leeward Koʻolau (windward) foothills, starting at Helemano Military Reservation and finishing by the end of Pūpūkea Rd. Built by the U.S. Army in 1937, the road was originally named after General Hugh A. Drum, a former commander of the Hawaiian Department.

Before you start the hike, a few cautions are in order. Walk gingerly over the narrow spots on the way to the dam. The trail past the dam is usually muddy and sometimes overgrown and obscure. Each bank at a stream crossing may be marked with surveyor's ribbon of various colors, but don't count on it. If you lose the trail, keep walking upstream until you find the route again. Watch your footing while crossing the stream. If possible, change to tabis (Japanese reef walkers) for better traction on the slippery rocks. As always, do not ford the stream if the water is much above your knees. Finally, look out for an occasional mosquito in the gulch.

On the trail, take the short access tunnel to see the underground ditch. It diverts water from Kawainui Stream and carries it to reservoirs in the Kawailoa area. The water once irrigated the cane fields of the Waialua Sugar Co. Now it waters mixed crops gradually taking over the former plantation fields. Later on in the hike you see the dam and the ditch intake.

Look for kukui trees by the side stream. Their large, pale green leaves resemble those of the maple, with several distinct lobes. Early Polynesian voyagers introduced kukui into Hawai'i. They used the wood to make gunwales and seats for their outrigger canoes. The flowers and sap became medicines to treat a variety of ailments. Early Hawaiians strung the nuts together to make *lei hua* (seed or nut garlands). The oily kernels became house candles and torches for night spearfishing.

After crossing the side stream, the trail passes through a grove of mountain apples ('ōhi'a 'ai). The trees have large, oblong, shiny leaves. In spring their purple flowers carpet the trail. The delicious pink or red fruit usually ripens in late July or early August. If none is in reach, shake the tree and try to catch the apples as they come down. The species is native to Malaysia and was brought over by early Hawaiians.

On the descent to the dam are native 'ōhi'a trees. They have oval leaves and clusters of delicate red flowers. Early Hawaiians used the flowers in *lei* (garlands) and the wood in outrigger canoes. The hard, durable wood was also carved into god images for *heiau* (religious sites).

Along the stream are tangled groves of hau trees with large, heart-shaped leaves. Their flowers are bright yellow with a dark red center and resemble those of a hibiscus. Early Hawaiians used the wood for kites and canoe outriggers, the bark for sandals, and the sap as a laxative.

The hike ends at a deep, circular pool surrounded by cliffs and kukui trees. Take a dip and then stretch out on the sunny, rocky ledges. If you feel ambitious, swim across the pool and climb out the other side. A short way upstream several large boulders wedged together have created two miniature waterfalls. Ease up below them for a cool shower and a soothing back rub.

Two other stream hikes, 'Ōpae'ula and Kawai Iki, share the same road access. Both of them follow irrigation ditches to inviting swimming holes.

44 'Ōpae'ula

Type:	Valley
Length:	2-mile round trip
Elevation Gain:	200 feet
Danger:	Low
Suitable for:	Novice
Location:	Kawailoa Forest Reserve above Hale'iwa
Topo Map:	Hau'ula
Access:	Conditional; open only to outdoor organizations with permission. Contact Bishop Estate, 567 S. King St., Honolulu, HI 96813 and Commander, U.S. Army Garrison, Hawai'i, Schofield Barracks, HI 96857 (attn: APVG-GWY-O).

Highlights
This short stroll follows an irrigation ditch along a meandering stream. En route and at the end are several refreshing swimming holes.

Trailhead Directions
At Punchbowl St. get on Lunalilo Fwy (H-1) heading 'ewa (west).

Near Middle St. keep left on Rte 78 west (exit 19B, Moanalua Rd.) to 'Aiea.

By Aloha Stadium bear right to rejoin H-1 to Pearl City.

Take H-2 freeway (exit 8A) to Wahiawā.

As the freeway ends, continue on Rte 99 north (Wilikina Dr.) bypassing Wahiawā.

Pass Schofield Barracks on the left.

The road narrows to two lanes, dips, and then forks. Take the right fork to the north shore (Kamananui Rd., but still Rte 99 north).

At the road end turn left on Kamehameha Hwy (Rte 99).

Pass Dole Plantation on the right.

Before entering Hale'iwa, reach an intersection. Keep right on Joseph P. Leong Hwy, better known as Hale'iwa Bypass (Rte 83). (To the left Kamehameha Hwy continues into Hale'iwa town.)

Take the first right after the intersection on Emerson Rd.

Turn right at the stop sign.

As the pavement ends, go through a locked gate.

Almost immediately turn sharp right on a paved road and go through another locked gate.

Take the first left on paved 'Ōpae'ula Rd. and reset your trip odometer (0.0 mile).

Ascend gradually through cropland.

The road forks (1.5 miles). Keep right on the paved main road paralleling 'Ōpae'ula Gulch.

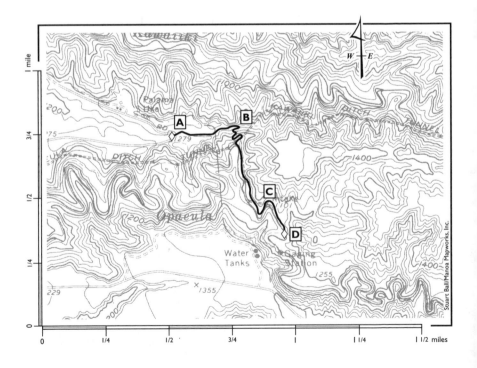

The road narrows, and the pavement deteriorates. Ignore side roads to the left.

As the pavement ends, go through a third locked gate (2.5 miles).

The road forks again (4.4 miles). Keep left on the main road.

'Ōpae'ula Rd. ends at a reservoir (5.2 miles). Continue straight on a military road, called Pa'ala'a Uka Pūpūkea.

Pass 'Ōpae'ula Lodge on the right in a grove of eucalyptus trees (5.3 miles).

At the top of the fields descend briefly into a small gulch.

As the road turns sharp left, reach a junction with a side road on the right (6.7 miles). Park on the right side of the main road just past the junction (elevation 1,279 feet) (map point A). Leave plenty of room for military vehicles to get by.

Bus: None, within reasonable walking distance of the trailhead.

Route Description
Take the rough side road at the turn.

At the road end continue straight on a trail along the ridge-line.

Descend briefly through a grove of eucalyptus trees.

As the eucalyptus end and the trail starts to climb, reach a junction (map point B). Turn right and down, into 'Ōpae'ula Gulch. (The trail straight ahead leads into Kawai Iki Gulch.)

Descend on a series of switchbacks through a stand of strawberry guava.

Reach the junction of the 'Ōpae'ula and Kawai Iki Ditches.

Cross the 'Ōpae'ula Ditch on a plank and turn left, heading upstream. If the plank across 'Ōpae'ula Ditch is gone, turn right and down, along the ditch, and walk underneath it through a short tunnel.

Contour above 'Ōpae'ula Stream, roughly paralleling the ditch. It tunnels through the side ridges, rather than going around them as the trail does. Look for native koa and 'ōhi'a trees across the stream.

Cross a ditch overflow channel on a short plank.

Break out into the open briefly. On the left an obscure trail climbs a side ridge to a grassy plateau and the start of the Kawai Iki Trail.

Pass a concrete dam and the ditch intake on the right (map point C).

Descend to the stream and cross it by some large, smooth rocks.

Cross the stream two more times and then pass a bamboo grove.

Reach a small clearing with a swimming hole (map point D). The trail continues briefly past an abandoned pumping station, through a bamboo grove, to a stream gauging station by another pool.

Notes

This short, pleasant walk winds along a stream and an irrigation ditch. Take your time, or the hike will be over before you know it. At the end is a small pool for a cooling dip on a hot summer day. The stream is named after the red 'ōpae, a native freshwater shrimp.

The drive to the trailhead is long and a bit rough. The last few miles are over a dirt military road, known as Pa'ala'a Uka Pūpūkea. Although rutted in spots, the road is passable for two-wheel-drive vehicles under dry conditions. Pa'ala'a Uka Pūpūkea Rd., formerly known as Drum Dr., winds through the leeward Ko'olau (windward) foothills, starting at Helemano Military Reservation and finishing by the end of Pūpūkea Rd. Built by the U.S. Army in 1937, the road was originally named after General Hugh A. Drum, a former commander of the Hawaiian Department.

'Ōpae'ula makes a good novice hike. The trail is well graded and easy to follow. Some sections, however, may be muddy or overgrown with introduced shrubs. As always, do not ford the stream if the water is much above your knees. Watch out for a few mosquitoes in the gulch.

Initially the trail descends into the gulch through a grove of strawberry guavas (waiawī 'ula'ula). They have glossy, dark green leaves and smooth brown bark. Their dark red fruit is delicious, with a taste reminiscent of strawberries. The guavas usually ripen in August and September. The strawberry guava is a native of

Brazil but was introduced to Hawai'i from England in the 1800s.

The route then crosses and roughly parallels the 'Ōpae'ula Ditch. It diverts water from 'Ōpae'ula Stream and carries it to the reservoir you passed on the drive up. The water once irrigated the cane fields of the Waialua Sugar Co. Now it waters mixed crops gradually taking over the former plantation fields. Later on in the hike you see the dam and the ditch intake.

In the gulch look upslope for native koa trees. They have sickle-shaped foliage and pale yellow flower clusters. Early Hawaiians made surfboards and outrigger canoe hulls out of the beautiful red brown wood. Today it is made into fine furniture.

For a longer, but similar hike, try Kawai Iki, which starts from the same trailhead. Take the ridge trail past the 'Ōpae'ula junction. After going around a small hump, reach another junction. Turn left and descend into Kawai Iki Gulch. Follow the irrigation ditch to several inviting swimming holes. The Kawai Iki Trail has received little use in recent years and so may be overgrown and hard to follow.

If you enjoyed 'Ōpae'ula, try the Kawainui hike. It shares the same road access and has better pools.

45 Dupont

Type:	Ungraded ridge
Length:	11-mile round trip
Elevation Gain:	4,100 feet
Danger:	High
Suitable for:	Intermediate, Expert
Location:	Mokulēʻia Forest Reserve and Kaʻala Natural Area Reserve above Waialua
Topo Map:	Haleʻiwa
Access:	Conditional; open only to outdoor organizations with permission. Contact

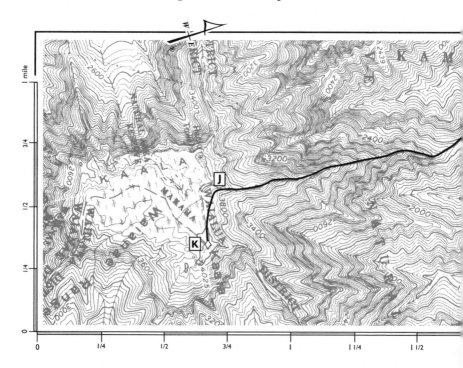

Dole Food Co. Hawai'i, 1116 Whitmore
Ave., Wahiawā, HI 96786; Waialua Ranch,
P.O. Box 922, Waialua, HI 96791 (phone
637-9441); and Kamananui Orchard,
P.O. Box 721, Waialua, HI 96791.

Highlights

This classic hike climbs to the summit plateau of Ka'ala from the
north-shore side. Along the rugged, sometimes narrow route is
an incredible variety of native dryland and rain forest plants. At
the top are commanding views and a misty bog.

Trailhead Directions

At Punchbowl St. get on Lunalilo Fwy (H-1) heading *'ewa* (west).

Near Middle St. keep left on Rte 78 west (exit 19B, Moanalua
Rd.) to 'Aiea.

By Aloha Stadium bear right to rejoin H-1 to Pearl City.

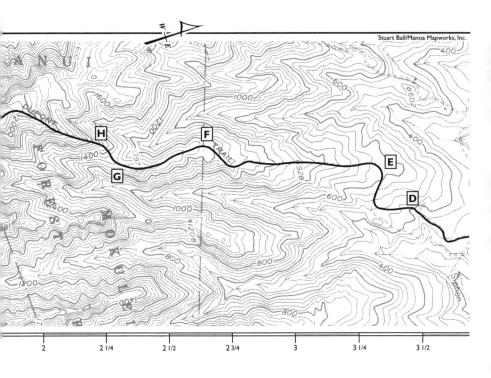

Take H-2 freeway (exit 8A) to Wahiawā.

As the freeway ends, continue on Rte 99 north (Wilikina Dr.) bypassing Wahiawā.

Pass Schofield Barracks on the left.

The road narrows to two lanes, dips, and then forks. Take the left fork toward Waialua (still Wilikina Dr., but now Rte 803).

Wilikina Dr. becomes Kaukonahua Rd. (still Rte 803).

At Thomson Corner (flashing yellow light) continue straight on Farrington Hwy (Rte 930).

At the small traffic circle bear left under the overpass to Mokulēʻia.

Look for Waialua Intermediate and High School on the left.

Park on the street near the school's last lot (elevation 43 feet) (map point A).

Bus: Route 76 to Farrington Hwy and Goodale Ave. Walk 0.4 mile along Farrington Hwy to the high school.

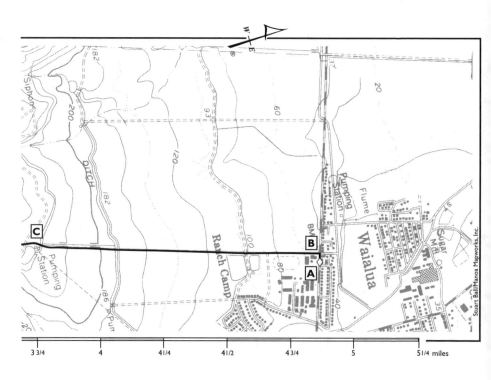

Route Description

Continue along Farrington Hwy toward Mokulē'ia on foot.

Just past the high school turn left on a semipaved road (map point B).

Climb over a locked yellow gate.

Pass the high school football field on the left.

Near the end of the cropland pass a small reservoir on the left (map point C).

As the pavement ends, go through a white gate.

The road bears right and begins to climb.

Another dirt road comes in on the right. Keep left.

As the road curves right past a macadamia nut orchard, bear left to a locked wooden gate (map point D). Use the ladder on the left side to climb over the fence.

Follow a grassy road through a pasture. The road swings left and then right toward a watering trough.

Just past the trough turn right and climb steadily up the side of a broad ridge. The rutted road is overgrown and indistinct in spots.

At the top of the ridge reach a junction with a more traveled dirt road (map point E). Turn left up it. Memorize that junction for the return trip.

Ascend steadily through pasture dotted with introduced trees.

In a large eroded area pass another watering trough on the right.

The road forks. Keep left through a band of Java plum trees.

The pasture becomes overgrown with guava and native 'a'ali'i trees.

Reach the Mokulē'ia Forest Reserve boundary marked by an old wood and wire fence at the road end (map point F). Use the built-in steps to climb over the gate.

Climb more gradually through a pleasant, mixed dryland forest. Look for native alahe'e trees and pūkiawe shrubs.

Descend briefly to a saddle in the ridge (map point G).

Curve right and climb steeply up an eroded slope.

At its end bear left along the ridge through strawberry guava trees (map point H).

Climb steeply past an open, bare spot with good views.

The angle of ascent eases through another section of dryland forest. Native lama trees make an appearance.

Cross a thin, eroded neck (map point I).

Begin serious climbing as the ridge narrows and becomes rocky.

Descend a 30-foot drop in the ridge with the help of a cable.

Negotiate numerous steep and narrow spots. Watch your footing on the loose rock and dirt. Between cables look for the native herb koʻokoʻolau.

Continue the steep, slippery climb, now through native forest with some thorny blackberry bushes. Along the trail are pūʻahanui (kanawao) and kūkaemoa (alani) shrubs.

Pass a shelter informally known as "the bus stop." Nearby are two derelict radars.

The trail becomes a stairway with handrails. Look for native olomea and ʻōhiʻa ʻāhihi trees.

On the right pass a shack with antennas.

Bear left and cross a small, green wooden bridge. Watch for a native *Lobelia*, koliʻi.

By a blind-spot mirror reach a junction with Mt. Kaʻala Rd. (map point J). Turn left up the paved road.

Another paved road comes in on the right. Keep left on the main road.

Reach the summit of Kaʻala (elevation 4,025 feet) (map point K) near the main entrance to an FAA radar installation.

For the best views, turn left along the outside of the perimeter fence just before reaching the main gate. Circle halfway around the fence to a grassy lookout. Do not enter the FAA installation, which is a secured area off-limits to the public.

To get to the boardwalk through the bog, turn right across a grassy helipad near the main entrance and go through an unlocked gate.

Notes

Dupont is the premier hike in the Waiʻanae (mullet water) Range. The trail climbs to the top of Kaʻala (the fragrance), the highest mountain on the island. On the way up the route passes through cropland, pasture, mixed dryland forest, and native rain forest. On the summit plateau is a cool, misty bog with some unusual native plants.

The Dupont Trail may have been part of an early Hawaiian route from Wai'anae Valley to Waialua. The first recorded use, however, occurred in 1920 during a descent of Ka'ala. The explorers named the rediscovered route De Ponte, in honor of an acquaintance, Mary De Ponte. Over the years the name changed to Dupont.

This rugged hike requires several cautions. The upper trail section is narrow, steep, and often slippery. Watch your balance and footing constantly, especially on the descent. Test all cables before using them. If you feel uneasy about the exposure, turn around. On the final climb blackberry bushes may overgrow the trail. Wear gloves and long pants for protection against the thorns. Finally, don't enter the FAA radar installation even though the main gate is sometimes open. The staff there does not welcome tourists!

In the dryland forest look for native 'a'ali'i shrubs and alahe'e trees. 'A'ali'i has shiny, narrow leaves and red seed capsules. Early Hawaiians used the leaves and capsules in making *lei* (garlands). When crushed or boiled, the capsules produced a red dye for decorating *kapa* (bark cloth). Alahe'e has shiny, oblong, dark green leaves. Its fragrant white flowers grow in clusters at the branch tips. Early Hawaiians fashioned the hard wood into farming tools, and hooks and spears for fishing.

Pū'ahanui (kanawao) and kūkaemoa (alani) are common native shrubs along the wet upper section of the trail. Pū'ahanui, a relative of hydrangea, has large, serrated, deeply creased leaves and clusters of delicate pink flowers. Early Hawaiians used the plants for medicinal purposes. Kūkaemoa (chicken dung) has curled, dark green leaves, which give off a slight anise odor. The fruits resemble miniature cauliflowers or chicken droppings.

After passing "the bus stop," look for the small native trees 'ōhi'a 'āhihi and olomea. 'Ōhi'a 'āhihi has narrow, pointed leaves with red stems and midribs. Its delicate red flowers grow in clusters and are similar to those of the more common 'ōhi'a, which you saw on the way up. Olomea has shiny leaves with serrated edges and red veins and stems.

On the last trail section, keep your eye out for koli'i, an unusual native *Lobelia*. It has a single woody stem with triangular leaf scars. Its long, slender leaves are arranged in a rosette resembling a dry mop head. A circle of horizontal stalks from the rosette bears the lovely scarlet tubular flowers. After flowering, the entire plant dies, leaving a ring of seed capsules.

In spite of its road and radars, the summit of Ka'ala is a fascinating place. The high plateau consists of thick, nearly horizontal beds of lava that are very resistant to erosion. As a result, the area is a little-changed remnant of the original surface of the old Wai'anae volcano. Over the years the poor drainage produced a bog, home to a special plant community.

From the lookouts along the perimeter fence at the summit you can see the beautiful north shore to Waimea (reddish water) Bay, the Wahiawā (place of noise) plain, and, in back, the Ko'olau (windward) Range. In the distance are Pearl Harbor, Honolulu, and Diamond Head. Along the Wai'anae summit ridge are the peaks of Kalena (the lazy one), Hāpapa (rock stratum), and Pu'u Kaua (war hill). If the view is obscured, wait a while because the mist may lift suddenly.

After enjoying the view, be sure to visit the summit bog. Stay on the one-lane boardwalk to keep reasonably dry and to avoid damaging the vegetation. Take your time and try to identify some of the native plants. Many of the ones you saw on the way up are also here.

The boardwalk is also part of the Wai'anae Ka'ala hike. To traverse the mountain, combine the Dupont and Wai'anae Ka'ala hikes. Do not use the paved Mt. Ka'ala Rd. as part of a traverse or a loop hike. The long, boring road is hard on the feet and knees and closed to the public.

46 Keālia

Type:	Graded ridge
Length:	7-mile round trip
Elevation Gain:	2,000 feet
Danger:	Low
Suitable for:	Intermediate
Location:	Kuaokalā and Mokulēʻia Forest Reserves above Mokulēʻia
Topo Map:	Kaʻena
Access:	Open

Highlights
This hot, dry hike ascends a steep *pali* (cliff) en route to the summit of the Waiʻanae Range. While climbing, you may see fixed-wing gliders soaring above the north shore of Oʻahu. At the end is a scenic overlook of an undeveloped leeward valley.

Trailhead Directions
At Punchbowl St. get on Lunalilo Fwy (H-1) heading *ʻewa* (west).

Near Middle St. keep left on Rte 78 west (exit 19B, Moanalua Rd.) to ʻAiea.

By Aloha Stadium bear right to rejoin H-1 to Pearl City.

Take H-2 freeway (exit 8A) to Wahiawā.

As the freeway ends, continue on Rte 99 north (Wilikina Dr.) bypassing Wahiawā.

Pass Schofield Barracks on the left.

The road narrows to two lanes, dips, and then forks. Take the left fork toward Waialua (still Wilikina Dr., but now Rte 803).

Wilikina Dr. becomes Kaukonahua Rd. (still Rte 803).

At Thomson Corner (flashing yellow light) continue straight on Farrington Hwy (Rte 930).

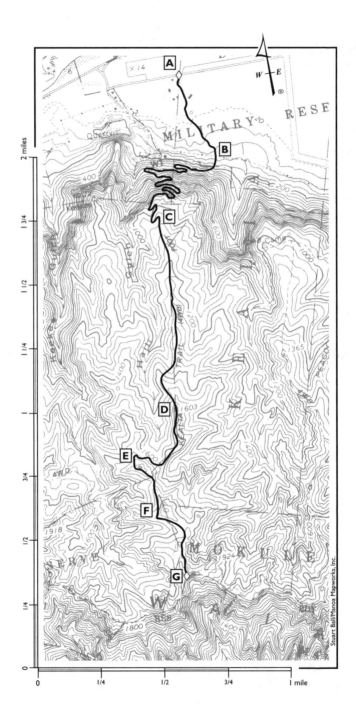

At the small traffic circle bear left under the overpass to Mokulē'ia.

Pass Waialua Intermediate and High School on the left.

Drive through Mokulē'ia.

On the left pass Dillingham Airfield and Glider Port, surrounded by a green fence.

At the far end of the runway turn left through an access gate in the fence by a low-flying aircraft warning sign. The gate is open from 7 A.M. to 6 P.M. daily.

Go around the end of the runway and head back along the other side.

Pass a low concrete building on the left.

Turn left into the paved lot in front of the airfield control tower and park there (elevation 20 feet) (map point A).

Bus: None, within reasonable walking distance of the trailhead.

Route Description

From the lot walk back across the access road and proceed along a wide, badly paved road heading *mauka* (inland).

By a trail sign go around a chain across the road.

Almost immediately the road forks. Take the left fork, keeping a large concrete building on your right.

The road narrows to a gravel track through koa haole trees.

Another road comes in on the left. Keep right.

Reach a low green fence with an unlocked gate (map point B).

Go through the gate and immediately bear left on the Keālia Trail.

Work toward the base of the cliffs through grass and koa haole.

Pass a utility pole on the right.

Ascend the *pali* gradually on nineteen switchbacks. Watch your footing on the loose rock. After the second switchback look for kukui and wiliwili trees. At the third is a lone noni shrub. After the fourth, views of the north shore begin to open up. On the upper switchbacks are large native wiliwili and alahe'e trees.

Reach the top of the cliff at an ironwood grove (map point C).

Pick up a dirt road at the far end of the grove.

Ascend gradually up the wide ridge through a forest of silk

oaks and Christmas berry. Look for the native shrub 'a'ali'i along the roadside.

Reach a junction by an old fence line. Turn right, still on the main road. (To the left a less-traveled road heads downhill.)

Continue climbing through introduced forest. Young pines line the road in the open sections.

Pass a rusted water tank on the left.

Enter Kuaokalā Public Hunting Area (map point D).

The road levels, dips briefly and then resumes climbing around a hump in the ridge.

As the road curves left in a eucalyptus grove, reach a junction (map point E). Continue left on the main road. (To the right a less-traveled dirt road heads downhill.)

Ascend steeply up the side of the hump and then descend just as steeply to a saddle on the ridge.

Climb steadily until the road ends at a signed T junction (map point F). Turn left on Kuaokalā Access Rd. toward Mākua Valley. (To the right the access road leads to Ka'ena Point Satellite Tracking Station.)

On the right pass a wildlife restoration project with a small water tank and trough.

Reach a signed four-way junction. Bear slightly right and up on the Kuaokalā Trail, a less-traveled dirt road. (Kuaokalā Access Rd. veers left and leads to an abandoned Nike missile site and the Mākua Rim Trail.)

Reach the road end at an overlook of Mākua Valley (elevation 1,960 feet) (map point G).

Notes

Keālia means salt encrustation. The name probably refers to sea salt along the coast, but it is also an apt description of your shirt after you finish the hike. Keālia is a hot, dry, unrelenting climb to the summit ridge of the Wai'anae Range. Switchbacks on the *pali* and a dirt road to the top ease the gradient somewhat. Magnificent views and interesting plants and birds make the effort worthwhile.

The best time to take this hike is from February to April. The weather is cooler then, and you miss the pig and bird hunting seasons. Whenever you go, drink plenty of water and use lots of sunscreen.

Built by the Civilian Conservation Corps in 1934, the initial switchback section is clear and well graded. You are hiking up a cliff, though, so watch your footing constantly. Don't sightsee and walk at the same time. On the road look out for the occasional four-wheel-drive vehicle. At the lookout don't even think of descending into Mākua Valley. It is a military range used for live-fire exercises.

On the switchbacks, look for native wiliwili trees. They have heart-shaped, leathery leaflets in groups of three. Flowers appear in the spring and are usually orange. Early Hawaiians used the soft, light wood for surfboards, canoe outriggers, and fishnet floats. The red seeds were strung together to form *lei hua* (seed or nut garlands).

Above the fourth switchback are superb views of the beautiful north shore of O'ahu. Along the coast are the towns of Waialua and Hale'iwa (house of the frigate bird). Beyond are Waimea (reddish water) Bay and Sunset Beach. In the distance is the Ko'olau (windward) Range. Directly below lies Dillingham Airfield. The large pond nearby is actually a quarry once used to mine rock for the airstrip and other construction projects. Look for fixed-wing gliders soaring above cliff and ocean. You may also see sky divers with their colorful parachutes.

Along the upper switchbacks is the native tree alahe'e. Its oblong leaves are shiny and dark green. Alahe'e has fragrant white flowers that grow in clusters at the branch tips. Early Hawaiians fashioned the hard wood into farming tools, and hooks and spears for fishing.

Along the switchbacks and the road is a variety of introduced birds. Much in evidence is the white-rumped shama, a Malaysian songbird with a chestnut-colored breast. Watch for the red northern cardinal from the mainland and the red-crested cardinal from South America. Listen for the cackling cry of the Erckel's Francolin, a brown game bird introduced from Africa. Look and listen for the iridescent peacock with its wailing call.

On the first road section look for native 'a'ali'i shrubs. They have shiny, narrow leaves and red seed capsules. Early Hawaiians used the leaves and capsules in making *lei*. When crushed or boiled, the capsules produced a red dye for decorating *kapa* (bark cloth).

After the uphill road walk, the summit lookout is a welcome sight. A thousand feet below lies the green expanse of Mākua (parents) Valley leading to the ocean. In back are the dark, sheer walls of ʻŌhikilolo (scooped out brains) Ridge. To the left the Waiʻanae (mullet water) summit ridge gradually rises to flat-topped Kaʻala (the fragrance), the highest peak on the island.

For a longer hike continue along the Kuaokalā (back of the sun) Trail to the right until turnaround time. The trail hugs the rim of Mākua Valley and then follows the coastal cliffs to Kaʻena (the heat) Point Satellite Tracking Station. The Kuaokalā Trail is also part of the hike with the same name.

LEEWARD SIDE

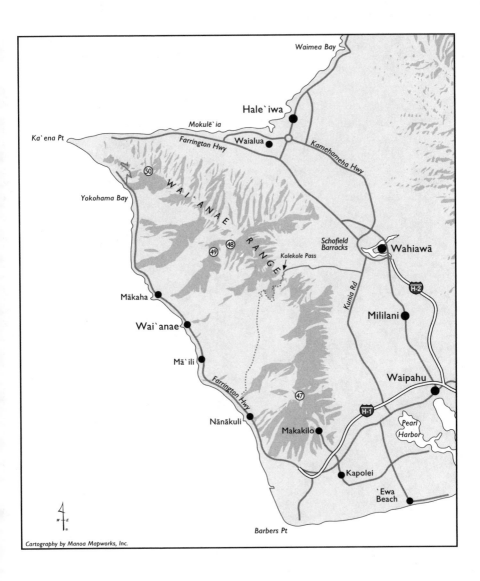

Cartography by Manoa Mapworks, Inc.

47 Pālehua-Palikea

Type:	Ungraded ridge
Length:	2-mile round trip
Elevation Gain:	400 feet
Danger:	Low
Suitable for:	Novice
Location:	Honouliuli Preserve above Makakilo
Topo Map:	Schofield Barracks
Access:	Conditional; open to individuals on a guided hike and outdoor organizations with permission. Contact The Nature Conservancy, 923 Nuʻuanu Ave., Honolulu, HI 96817 (phone 537-4508).

Highlights
This short, superb hike follows the Waiʻanae summit to Palikea peak. Along the ridge route are glorious views and an incredible variety of native plants. You may also see the endangered Hawaiian land snail.

Trailhead Directions
At Punchbowl St. get on Lunalilo Fwy (H-1) heading ʻewa (west).

Near Middle St. keep left on Rte 78 west (exit 19B, Moanalua Rd.) to ʻAiea.

By Aloha Stadium bear right to rejoin H-1 to Pearl City and on toward Waiʻanae.

Take exit 2, marked Makakilo-Kapolei.

At the top of the off-ramp turn right on Makakilo Dr.

Pass Makakilo Fire Station on the right and Makakilo Community Park on the left.

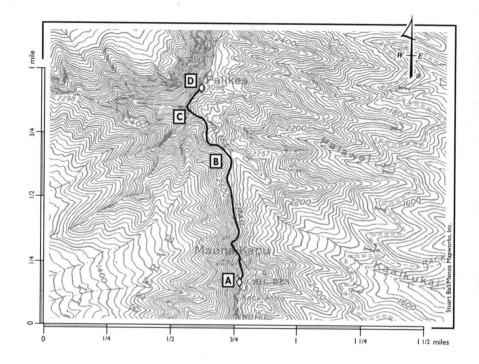

As the road curves right and down, turn left on Kīkaha St.

At the road end turn left on 'Umena St.

As 'Umena ends, continue straight on narrow, but paved Pālehua Rd.

Almost immediately reach a locked gate.

Contour through pasture land dotted with kiawe trees.

After curving right, the road splits. Take the right fork uphill. (The left fork, marked Camp Timberline, continues to contour.)

Reach another locked gate at the forest reserve boundary.

Climb steadily through eucalyptus forest. Ignore private driveways to the left and right.

On the right pass the lower communications site, consisting of building no. 203 and two towers.

The road forks by a light green building. Keep right along the Wai'anae summit ridge.

The road narrows, and the pavement deteriorates.

Park in the small dirt lot on the right just before the road ends at the upper communications site (elevation 2,720 feet) (map point A).

Bus: None, within reasonable walking distance of the trailhead.

Route Description

Walk past the upper communications site at the road end.

Climb some steps and turn left by a radar tower on the Palikea Summit Trail.

Go around the top of Mauna Kapu through a bamboo grove.

Keep left by a utility pole and then turn right on the leeward side of the hill.

Switchback twice down the steep flank of Mauna Kapu. The trail is narrow and slippery in spots.

Traverse a rocky section of the ridge. Look for native maile shrubs among the ironwood trees.

Scramble through a tunnel of large boulders.

Stroll through a flat, grassy stretch dotted with native koa and ʻōhiʻa trees.

Reach a junction (map point B). Continue straight along the Waiʻanae summit ridge. (The trail to the right descends Kaʻaikukui Gulch to the Honouliuli Contour Trail.)

Almost immediately cross an eroded spot. Watch for native ʻaʻaliʻi and koʻokoʻolau shrubs.

Contour to the right of a knob on the ridge through sugi cedars and Cook pines. Past the introduced evergreens, look for native pānaunau (Lobelia) shrubs.

After a short level stretch, climb steeply up a second knob, keeping to the right side of the ridge. Along the trail are small native manono and pilo trees. Watch for Hawaiian land snails on the manono.

Dip into a notch, possibly made by early Hawaiians.

Reach the top of the knob (map point C). Turn right to continue along the summit ridge.

Reach Palikea (elevation 3,098 feet) (map point D). Its summit is marked by a group of kī (ti) plants.

Notes

Pālehua-Palikea is a gem of a hike—short and instantly reward-ing. Your car does most of the climbing through the Wai'anae (mullet water) foothills to the summit ridge. A brief walk along the crest leads you to magnificent viewpoints and intriguing native plants. Watch your step, however, in a few narrow, slip-pery spots.

The route lies entirely within the Honouliuli (dark bay) Preserve managed by The Nature Conservancy (TNC). Volunteers for TNC conduct monthly hikes along the ridge trail. For individuals, those guided tours are the best and only way to hike in the preserve. Call TNC for schedule information and reservations.

Along the trail are over fifty species of native plants and sev-eral species of land snails. The notes below describe a few of the more common and easily identified plants and snails.

In the initial rocky section is maile, a native twining shrub. It has shiny, pointed leaves, tangled branches, and fruit resembling a small olive. The fragrant leaves and bark make a distinctive open-ended *lei* (garland), in both ancient and modern Hawai'i.

Near the junction with the Ka'aikukui Gulch Trail, watch for the native shrub 'a'ali'i. It has shiny, narrow leaves and red seed capsules. Early Hawaiians used the leaves and capsules in making *lei*. When crushed or boiled, the capsules produced a red dye for decorating *kapa* (bark cloth).

After passing the Cook pines, look for native pānaunau (*Lobelia*) shrubs on the hillside. They have a single woody stem with triangular leaf scars. Their long, slender leaves are arranged in a rosette resembling a dry mop head. The pānaunau produces lovely white flowers that are curved and tubular.

On the approach to the second knob are native pilo and manono shrubs. Pilo has reddish orange berries and narrow leaves in a cluster at the branch tips. Manono has thick, glossy, oblong leaves with purple stems, small yellow green flowers, and purple black fruits.

Manono is a favorite habitat of endangered Hawaiian land snails. Look carefully for them on both sides of the leaves. One variety has a white, spiral shell, and another has a brown, rounded shell. Do not disturb the snails or allow them to fall to the ground. Years ago many valleys on Oʻahu had their own species of snail. Now most are gone because of shell collecting, habitat loss, and predation from introduced snails and rats.

The deep notch near the top may have been a defensive position dug by early Hawaiians. The unexpected downslope forced attacking warriors coming up the ridge to slow down and bunch up. The defenders on the ridge above could then hurl stones and spears down on the hapless attackers.

All along the ridge and at the Palikea (white cliff) summit are awesome views. To leeward are Nānākuli (look at knee) and Lualualei Valleys separated by Heleakalā (snare by the sun) hill. To windward are the Koʻolau Range, Pearl Harbor, and, in the distance, Honolulu and Diamond Head. To the north along the Waiʻanae summit ridge are the peaks of Puʻu Kaua (war hill), Hāpapa (rock stratum), Kalena (the lazy one), and flat-topped Kaʻala (the fragrance). Leeward of Kaʻala is Waiʻanae Valley backed by massive Kamaileʻunu (the stripped maile) Ridge.

48 Wai'anae Ka'ala

Type:	Ungraded ridge
Length:	8-mile round trip
Elevation Gain:	3,500 feet
Danger:	Medium
Suitable for:	Intermediate, Expert
Location:	Wai'anae Kai Forest Reserve and Ka'ala Natural Area Reserve above Wai'anae town
Topo Map:	Wai'anae, Ka'ena, Hale'iwa
Access:	Open

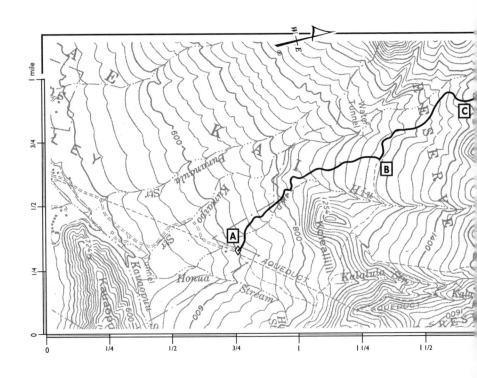

Highlights

The highest mountain on Oʻahu is flat-topped Kaʻala. This rugged hike climbs to its misty summit from the hot leeward side. En route and in the bog at the top is an amazing assemblage of native forest plants.

Trailhead Directions

At Punchbowl St. get on Lunalilo Fwy (H-1) heading ʻewa (west).

Near Middle St. keep left on Rte 78 west (exit 19B, Moanalua Rd.) to ʻAiea.

By Aloha Stadium bear right to rejoin H-1 to Pearl City and on toward Waiʻanae.

As the freeway ends near Campbell Industrial Park, continue along the leeward coast on Farrington Hwy (Rte 93).

Drive through Nānākuli and Māʻili to Waiʻanae town.

Pass Waiʻanae Mall on the right.

Turn right on Waiʻanae Valley Rd.

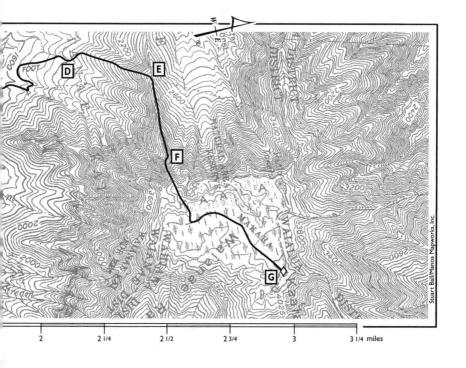

Turn left on a one-lane paved road (still Wai'anae Valley Rd.) by a bus turnaround marked with white curbs.

Pass several houses.

A locked gate blocks the road at the forest reserve boundary (elevation 580 feet) (map point A). Park in the dirt lot on the left across from a house.

Bus: Route 75 to the turnaround. Walk 1.1 miles along Wai'anae Valley Rd. to the forest reserve boundary.

Route Description

Go around the locked gate and continue up the one-lane paved road on foot through scrub koa haole trees.

Pass a water tank on the left.

In a wooded area the road levels off momentarily and passes Wai'anae Well I surrounded by a chain-link fence (map point B).

Ascend steeply through a mixed forest of kukui, silk oak, and coffee. Listen for the Japanese bush warbler.

The pavement ends by Wai'anae Well II (map point C). Continue up a dirt road through Formosa koa trees.

Reach the end of the road by a covered picnic table. Take the trail on the right marked by several boulders. Nearby are some macadamia nut trees.

Ascend gradually along a broad ridge, keeping to its right edge. On the left are several terraces once used for growing kalo (taro).

Bear right around a large rock outcrop and pass a utility pole.

After the ridge narrows, turn left down into a gully.

Cross the streambed and turn left downstream past some kukui trees.

Climb out of the gully and traverse a side ridge through strawberry guava and Christmas berry trees.

Work right, up a partially open ridge. Ignore a side trail on the left.

Bear left off the ridgeline into a broad gully.

Cross a very small streambed and reach an obscure junction (map point D). Take the right fork up the gully past some kī (ti) plants. (The trail to the left is the return leg of the Wai'anae Kai loop.)

Work left out of the gully onto a side ridge and climb steeply up its left side.

The trail switchbacks twice and then resumes going straight up.

Switch to the right edge of the ridge through native koa and 'ōhi'a trees and uluhe ferns. Look for maile, a native twining shrub.

Work left across the ridge face and ascend very steeply.

Reach the top of Kamaile'unu Ridge and a trail junction (map point E). Turn right up the ridge. (The trail down the ridge to the left is the return leg of the Wai'anae Kai loop.)

Almost immediately reach an overlook of Wai'anae Valley by some metal utility poles (elevation 2,720 feet). In front of the overlook are native 'a'ali'i shrubs.

Climb steadily up the ridge through open native vegetation. Look for the native shrub pilo.

The ridge broadens and levels through a stand of 'ōhi'a 'āhihi.

Negotiate a series of large boulders on a steep and narrow section of the ridge. The last boulder is notorious. Scramble up to the right initially and then back to the left. A cable provides some security.

Climb very steeply on the now-broad ridge through native forest. Between cables look for olomea trees with their red-veined leaves.

Cut right, across the face of the ridge and then resume steep scrambling. Several more cables ease the climb.

Enter Ka'ala Natural Area Reserve, marked by a sign.

The ridge narrows and the angle of ascent decreases as the top nears. Watch for a native *Lobelia*, koli'i.

Reach the Ka'ala plateau and bog (map point F).

Cross the bog on a narrow boardwalk through diverse native vegetation. Common are lapalapa trees and kūkaemoa (alani) and pū'ahanui (kanawao) shrubs.

Go through an unlocked gate and cross a helipad.

Reach paved Mt. Ka'ala Rd. and the summit (elevation 4,025 feet) (map point G) near an FAA radar installation.

For the best views turn right on the road. Just before reaching the main gate of the installation, turn left along the outside of the perimeter fence. Circle halfway around the fence to a grassy lookout. Do not enter the FAA installation, which is a secured area off-limits to the public.

Notes

The Waiʻanae Kaʻala hike climbs to the summit of the highest peak on Oʻahu from the leeward side. The route starts in a hot, dry valley and ends in a cool, wet bog. The misty walk through the native forest in the bog is one of the great hiking experiences on the island. After that, the summit, with its road, radars, and fleeting views is an anticlimax.

This rugged hike requires a number of cautions. The section through the boulders to the summit plateau is very steep and usually slippery. Watch your balance and footing constantly, especially on the descent. Test all cables before using them. If you feel uneasy about the exposure, turn around. On the final climb blackberry bushes may overgrow the trail. Wear gloves and long pants for protection against the thorns. While crossing the bog, stay on the boardwalk to avoid damaging the vegetation. Finally, don't enter the FAA radar installation even though the main gate is sometimes open. The staff there does not welcome tourists!

On the ascent to the Waiʻanae Valley overlook watch for the native shrubs ʻaʻaliʻi and maile. ʻAʻaliʻi has shiny, narrow leaves and red seed capsules. Maile has glossy, pointed leaves, tangled branches, and fruit resembling a small olive. Its fragrant leaves and bark make a distinctive open-ended *lei* (garland), in both ancient and modern Hawaiʻi.

From the overlook you can see Waiʻanae (mullet water) and Lualualei Valleys to the right. On the left is Mākaha (fierce) Valley backed by ʻŌhikilolo (scooped out brains) Ridge. Ahead along Kamaileʻunu (the stripped maile) Ridge are the imposing ramparts of Kaʻala (the fragrance).

On the final climb take a break between cables and look for the small native trees ʻōhiʻa ʻāhihi, pilo, and olomea. ʻŌhiʻa ʻāhihi has narrow, pointed leaves with red stems and midribs. Its delicate red flowers grow in clusters and are similar to those of the more common ʻōhiʻa, which you saw on the way up. Pilo has reddish orange berries and narrow leaves in a cluster at the branch tips. Olomea has shiny leaves with serrated edges and red veins and stems.

Olomea is a favorite habitat of endangered Hawaiian land snails. Look carefully for them on both sides of the leaves. One variety has a white, spiral shell, and another has a brown, rounded shell. Do not disturb the snails or allow them to fall to the ground. Years ago many valleys on O'ahu had their own species of snail. Now most are gone because of shell collecting, habitat loss, and predation from introduced snails and rats.

After entering the natural area reserve, keep your eye out for koli'i, an unusual native *Lobelia*. It has a single woody stem with triangular leaf scars. Its long, slender leaves are arranged in a rosette resembling a dry mop head. A circle of horizontal stalks from the rosette bears the lovely scarlet tubular flowers. After flowering, the entire plant dies, leaving a ring of seed capsules.

The one-lane boardwalk makes for easy and reasonably dry walking through the misty bog. Take time to enjoy the incredible variety of native plants there. See if you can identify these three common ones—lapalapa, pū'ahanui (kanawao), and kūkaemoa (alani). Lapalapa trees have roundish leaves that are arranged in groups of three and flutter in the slightest wind. Pū'ahanui, a relative of hydrangea, has large, serrated, deeply creased leaves and clusters of delicate pink flowers. Kūkaemoa (chicken dung) shrubs have curled, dark green leaves, which give off a slight anise odor. The fruits resemble miniature cauliflowers or chicken droppings.

From the lookouts along the perimeter fence at the summit you can see the beautiful north shore, the Wahiawā (place of noise) plain, and, in back, the Ko'olau (windward) Range. In the distance are Pearl Harbor, Honolulu, and Diamond Head. Along the Wai'anae summit ridge are the peaks of Kalena (the lazy one), Hāpapa (rock stratum), and Pu'u Kaua (war hill). If the view is obscured, wait a while because the mist may lift suddenly.

For a shorter hike, try the Wai'anae Kai loop that starts from the same trailhead. To traverse Ka'ala, combine the Dupont and Wai'anae Ka'ala hikes.

49 Wai'anae Kai

Type:	Foothill
Length:	6-mile loop
Elevation Gain:	2,200 feet
Danger:	Low
Suitable for:	Intermediate
Location:	Wai'anae Kai Forest Reserve above Wai'anae town
Topo Map:	Wai'anae, Ka'ena
Access:	Open

Highlights

This hot, dry hike climbs around the back of Wai'anae Valley in the shadow of Ka'ala, the tallest peak on the island. Along the loop portion are a variety of native plants and good views of the Wai'anae Range and coast. The return route follows an old Hawaiian trail.

Trailhead Directions

At Punchbowl St. get on Lunalilo Fwy (H-1) heading *'ewa* (west).

Near Middle St. keep left on Rte 78 west (exit 19B, Moanalua Rd.) to 'Aiea.

By Aloha Stadium bear right to rejoin H-1 to Pearl City and on toward Wai'anae.

As the freeway ends near Campbell Industrial Park, continue along the leeward coast on Farrington Hwy (Rte 93).

Drive through Nānākuli and Mā'ili to Wai'anae town.

Pass Wai'anae Mall on the right.

Turn right on Wai'anae Valley Rd.

Turn left on a one-lane paved road (still Wai'anae Valley Rd.) by a bus turnaround marked with white curbs.

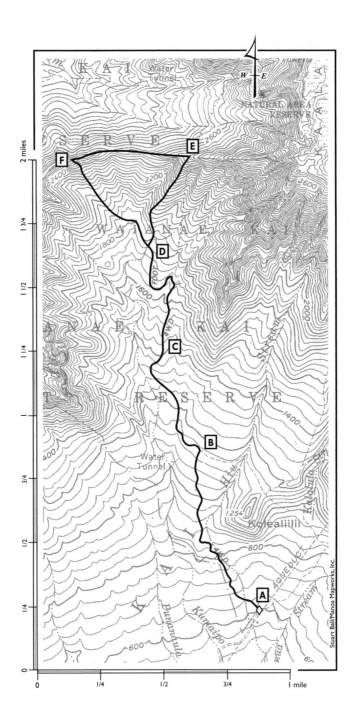

Pass several houses.

A locked gate blocks the road at the forest reserve boundary (elevation 580 feet) (map point A). Park in the dirt lot on the left across from a house.

Bus: Route 75 to the turnaround. Walk 1.1 miles along Wai'anae Valley Rd. to the forest reserve boundary.

Route Description

Go around the locked gate and continue up the one-lane paved road on foot through scrub koa haole trees.

Pass a water tank on the left. Ahead, Kamaile'unu Ridge climbs to massive Ka'ala. Along the ridge to the left is the prominent peak of Kawiwi.

In a wooded area the road levels off momentarily and passes Wai'anae Well I surrounded by a chain-link fence (map point B).

Ascend steeply through a mixed forest of kukui, silk oak, and coffee. Listen for the Japanese bush warbler.

The pavement ends by Wai'anae Well II (map point C). Continue up a dirt road through Formosa koa trees.

Reach the end of the road by a covered picnic table. Take the trail on the right marked by several boulders. Nearby are some macadamia nut trees.

Ascend gradually along a broad ridge, keeping to its right edge. On the left are several terraces once used for growing *kalo* (taro).

Bear right around a large rock outcrop and pass a utility pole.

After the ridge narrows, turn left down into a gully.

Cross the streambed and turn left downstream past some kukui trees.

Climb out of the gully and traverse a side ridge through strawberry guava and Christmas berry trees.

Work right, up a partially open ridge. Ignore a side trail on the left.

Bear left off the ridgeline into a broad gully.

Cross a very small streambed and reach an obscure junction (map point D). Take the right fork up the gully past some kī (ti) plants. (The trail to the left is the return leg of the loop.)

Work left out of the gully onto a side ridge and climb steeply up its left side.

The trail switchbacks twice and then resumes going straight up.

Switch to the right edge of the ridge through native koa and 'ōhi'a trees and uluhe ferns. Look for maile, a native twining shrub.

Work left across the ridge face and ascend very steeply.

Reach the top of Kamaile'unu Ridge and a trail junction (map point E). For now, turn right up the ridge toward Ka'ala. (The trail down the ridge to the left is the return leg of the loop.)

Almost immediately reach an overlook of Wai'anae Valley by some metal utility poles (elevation 2,720 feet). Near the overlook are native 'ōhi'a 'āhihi trees and 'a'ali'i shrubs.

Backtrack briefly down the ridge and keep right at the junction. (The trail on the left was the route up.)

Descend, steeply at first, and then more gradually along Kamaile'unu Ridge. Look for native alani trees and ko'oko'olau herbs.

Cross a relatively flat section of the ridge.

As the trail begins to climb toward a sharp peak, reach a junction (map point F). Turn left and down into Wai'anae Valley on Kūmaipō, an ancient Hawaiian trail. (The ridge trail continues straight.)

Descend steeply along a side ridge. Look for native alahe'e trees among the strawberry guava.

Reach the end of the side ridge where two streambeds converge by several mango trees. The gully is lined with huge kukui trees.

Walk down the right side of the gully very briefly and cross the rocky streambed to the left.

Angle up out of the gully.

Contour around a side ridge and curve left into another gully.

Reach the familiar junction with the route going up (map point D). Turn right and retrace your steps back to the road and your car.

Notes

Wai'anae Kai is all ups and downs. The hike initially follows a hot, dry road to the back of Wai'anae Valley. The loop portion then climbs steeply to a breezy overlook and enters a lovely native forest along Kamaile'unu Ridge. The return route traces an old Hawaiian trail.

The trails making up this hike are steep, rough, and unimproved. The route is poorly defined in spots, and the junctions may be obscure. Follow the narrative closely and watch your step. Start early to avoid the intense sun on the access road.

On the road look up to Kamaile'unu (the stripped maile) Ridge. Slightly to the left is a prominent peak, known as Kawiwi. According to legend, a lonely and bitter woman lived alone at the summit. When hungry, she cried out to the birds, who gave her scraps to eat. In later times the *kāhuna* (priests) heard about the legend and designated Kawiwi as a *pu'uhonua* or place of refuge during war.

From the overlook you can see Wai'anae (mullet water) and Lualualei Valleys to the right. On the left is Mākaha (fierce) Valley backed by 'Ōhikilolo (scooped out brains) Ridge. Ahead, Kamaile'unu Ridge rises toward the imposing ramparts of Ka'ala (the fragrance).

At the overlook are native 'a'ali'i shrubs and 'ōhi'a 'āhihi trees. 'A'ali'i has shiny, narrow leaves and red seed capsules. Early Hawaiians used the leaves and capsules in making *lei* (garlands). When crushed or boiled, the capsules produced a red dye for decorating *kapa* (bark cloth). 'Ōhi'a 'āhihi has narrow, pointed leaves with red stems and midribs. Its delicate red flowers grow in clusters and are similar to those of the more common 'ōhi'a, which you saw on the way up. 'Ōhi'a 'āhihi is found only in the Ko'olau (windward) and Wai'anae Mountains on O'ahu.

Along Kamaile'unu Ridge look for native ko'oko'olau herbs and alani trees. Related to the daisy and sunflower families, ko'oko'olau has pointed, serrated leaves and flower heads with yellow petals. Early Hawaiians steeped the leaves to make a tea used as a tonic. Alani has oval, opposite leaves, which give off a strong anise odor. Its yellow green flowers turn into four-lobed seed capsules.

The route down roughly follows an old Hawaiian trail, called Kūmaipō. The footpath started at the back of Wai'anae Valley, crossed over Kamaile'unu Ridge, and then descended into upper Mākaha Valley.

Among the strawberry guava on the way down is the small native tree alahe'e. Its oblong leaves are shiny and dark green. Alahe'e has fragrant white flowers that grow in clusters at the branch tips. Early Hawaiians fashioned the hard wood into farming tools, and hooks and spears for fishing.

For more open views continue along Kamaile'unu Ridge from the Kūmaipō Trail junction to an unnamed peak short of Kawiwi. That extension quickly becomes an expert hike because of several narrow spots. For more climbing and more native plants, try the Wai'anae Ka'ala hike that starts from the same trailhead.

50 Kuaokalā

Type:	Foothill
Length:	6-mile loop
Elevation Gain:	1,200 feet
Danger:	Low
Suitable for:	Novice, Intermediate
Location:	Kuaokalā Forest Reserve above Kaʻena Point
Topo Map:	Kaʻena
Access:	Conditional; open to individuals and outdoor organizations with a permit. Obtain one from the State Division of Forestry and Wildlife, Room 131, 1151 Punchbowl St., Honolulu (phone 587-0166).

Highlights

This loop hike initially tracks the crest of the Waiʻanae summit ridge above Kaʻena Point. Along the trail are lofty views of the rugged leeward coast, Mākua Valley, and Kaʻala, the highest peak on the island. The return portion follows a dirt road through the foothills on the Mokulēʻia side of the ridge.

Trailhead Directions

At Punchbowl St. get on Lunalilo Fwy (H-1) heading ʻewa (west).

Near Middle St. keep left on Rte 78 west (exit 19B, Moanalua Rd.) to ʻAiea.

By Aloha Stadium bear right to rejoin H-1 to Pearl City and on toward Waiʻanae.

As the freeway ends near Campbell Industrial Park, continue along the leeward coast on Farrington Hwy (Rte 93).

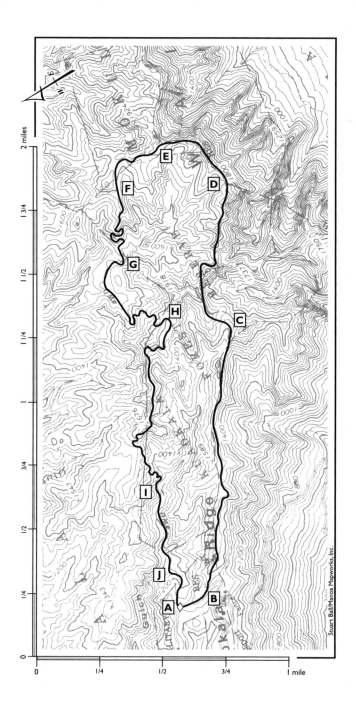

Stuart Ball/Manoa Mapworks, Inc.

Pass Kahe Point power plant on the right.

Drive through Nānākuli, Māʻili, and Waiʻanae town.

The road narrows to two lanes.

Drive through Mākaha and pass Keaʻau Beach Park on the left.

On the right pass ʻŌhikilolo Mākua Ranch and then Mākua Military Reservation with its observation post.

Reach the end of the paved highway at Keawaʻula (Yokohama) Bay.

Turn right on the access road to Kaʻena Point Satellite Tracking Station.

Show your permit to the guard at the station and get a visitor pass.

Switchback up Kuaokalā Ridge.

At its top turn right at the T intersection on Road B.

Curve left past the main administration building.

Pass a paved one-lane road coming in on the right through some ironwood trees.

After a short descent look for a dirt lot on the right. It's just after another paved side road comes in on the right.

Park in the lot (elevation 1,300 feet) (map point A).

Bus: None, within reasonable walking distance of the trailhead.

Route Description

From the lot walk across the side road and pick up the signed Kuaokalā Trail.

Contour around a hill topped by ironwood trees.

Reach a junction at the crest of Kuaokalā Ridge (map point B). Turn left on a dirt road along the ridge. (To the right the road leads down to the main administration building.)

Stroll through ironwoods and introduced pines.

Pass a covered picnic table on the right.

Contour on the right side of the ridge below its top. Way below is the guard station at the foot of a small valley.

Descend briefly into a shallow ravine lined with kukui trees. Climb alongside it.

At the head of the ravine turn left along the edge of the ridge (map point C).

At the road end ascend along a rocky, eroded strip and then swing right.

Traverse a narrow, bare section. Watch your step if the trail is wet.

Climb briefly to a copse of ironwood trees.

Ascend a small knob in the ridge. Look for native pūkiawe shrubs and dwarf 'ōhi'a trees in the bare patches.

Climb a second knob to an awesome overlook of Mākua Valley (map point D). On the way up watch for the native ko'oko'olau herb with its yellow flowers.

Bear left along the rim of the valley.

Cross an open, grassy stretch with views in all directions.

Pass another overlook with rock slabs. From here you can look over the main ridge to see the north shore. Farther along the crest of the Wai'anae Range is an abandoned Nike missile site.

Descend briefly and then climb steeply to reach another overlook and a junction (elevation 1,960 feet) (map point E). Turn left, away from the rim, on a dirt road. (The obscure trail to the right leads to Kuaokalā Access Rd. and the Mākua Rim Trail.)

Reach a four-way junction. Continue straight across and downhill on the well-traveled Kuaokalā Access Rd.

Reach a junction with the Keālia Trail (map point F). Keep left and down on the main road. (To the right, the Keālia Trail, which is actually a road, leads down to Dillingham Airfield on the Mokulē'ia side.)

At the next fork, turn sharp left on a section of the old road.

Descend steeply into Ke'eke'e Gulch.

At the bottom of the gulch bear left to rejoin the through road (map point G).

As the road splits again, keep left uphill on the through road.

The old road comes in on the right.

Reach the top of a ridge (map point H).

Descend and then bear left on a section of the old road.

Rejoin the through road.

At the next fork keep right on the through road.

The old road comes in on the left.

The road forks again by some gateposts. Bear left and down on a section of the old road.

Descend into Manini Gulch (map point I).

Rejoin the through road and parallel the streambed.

Reach the end of a paved road by a water pump (map point J).

Take the road up out of the gulch.

Reach the dirt parking lot on the right (map point A).

Notes

The Kuaokalā (back of the sun) hike loops around the cliffs, ridges, and gulches of the Wai'anae (mullet water) Range in back of Ka'ena (the heat) Point. Outbound are impressive views of the leeward coast and Mākua (parents) Valley. On the return you can watch fixed-wing gliders soaring above the beautiful north shore of O'ahu.

The best time of year to take this hike is February through April. The weather is cooler then, and you avoid the pig and bird hunting seasons. Whenever you go, drink plenty of water and use lots of sunscreen.

The footing on the hike varies from solid to slippery. Much of the trail and road making up the loop is wide and graded. Watch your step, however, on the narrow, bare trail sections, which can be slick when wet. Also, do not descend into Mākua Valley because it is a military range used for live-fire exercises.

Initially, the route passes through stands of introduced pine trees planted for erosion control and reforestation. Interspersed among the pines are the native dryland shrubs pūkiawe and 'ilima. Pūkiawe has tiny, rigid leaves and small white, pink, or red berries. 'Ilima has oblong, serrated leaves, about 1 inch long. The yellow orange flowers strung together make a regal *lei* (garland), in both ancient and modern Hawai'i.

Listen for a cackling cry in the gulches below. The sound is made by the Erckel's francolin, a game bird originally from Africa. Although you probably won't see it, the francolin is brown with white spots on its breast and belly.

Before reaching the first overlook of Mākua Valley, watch for the native herb ko'oko'olau, related to the daisy and sunflower families. It has pointed, serrated leaves and flower heads with yellow petals. Early Hawaiians steeped the leaves to make a tea used as a tonic.

The Mākua overlook is an awesome spot. A thousand feet below lie the green slopes of the valley leading to the beach and the Pacific Ocean. In back are the dark, sheer walls of ʻŌhikilolo (scooped out brains) Ridge. On the left the spine of the Waiʻanae Range rises to the flat summit of Kaʻala (the fragrance), the tallest peak on the island at 4,025 feet.

On the return portion of the loop, the narrative refers to the main or through road and the old road. The main road is the well-graded and traveled road. The old road consists of rough, eroded sections, which leave and then rejoin the main road. The route description follows the old sections where possible because they are shorter and have less traffic. You can, of course, take the main road all the way back. Whichever way you go, watch out for four-wheel-drive vehicles and mountain bikes.

The initial road section on the way back is also the final stretch of the Keālia (salt encrustation) hike. It climbs to the overlook at map point E from the Mokuleʻia side. Unlike Kuaokalā, Keālia does not require a permit.

The Kuaokalā route is described as a counterclockwise loop. You can, of course, do the hike in reverse. If you don't like road walking, return the way you came, along the trail. For a longer hike, take the Kuaokalā Access Rd. from map point E toward an abandoned Nike missile site. As the road swings left around the site, turn right on a dirt road that climbs to a lookout near the start of the Mākua Rim Trail. Total distance is about 10 miles.

APPENDIX 1: CLOSED HIKES

Listed below with a short description are hikes that are NOT open to the general public. They are classified as CLOSED for one or more of the following reasons.

1. The landowner does not grant access under any circumstance.
2. The landowner may grant access but with such onerous conditions attached as to make the hike impractical to do.
3. The landowner does grant access but getting the necessary permission is too complicated and time consuming for the average person. The outdoor organizations mentioned in Appendix 2: Hiking and Camping Information Sources can sometimes get permission to do hikes in this category.
4. The trail is not maintained and has become impassable for the average hiker.

Castle
Castle is the finest hike on the island. The route climbs the steep west wall of Punalu'u Valley by a series of spectacular switchbacks. The trail then crosses Kaluanui Stream well above Sacred (Kaliuwa'a) Falls and continues to the top of the Ko'olau Range and a junction with the Ko'olau Summit Trail.

Ha'ikū Stairs
The Ha'ikū Stairs is a metal stairway that ascends the windward Ko'olau cliffs in back of Kāne'ohe. The stairs start from the south side of Ha'ikū Valley and top out near the summit of Pu'u Keahi a Kahoe. The climb is near vertical in spots.

Hālawa Ridge
Hālawa Ridge is another long, graded hike in the leeward Ko'olau Range. The route begins in North Hālawa Valley near H-3 freeway and ascends steeply to the ridge separating the north

and south valleys. The trail then follows that ridge all the way to the Koʻolau summit.

Heleakalā

Heleakalā is a peak on the ridge between Nānākuli and Lualualei Valleys. The steady climb to its summit is hot and dry.

Hidden (Makaua) Valley

The Hidden Valley hike climbs the precipitous cliffs in back of Swanzy Beach Park in Kaʻaʻawa. The trail ends at the top of a waterfall in the small lush valley of Makaua.

Kaʻau Crater

Kaʻau is a little-known crater nestled against the Koʻolau summit. The hike initially follows Waiʻōmaʻo Stream in Pālolo Valley. A difficult climb past three waterfalls leads to the rim of the crater and to the top of the Koʻolau Range.

Kahuku

Kahuku is an ungraded ridge hike in back of Kahuku town. The trail climbs to the top of the Koʻolau Range and a junction with the Koʻolau Summit Trail.

Kaipapaʻu Gulch

Kaipapaʻu is a long gulch hike near Hauʻula. The route follows Kaipapaʻu Stream to a pool and a waterfall.

Kaʻiwa Ridge

Kaʻiwa Ridge is a short, windy hike in the hills above Lanikai.

Kaluanui Ridge

Kaluanui Ridge is the easiest hike to the Koʻolau summit. The route starts in back of Mariners Ridge subdivision in Hawaiʻi Kai.

Kamaileʻunu

Kamaileʻunu is the most rugged hike on the island. The hot, steep route climbs partway up the ridge separating Waiʻanae and Mākaha Valleys.

Kapālama
Kapālama is a beautiful loop hike in the Koʻolau foothills above the Kamehameha Schools and the Oʻahu Country Club.

Kawailoa Ridge
Kawailoa Ridge is a long, little-used hike that starts above Haleʻiwa. The graded route eventually reaches the top of the Koʻolau Range and a junction with the Koʻolau Summit Trail.

Kīpapa Ridge
Kīpapa Ridge is the longest, wildest hike on Oʻahu. The route begins near Mililani Memorial Park and climbs the ridge south of Kīpapa Stream. The hike ends at the top of the Koʻolau Range just beyond the junction with the Koʻolau Summit Trail.

Kōnāhuanui
Kōnāhuanui is the highest peak in the Koʻolau Range. The steep climb to its twin summits starts at the Nuʻuanu Valley overlook.

Kūlepeamoa
Kūlepeamoa is a ridge and valley loop in back of Niu Valley subdivision. A short section of the hike follows the Koʻolau summit.

Kuolani-Waianu
Kuolani-Waianu is an intricate loop hike that wanders around the back of Waiāhole Valley. The route crosses two major streams, Waianu and Uwao.

Māʻeliʻeli
Māʻeliʻeli is the hill overlooking Kāneʻohe Bay in front of ʻĀhuimanu. The climb to its top is short, but steep.

Makapuʻu-Tom-Tom
Makapuʻu-Tom-Tom offers summit hiking at its best. The route along the Koʻolau cliffs starts near Makapuʻu lookout and ends in Waimānalo. The descent is via the Tom-Tom Trail.

Mālaekahana

Mālaekahana is an ungraded ridge hike in back of Lā'ie town. The trail climbs to the top of the Ko'olau Range and a junction with the Ko'olau Summit Trail.

Mauna 'Ōahi

Mauna 'Ōahi is a complicated valley and ridge combination in back of Hawai'i Kai. The hike has a short section along the Ko'olau summit.

Mokulēi'a

Mokulēi'a is a pleasant graded hike to the top of the Wai'anae Range. The route begins in pastureland near Mokulēi'a and ends at an overlook of Mākua Valley.

'Ōhikilolo

'Ōhikilolo is a hot, steep climb with several narrow sections. The route parallels a fence line along 'Ōhikilolo Ridge above Mākua Valley.

Palikea

Palikea is a peak on the Wai'anae summit above Lualualei Valley. This hike climbs the Kunia side of the mountain from the Honouliuli Contour Trail. See the Pālehua-Palikea hike for the main route to the top.

Pe'ahināi'a

Pe'ahināi'a is a long, rugged ridge hike that starts above Hale'iwa. The ungraded route eventually reaches the top of the Ko'olau Range and a junction with the Ko'olau Summit Trail.

Pu'u 'Ōhulehule

Pu'u 'Ōhulehule is the craggy peak that dominates the windward coast from Kahalu'u to Punalu'u. The climb to its summit along the southeast ridge is the most dangerous hike on the island.

Pu'u o Hulu
Pu'u o Hulu is a hill overlooking the leeward coast near Nānākuli. This hot, dry hike climbs to its twin summits.

Sacred (Kaliuwa'a) Falls
This popular hike winds through a narrow gorge to sacred Kaliuwa'a Falls. The route is closed indefinitely because of a rock fall that killed eight hikers on 9 May 1999.

Tripler (Kauakaulani) Ridge
Tripler Ridge is a long, ungraded hike in back of Tripler Hospital. Much of the original route is now included in the Pu'u Keahi a Kahoe loop.

Ulupaina
Ulupaina is a short loop hike in the Ko'olau foothills near 'Āhuimanu.

Wai'alae Nui
Wai'alae Nui is a superb ungraded ridge hike to the Ko'olau summit. The trail starts in back of Wai'alae Nui subdivision.

Waiau
Waiau is a rough, ungraded ridge hike to the Ko'olau summit. The unfinished route begins above Newtown Estates subdivision.

Waiawa Ditch
Waiawa Ditch is a graded hike that roughly parallels Waiāhole Ditch and Waiawa Stream. The trail starts in back of Waiawa Correctional Facility.

Waikakalaua
Waikakalaua is a short valley loop in the East Range of Schofield Barracks. The route ends at a swimming hole along Waikakalaua Stream.

Waikāne

Waikāne is the windward continuation of the Schofield-Waikāne Trail. The route winds through Waikāne Valley and then climbs to the top of the Koʻolau Range and a junction with the Koʻolau Summit Trail.

Wailupe Gulch

Wailupe Gulch is a ridge and valley loop in back of ʻĀina Haina. A short section of the hike follows the Koʻolau summit.

Waimalu Ditch

Waimalu Ditch is a valley hike with some great swimming holes. The trail starts above Pearlridge and follows Waimalu Stream.

APPENDIX 2: HIKING AND CAMPING INFORMATION SOURCES

Division of Forestry and Wildlife
1151 Punchbowl St., Room 131
Honolulu, HI 96813
Phone: 587-0166

For: Oʻahu Recreation Map, individual trail maps, and hiking and backcountry camping permits

Division of State Parks
P.O. Box 621
(1151 Punchbowl St., Room 131)
Honolulu, HI 96809
Phone: 587-0300

For: state parks brochure, park camping permits

Hawaiian Trail and Mountain Club
P.O. Box 2238
Honolulu, HI 96804
Phone: 674-1459 or 377-5442 or 596-4864
Internet: www.geocities.com/yosemite/trails/3660/ or htmc.u4l.com

For: guided hikes on Oʻahu

Sierra Club, Hawaiʻi Chapter
P.O. Box 2577
Honolulu, HI 96803
Phone: 538-6616
Internet: www.hi.sierraclub.org

For: guided hikes on Oʻahu

The Hawai'i Nature Center
2131 Makiki Heights Dr.
Honolulu, HI 96822
Phone: 955-0100

For: guided hikes on O'ahu

The Nature Conservancy
1116 Smith St. Suite 201
Honolulu, HI 96817
Phone: 537-4508

For: guided hikes in Honouliuli Preserve

Moanalua Gardens Foundation
1352 Pineapple Pl.
Honolulu, HI 96819
Phone: 839-5334

For: guided hikes in Moanalua (Kamananui) Valley

SUGGESTED REFERENCES

Ball, Stuart M., Jr. *The Backpackers Guide to Hawai'i*. Honolulu: University of Hawai'i Press, 1996.

————. *The Hikers Guide to the Hawaiian Islands*. Honolulu: University of Hawai'i Press, 2000.

Berger, Andrew J. *Hawaiian Birdlife*, 2d ed. Honolulu: University of Hawai'i Press, 1988.

Bier, James A. Map of O'ahu, 5th ed. Honolulu: University of Hawai'i Press, 1992.

————. O'ahu Reference Maps, 3d ed. Champaign, Illinois.

Bryan's Sectional Maps of O'ahu, 2000 ed. Honolulu: EMIC Graphics, 1993.

Carlquist, Sherman. *Hawaii, a Natural History*, 2d ed. Lāwai, Hawai'i: Pacific Tropical Botanical Garden, 1980.

City and County of Honolulu. *Hiking on O'ahu* (pamphlet). Honolulu.

Gutmanis, June. *Pohaku Hawaiian Stones*. Lā'ie: Brigham Young University, 1986.

Hawaii Audubon Society. *Hawaii's Birds*. Honolulu, 1989.

Hawai'i Nature Center. *Mānoa Cliff Trail Plant Guide* (pamphlet), rev. ed. Honolulu, 1996.

Hazlett, Richard W., and Donald W. Hyndman. *Roadside Geology of Hawai'i*. Missoula, Montana: Mountain Press Publishing Company, 1996.

James, Van. *Ancient Sites of O'ahu*. Honolulu: Bishop Museum Press, 1991.

Krauss, Beatrice H. *Plants in Hawaiian Culture*. Honolulu: University of Hawai'i Press, 1993.

Little, Elbert L., Jr., and Roger G. Skolmen. *Common Forest Trees of Hawaii*. Washington: U.S. Department of Agriculture, 1989.

Macdonald, Gordon A., Agatin T. Abbott, and Frank L. Peterson. *Volcanoes in the Sea: The Geology of Hawaii*, 2d ed. Honolulu: University of Hawai'i Press, 1990.

McMahon, Richard. *Camping Hawai'i: A Complete Guide*. Honolulu: University of Hawai'i Press, 1994.

Merlin, Mark. *Hawaiian Forest Plants*. Honolulu: Pacific Guide Books, 1995.

Miller, Carey D., Katherine Bazore, and Mary Bartow. *Fruits of Hawaii*. Honolulu: University of Hawai'i Press, 1991.

O'Connor, Maura. *A Walk into the Past* (pamphlet). Honolulu: Moanalua Gardens Foundation, 1992.

Pukui, Mary Kawena, and Samuel H. Elbert. *Hawaiian Dictionary*, revised and enlarged ed. Honolulu: University of Hawai'i Press, 1986.

Pukui, Mary Kawena, Samuel H. Elbert, and Esther T. Mookini. *Place Names of Hawaii*, revised and enlarged ed. Honolulu: University of Hawai'i Press, 1981.

Roelofs, Faith. *'Aiea Loop Trail and Keaīwa Heiau: Field Site Guide* (pamphlet). Honolulu: Moanalua Gardens Foundation, 1996.

———. *Hau'ula Loop Trail: Field Site Guide* (pamphlet). Honolulu: Moanalua Gardens Foundation, 1996.

Scott, Edward B. *The Saga of the Sandwich Islands*. Lake Tahoe: Sierra-Tahoe Publishing Co., 1968.

Sohmer, S. H., and R. Gustafson. *Plants and Flowers of Hawai'i*. Honolulu: University of Hawai'i Press, 1987.

State of Hawai'i, Department of Health. *What Is Leptospirosis?* (pamphlet). Honolulu, 1992.

State of Hawai'i, Department of Land and Natural Resources. Hawai'i State Parks (pamphlet). Honolulu, 1997.

———. O'ahu Recreation Map. Honolulu, 1994.

———. O'ahu Hiking Trails (individual trail maps). Honolulu.

Sterling, Elspeth P., and Catherine C. Summers. *Sites of Oahu*. Honolulu: Bishop Museum Press, 1978.

University of Hawaii. *Atlas of Hawaii,* 2d ed. Honolulu: University of Hawai'i Press, 1983.

Wagner, Warren L., Derral R. Herbst, and S. H. Sohmer. *Manual of the Flowering Plants of Hawai'i.* 2 vols. Honolulu: University of Hawai'i Press and Bishop Museum Press, 1990.

INDEX

References to maps are in **boldface**.